consuming
mexican labor

consuming
mexican labor

FROM THE BRACERO PROGRAM TO NAFTA

RONALD L. MIZE AND ALICIA C.S. SWORDS

UTP

University of Toronto Press

LIBRARY AND ARCHIVES CANADA CATALOGUING IN PUBLICATION

Mize, Ronald L., 1970–
    Consuming Mexican labor : from the Bracero Program to NAFTA / Ronald L. Mize and Alicia C.S. Swords.

Includes bibliographical references and index.
Also available in electronic format.

ISBN 978-1-4426-0157-4 (pbk.). — ISBN 978-1-4426-0158-1 (bound)

    1. Foreign workers, Mexican — United States.
2. Mexicans — Employment — United States. 3. Mexicans — United States — Social conditions.
4. Mexicans — Civil rights — United States. 5. United States — Emigration and immigration-
Government policy. 6. Mexico — Emigration and immigration. I. Swords, Alicia C.S., 1974– II. Title.

E184.M5M59 2010   331.6'272073   C2010-905101-7

We welcome comments and suggestions regarding any aspect of our publications—
please feel free to contact us at news@utphighereducation.com or visit our Internet site at
www.utphighereducation.com.

North America
5201 Dufferin Street
North York, Ontario, Canada, M3H 5T8

2250 Military Road
Tonawanda, New York, USA, 14150
ORDERS PHONE: 1-800-565-9523
ORDERS FAX: 1-800-221-9985
ORDERS EMAIL: utpbooks@utpress.utoronto.ca

UK, Ireland, and continental Europe
NBN International
Estover Road, Plymouth, PL6 7PY, UK
ORDERS PHONE: 44 (0) 1752 202301
ORDERS FAX: 44 (0) 1752 202333
ORDERS EMAIL: enquiries@nbninternational.com

The University of Toronto Press acknowledges the financial support for its publishing activities of the Government of Canada through the Canada Book Fund.

Cover design: Pam Woodland
Text design by Daiva Villa, Chris Rowat Design.

Printed in Canada

Contents

List of Tables

List of Acronyms

AFL-CIO	American Federation of Labor-Congress of Industrial Organizations
AFSCME	American Federation of State, County, and Municipal Employees
ALRB	Agricultural Labor Relations Board of California
AWA	Agriculture Workers' Alliance (Canada)
AWOC	Agricultural Workers Organizing Committee
BWICLO	British West Indies Central Labor Organization
CAFÉ	Carolina Alliance for Fair Employment
CASA	Centers for Autonomous Social Action/*Centros de Acción Social Autónomo*
CFU	Canadian Farmworkers' Union
CIW	Coalition of Immokalee Workers
CNSM	Mexico's National Commission on Minimum Wages (*Comisión Nacional de los Salarios Mínimos*)
CTW	Change to Win Federation
CWA	Communication Workers of America
DHS	Department of Homeland Security
DREAM Act	Development, Relief, and Education for Alien Minors Act
EZLN	Zapatista Army of National Liberation/*Ejército Zapatista de Liberación Nacional*
FAIR	Federation for American Immigration Reform
FARMS	Federal Agricultural Research Management Services (Canada)
FAT	*Frente Autentico del Trabajo*
FERME	*Fondation des Entreprises en Recrutement de Main-d'œuvre Agricole Etrangère*

FIOB	*Frente Indígena de Organizaciones Binacionales/* Binational Front of Indigenous Organizations
FLOC	Farm Labor Organizing Committee
HTAs	Hometown Associations/*Clubes de Oriundos*
IBP	Iowa Beef Processors
IBT	International Brotherhood of Teamsters
ICE	US Immigration and Customs Enforcement, formerly known as INS
IDB	Inter-American Development Bank
IIRIRA	Illegal Immigration Reform and Immigrant Responsibility Act 1996
INA	Immigration and Nationality Act 1965
INS	US Immigration and Naturalization Service, renamed ICE
IRCA	Immigration Reform and Control Act 1986
ISI	Import Substitution Industrialization
J4J	Justice for Janitors
J4MW	*Justicia* for Migrant Workers
JBGs	Good Government Councils/*Juntas de Buen Gobierno*
LIC	Low Intensity Conflict doctrine
LMO	*La Mujer Obrera* of El Paso
OECD	Organization for Economic Co-operation and Development
NAACP	National Association for the Advancement of Colored People
NAFTA	North American Free Trade Agreement
NFLU	National Farm Labor Union
NFWA	National Farm Workers Association
NLRB	National Labor Relations Board
NOII	No One is Illegal Campaign
PATCO	Professional Air Traffic Controllers Organization
PPP	Plan Puebla-Panamá
PROCAMPO	*Programa de Apoyos Directos al Campo/*Program for Direct Rural Assistance
PROGRESA	*Programa de Educación, Salud y Alimentación/*Education, Health, and Nutrition Program

PRONASOL	*Programa Nacional de Solidaridad*/National Solidarity Program of Mexico
RAW	Replenishment Agricultural Worker program (US)
RI	Index of Representation
SANDAG	San Diego Association of Governments
SAW	Seasonal Agricultural Workers (US)
SAWP	Seasonal Agricultural Worker Program (Canada)
SEIU	Service Employees International Union
TDU	Teamsters for a Democratic Union
TNCs	Transnational corporations
UCAPAWA	United Cannery, Agricultural, Packing, and Allied Workers of America
UFCW	United Food and Commercial Workers
UFW	United Farm Workers of America, formerly known as National Farm Labor Union (NFLU) and Agricultural Workers Organizing Committee (AWOC)
UFW	United Farm Workers
UNITE-HERE	Union of Needle Trades, Industrial, and Textile Employees-Hotel Employees and Restaurant Employees Union, formerly known as International Ladies' Garment Workers' Union (ILGWU) and Amalgamated Clothing and Textile Workers' Union (ACTWU)

Preface

The 2004 mockumentary A Day Without a Mexican satirized omnipresent anti-immigrant sentiments by challenging us to seriously think about how our economy would operate without Mexican immigrants in our midst. Instead of mass deportations or other tried and true measures of temporarily removing the Mexican-origin population from US shores, the movie identifies a mysterious fog (a metonymic criticism of anti-immigrant sentiments) that removes all Mexicans from California and dramatizes the economic standstill that would result if nobody was present to pick crops, clean houses, operate leafblowers, tend lawns, build roads and structures, and provide childcare. Our aim is similar. In pursuit of providing clarity to an often obscured and obfuscating debate, we critically examine how North American consumption patterns are shaping Mexican immigrant labor in the provision of goods and services. We posit that consumption and production are inextricably tied, and if one seeks to understand the immigration patterns of the postwar period, we are best served by examining how North American consumption practices are shaping particular labor needs in terms of low-wage and marginalized conditions where Mexican immigrant workers are increasingly recruited to work.

Alicia Swords' grandfather John Swords and his brother Herbert left Germany at 17 and 18 to avoid the draft. John's father, Albert, was a minister and spoke out from the pulpit against Hitler's fascist regime. On the other side of the family, Swords' maternal great-grandparents, Saul and Ethel Kaufman, were Jews in Canada, further from the war, but close to the fear that there might be no one to stand up for them.

Swords has always been on the lookout for people standing up for each other, for deep forms of solidarity. At first, she looked outside the United States (US). In the Dominican Republic, she worked in a migrant workers' community where anti-Haitianism was so thick that Dominicans said they couldn't leave their children home alone because Haitians would eat them. But only two years later, Dominicans and Haitians began caring for each other's children in daycare cooperatives and hiding each other when police came to deport undocumented workers. When Swords heard about the Zapatista uprising in Mexico, she, like many others, was inspired by the people's bold stance against corporate and state power. Their leadership ideal of "rule by obeying," in which leaders listen to and are accountable to the people, spoke to her. Their emphasis on popular education suggested that anyone could develop critical awareness about neoliberalism and stand up to challenge it. Infuriated by the military response to their demands, Swords organized a human rights delegation to Chiapas. During that year (1998–99), the Mexican government expelled more than 100 foreigners, mostly on charges of political participation. Swords saw why the government did not want any extra eyes watching: it had militarized the state to break down the Zapatistas' challenges to free trade ideology. The Zapatistas deepened Swords' understanding of solidarity and of neoliberal policies. "Don't come here because you want to help us," they said. "Come because we form part of the same struggle and you are going to carry on the struggle at home." They charged their visitors to resist all forms of neoliberalism and injustice in their home communities.

Back in the US, Swords got involved with the national poor people's movement, a movement led by the poor to unite people across color lines to end poverty. Willie Baptist, one of its leaders, explains that social movements begin when untold stories are told and the invisible is made visible. Swords joined this national networked campaign to share untold stories about poverty in the "land of plenty." With her encouragement, the Workers Rights Center, Immigrant Rights Center, and Living Wage Campaign in Ithaca joined this movement.

Swords hopes to build a deep internationalism. In Mexico, she explains that in the US "there are poor people and some of them are organizing too! They are your allies." For her, writing this book is about standing with people whose lives are deeply intertwined with her own. Sharing untold stories of injustices committed against Mexican immigrant workers in the US, and of resistance to these injustices, brings us all closer to having people stand with us when we need them. Challenges to neoliberal injustices anywhere make it easier to challenge elsewhere.

In the not too distant past, Mize's maternal family was irrevocably altered after a workplace incident that permanently disabled his late maternal grandfather, Theodore Herrera. After being displaced from the land near Gallup and Chimayo, New Mexico, the Herrera family had followed the migrant trail to work sugar beets in Central Wyoming. Far, far from home, they were one of several Mexican American (they likely would have referred to themselves as Hispano) families that left Northern New Mexico during the Depression (and earlier) as land speculators and White squatters utilized a legal system, fully designed with White interests in mind, to wrest control over the land and its resources. Census records confirm that the family had lived in New Mexico since at least 1820 when Patricio Herrera was born in Socorro County. Family records are difficult to trace before that time. The Herreras were one of several thousand Mexicans who did not cross the border to enter the US. The border crossed them with the signing of the Treaty of Guadalupe Hidalgo in 1848 when Mexico was forced to cede nearly one-half of its territory to the US. Mize's family does not share details about the land loss but still talks of the *enganchadores* (labor contractors) who represented the Great Western Sugar Company. The contractors waited for local economic downturns to start recruiting the resident Mexican population with the promise of good steady wages and housing. Sarah Deutsch (1987) has eloquently detailed these practices in *No Separate Refuge.* After returning from World War II and a short stint laying railroad track, rather than working in the sugar refinery in Wheatland or using *un cortito* (short-handled hoe) in the surrounding fields, Mize's grandfather relied upon the long family history as miners to become employed by the Rockefeller-owned Colorado Fuel and Iron (CF&I) iron-ore mine in Sunrise, Wyoming.[1] Unlike the seasonal and temporary nature of agricultural work, the mining operations were constant — with the exception of production downturns, intermittent strikes, and work stoppages to protest unsafe workplace conditions — and the pay was low but dependable. But for the Herrera family, all that changed at precisely 8:00 a.m. on September 12, 1946.

Town residents knew an accident had occurred because an alarm sounded whenever a worker was injured in the mine. Mine injuries happened all too often in Sunrise. The first two weeks of September 1946 bore witness to 15 accidents (CF&I Archives, Box MIN-0004). When Mize's eldest uncle graduated from high school, 11 of his 13 fellow senior classmates either lost their fathers in a mine accident (three), had fathers seriously injured (two) or had an injury that prevented them from working for a significant period of time (six). The two unscathed fathers were employed as a railroad engineer and a farmer. Operating a jackhammer, Theodore Herrera unknowingly hit unexploded dynamite; the resulting explosion embedded iron ore pellets under his exposed skin, in his lungs, and in one eye that eventually went blind. The company reported the accident in the worker injury ledger as "Injuries both eyes, contusions both hands and chest; Drilled into misfired shot; 75% loss vision both eyes" (CF&I Archives, Box MIN-0004). His accident was preceded by his brother-in-law losing his hand in a mine accident in New Mexico and followed by his son (Mize's Uncle Trinidad or "Doc" Herrera) breaking his back after falling 50 feet down a mineshaft. These abhorrent, dangerous working conditions were coupled with substandard housing. Mexican mine workers' families lived in three or four rooms, but their pay was not enough to meet expenses. Summertime was reserved for sugar-beet harvesting by wives and children. Differential treatment was integral to the everyday practices in a town defined by corporate ownership. The mine-owned school enforced a rule that speaking Spanish was strictly forbidden, and Mexican students were beaten if they strayed into their home language.

Fast-forward to March 15, 2004 — the Associated Press ran an investigative article summarizing their analysis of federal safety and labor statistics. They found that Mexican immigrant workers are 80 per cent more likely to die on the job than native workers. Mexicans were twice as likely as all other immigrant groups to die on the job, thus making them the immigrant group with the highest occupational death rate. "Mexicans died cutting North Carolina tobacco and Nebraska beef, felling trees in Colorado and welding a balcony in Florida, trimming grass at a Las Vegas golf course and falling from scaffolding in Georgia" (Pritchard 2004, C1). The most egregious characteristic of the forms of exploitation of Mexican labor for North American consumption is unquestionably the callous view that labor is disposable. One of the major themes in the story of Mexican immigrant labor is the degrading, dangerous, dirty, and downright deadly nature of the lowest-paid sectors of the US economy to which they are relegated.

When scholars, particularly economists, talk about labor markets and labor more generally, their discourse often implicitly refers to "native" or "domestic" labor and views the labor market as either wholly determinative of or unrelated to other forces in society. *Consuming Mexican Labor* is designed to problematize both these assumptions and examine the relationships of immigrant labor to the (post-)industrialization of the US economy. In particular, Mexican immigrant labor has been central to the settlement and development of the Western states. The US government's role in managing this labor flow is paramount. The history of US immigration law informs the current strategies that regulate the immigrant labor pool.

The central basis for *Consuming Mexican Labor* is that relations between the US, Canada, and Mexico have always been inextricably intertwined. Initially they were intertwined in colonial projects and today are more fully interconnected because major US production sectors depend on Mexican labor. In the postwar period, Mexican immigrants are employed in sectors outside the traditional employment in agriculture, railroads, and mining. Industrial (factory) production, textiles, service sector, meat-packing, construction, and to a much lesser extent management and other white-collar occupations currently employ the largest proportion of Mexican American and immigrant workers. We examine the postwar experiences of Mexican laborers in the US economy and how commodities and services bought by US consumers are increasingly, though not exclusively, built on the backs of Mexican laborers. The situation in Canada is much more complicated but most recently, with the passage of NAFTA, is quickly catching up with the US historical pattern of Mexican labor exploitation.

Note

1. Mize is sure that it is with a quip of irony that he writes many of these lines from his Latino Studies office at Cornell's Rockefeller Hall. What is often left out of the story of the robber barons is the literal blood, sweat, and tears of everyday laborers that were shed in the making of these vast fortunes that enabled the philanthropic efforts that keep names like Rockefeller in the eternal, valorized, common, and elite vernacular, while names like Herrera remain unappreciated, unnoticed, and unrecognized to this day.

Acknowledgments

This book began over five years ago. As a result, earlier versions of parts of Chapters 3 and 4 were initially penned by Chris Zepeda. Although he was not able to continue on the project, we thank him for his early commitment to the book. Research for Chapters 7 and 8 was partially funded by USDA Hatch Grant 2005–06–044 (Mize). Earlier comments by Fouad Makki, Suyapa Portillo, Sergio Chavez, Angela Gonzales, Phil McMichael, Lindy Williams, and Whitney Mauer were most helpful, and for those early inputs we are very grateful. Mary Jordan as always provided tremendous assistance in tracking references and formatting. The anonymous reviewers were essential for identifying the most important contributions of our hemispheric regional approach, and we are thankful for their insights; any remaining errors remain squarely with the authors. Additional thanks to those who commented on previous versions of the book that were presented to the School of Justice and Social Inquiry at Arizona State University, the Department of Human and Community Development at University of California Davis, the DC Chapter of the Cornell Latino Alumni Association, Puerto Rican Studies Association, Rural Sociological Society, and Latin American Studies Association. We would particularly like to thank our editor, Anne Brackenbury, as she has masterfully led this project through to successful completion. Words cannot express our depth of gratitude to Anne as she has shepherded this project with grace, wit, determination, and unbelievable efficiency. At the same time, our intellectual vision was never lost, and Anne's determined working style served as an inspiration to both of us.

Ron would like to thank first and foremost his family, nuclear and extended, for their unwavering support through the best and worst of times. The ability to complete this book is fully credited to his inspirations in life: Chris, Tori, and Theo. *A mis padres, hermanas, tías y tíos, primas y primos, sobrino y sobrinas, mil gracias.* He would also like to thank former colleagues at Colorado State University, University of Wisconsin Madison, University of California San Diego, and University of Saint Francis Fort Wayne, Indiana. He is particularly indebted to the unbelievable support and collegial environment fostered by Cornell's Latino Studies colleagues Mary Pat Brady, Maria Cristina Garcia, Michael Jones-Correa, Eloy Rodriguez, Vilma Santiago-Irizarry, Sofia Villenas, and Helena Viramontes.

Alicia is grateful to family, friends, colleagues, and mentors who supported her in working on this book. Especially, she wishes to thank her Granny, Alison Swords, who taught her to imagine doing what she never imagined, and her parents and brother who are about the world's best listeners. She is deeply grateful to Tim for his love, for listening to her think aloud, and for challenging her to be precise. She wishes to thank her *compañeros* from the Poverty Initiative, the Tompkins County Workers' Center, and *Justicia Global* for sharing their inspiration, clarity, and commitment.

Introduction

Why people move is a perennial question that has intrigued social scientists since their origins in the European Enlightenment. When the first political economists (Adam Smith, David Ricardo, John Stuart Mill, etc.) sought to understand the shift from traditional to modern society, rural-to-urban migration was already present, but it was not central to their explanation of these forces of socio-economic change. Yet the relevance of migration (rural-to-urban and international) to the advent of capitalism cannot be understated, nor can the preoccupation with immigration by scholars that sought to explain the great transformation. Marx's (1976 [1867]) discussion of the industrial reserve army of surplus labor was predominately concerned with Irish proletarians migrating to England's industrializing cities. Ravenstein's (1889) laws of migration were the first attempt to define the push-and-pull factors in a general theory of population distribution in equilibrium.

For Marx, the shift from feudalism to capitalism was experienced by the English peasantry as a shift from an agricultural subsistence lifestyle to the factory life of a wage laborer. In effect, the industrial proletariat, or working class, was formed by the displaced peasants who migrated to the city in search of wages. An often neglected, but extremely important, element of the process of proletarianization is the massive movement of people that is required in order to meet the labor demands of capitalists.

> The intermittent but constantly renewed expropriation of and expulsion of the agricultural population supplied the urban industries, as we have seen, with a mass of proletarians standing entirely outside the corporate guilds and unfettered by them.... The peasant, expropriated and cast adrift, had to obtain the value of the means of subsistence from his new lord, the industrial capitalist, in the form of wages. (Marx 1976 [1867], 908–9; all further citations from Marx below come from this source)

Table 0.1: *Timeline of Consuming Mexican Labor, 1942–2009*

Date	Event
1942–64	US-Mexico Bracero Program is a binational arrangement that operates for 22 years, bringing more than 2 million Mexican temporary workers to the US.
1954	Operation Wetback begins a mass repatriation campaign of undocumented workers, resulting in return of 1.3 million workers to Mexico, according to INS estimates.
1965	Hart-Celler Immigration and Nationality Act is passed. It ends discriminatory quotas but places a cap on Western Hemisphere immigrants and a premium on education and job skills, creates admissible class via family reunification, and strengthens the H-2 temporary visa program.
Spring–Summer 1966	A strike and boycott of the DiGiorgio Fruit Corporation results in a union recognition election. DiGiorgio enlists the Teamsters Union to oppose Chávez's NFWA. Soon, NFWA and AWOC merge to form the UFW, and DiGiorgio workers vote for the UFW representation.
1974	Canadian government initiates the Mexican Seasonal Agricultural Worker Program (SAWP) to allow for temporary labor migration from Mexico.
1986	Immigration Reform and Control Act (Simpson-Mazzoli) for the first time holds employers accountable for knowingly hiring undocumented workers. The first attempt at comprehensive reform, its aspects include employer sanctions, anti-discrimination, legalization for those undocumented residing in US continuously since 1982, funds for border enforcement, and expansion of H-2 program to include H-2A (agriculture), H-2B (non-agricultural temporary), and H-1B (specialty).
1993	INS Border operations begin in El Paso, Texas. The Border Patrol expands enforcement and fortification along the 2,000-mile border (particularly in San Diego, El Paso, and Arizona).
January 1, 1994	NAFTA is ratified by the US, Canada, and Mexico to remove national barriers to trade, allowing the free flow of capital. None of the agreement's chapters address labor migration.
January 1, 1994	In Chiapas, the Zapatista Army of National Liberation (*Ejército Zapatista de Liberación Nacional* or EZLN), a movement of indigenous Mexicans or Zapatistas declare "*¡Basta ya!*" — for indigenous people, 500 years of oppression was enough! The EZLN condemned NAFTA and threatened the ideological underpinnings that cemented the elite Mexican and North American alliance.

November 9, 1994	Proposition 187, the "Save Our State" initiative, is passed by California voters (59 per cent approval rate) to prohibit undocumented immigrants from gaining access to public services in the state. The initiative was struck down as unconstitutional five years later.
January 21, 2003	For the first time, Latinos are identified by the US Census as the largest minority group in the US.
Spring 2006	The largest series of protests since the Vietnam era arise in response to Sensenbrenner Bill 4437. The Immigrant Rights Marches bring out 5 million immigrants and their supporters over a three-month period.
2006–09	Immigration and Customs Enforcement implement a series of workplace raids and mass firings at meat-packing plants and apparel manufacturers based on "no-match" lists.
March 2010	Arizona SB1070 is signed into law. The law requires law enforcement to detain those suspected of being in the state unlawfully. A tremendous amount of controversy arises over its constitutionality as well as its message to all members of communities identified as potentially "illegal immigrants."

The "freedom" of the peasantry consisted of a rural-to-urban migration that cut the ties that bound them to their feudal lords. Concurrently, this freedom also required migrants to find new means of subsistence. This new need gave rise to the wage-laborer, the growth of cities, and the capitalist mode of factory production.

In addition to the rural-urban migration, international migration also played a key factor in the development of capitalist social relations in Britain. Migration is important because it maintains the ability of capitalists to reproduce their workforce over time. According to Marx, "We have heard how over-work has thinned the ranks of the bakers in London. Nevertheless, the London labour-market is always over-stocked with German and other candidates for death in the bakeries" (378). He expands this analysis in his chapter entitled "The General Law of Accumulation" (762–870) into what has become known as his industrial reserve army thesis. He sees the working class as being in competition for jobs with the unemployed sectors of society, which he terms the "surplus population." His description of this surplus population has a much more limited applicability in contemporary times.[1] Nevertheless, it is relevant that in this era of neoliberal globalization, migrants from less industrialized nations move to fill the worst jobs available in advanced capitalist societies.

Transnational Approaches to Migration Studies

Today we are impelled to examine the experiences of Mexican labor immigrants within the political economy of **neoliberalism**, the policies and practices that privilege free markets to govern political and economic relations. Migrants have responded very creatively to the evisceration of the public sphere in the United States and Mexico and increasing precariousness in Canada. In response, migrants send remittances, while forming **hometown associations**, immigrant rights organizations, and worker centers. In this way, their adaptability has facilitated development and some stability even in inherently unstable and marginal social locations. The multidisciplinary literatures on **transnationalism** and globalization provide helpful descriptions, analyses, and theories of migrant adaptations.

The key contribution of transnational anthropology has been around the relationship between **consumption** (both material and symbolic) and **production**. Appadurai (2001, 1996, 1986) has been particularly generative in theorizing the production–consumption linkage that best explains the process that brings Mexicans to the US and the vital services they are producing that are both dependent upon and bolster (by providing cheap labor inputs) US consumption practices.

The transnational turn in Chicano/a Studies builds upon a long history of exploring the linkages between migration and identity, labor and **exploitation**, second-class citizenship and racialization, and Mexican American community formation.[2] The contemporary relevance of Mexican migration can be understood only through an historical grounding in the aforementioned topics. Finally, we posit that the role of the **state** (US, Canadian, and Mexican) cannot be understated in the shaping of Mexican labor migration to meet the wants of US consumers' and industries' demands for exploitable labor. Here, the increasing precariousness of the Canadian welfare state means fewer protections are in place, as the social contract is eroded in favor of hemispheric trade agreements, transnational corporate dominance, and an immigration system that is increasingly providing temporary labor for firms catering to consumer tastes. The dual role of the state and direct employer recruitment, in both constructing and managing immigrant labor markets, shape the social networks that migration scholars view as so important in sustaining migrant streams over time (see Krissman 2006).

A key issue that sociological approaches to immigration have not adequately examined is how neoliberal globalization institutionalizes inequalities through ideologies and practices that require countries to espouse free markets and privatize state interests. Studies of transnationalism tend to be overly celebratory in promising development. Yet scholars do not fully examine the class and racial inequalities that shape the transnational experiences of migrants. Robert Courtney Smith's (2005, 2006a, 2006b) romanticization of transnationalism and Saskia Sassen's (2005) suggestive but underdeveloped "serving classes" metaphor for Latino immigrants in global cities point to the challenges sociologists face in moving beyond world systems approaches and in cultivating new theories of transnationalism and the deepening of class and racialized injustices. By using an historically grounded, multidisciplinary approach, we understand transnationalism as both a response to globalization and as evidence of long-standing exploitative North-South capitalist relations. We identify that consumption in the era of **global capital accumulation** is heavily rooted in the marginalization and exploitation of immigrant labor.

We concur with Robert Courtney Smith that "Transnational life includes those practices and relationships linking migrants and their children with the home country, where such practices have significant meaning, are regularly carried out, and are embodied in identities and social structures that help form the life world of immigrants or their children" (Smith 2005, 211). But we advise against the overly optimistic version of transnationalism that equates upward social mobility with transnational living or transnationalism from below. The following two quotes demonstrate the celebratory view of transnationalism that is all too common.

> Yet, the most active transnational immigrants are often among the most successful in their jobs, their careers, and education. (Smith 2005, 215)

> One sign of this convergence is the tendency to conceive of transnationalism as something to celebrate, as an expression of subversive popular resistance "from below." Cultural hybridity, multi-positional identities, border-crossing by marginal "others," and transnational business practices by migrant entrepreneurs are depicted as conscious and successful efforts by ordinary people to escape control and domination "from above" by capital and the state. (Guarnizo and Smith 1998, 5)

Remittance economies, or an economic base funded by immigrants sending monies home to families or the community, are not the panacea for the ills of neoliberalism. It should not come as a surprise to the champions of transnationalism that neoliberal adherents, such as former Mexican president Vicente Fox, prefer privately funded development from remittances to the state financing of public infrastructure projects. Often, hometown associations engage in patronage politics in the same way that corrupt local politicians have gained power in Mexican politics since the Partido Revolucionario Institucional (PRI) had a stranglehold. We pay very close attention to the continued political, economic, and social inequalities in our discussions of Mexican immigrant social formations.

The Hemispheric Politics of Production and Consumption

Production and consumption are deeply political processes, and in an increasingly neoliberal era they are both built upon the backs of those whose labor makes them possible. The ratification of the North American Free Trade Agreement (NAFTA) has increasingly bound the production and consumption practices of each nation to one another. In all three NAFTA nations, it is the most marginalized of Mexican laborers who do the hard work of production for the consumer-driven economy. The scholarly literature on consumption[3] is widely varied in its approaches, but a most prominent perspective is advanced by Appadurai (1996, 83) who claims the work of consumption "... is the hardest sort of work, the work of the imagination."[4] It seems egregious to us to claim consuming imaginations are the hardest sort of work when compared to the sheer dangers associated with back-breaking, physical, manual labor in construction, day labor jobs, farming, mining, and factories. Even in service jobs, the face work needed to maintain a subservient role in power relations, along with the arduous aspects of cleaning, childcare, landscaping, repetitive service tasks, and stroking the egos of the privileged, is certainly more taxing than the mental work of consuming imaginations. Clearly, consumption is built upon the backs of those who produce goods and services. To privilege the work of consumption belies the social relations that shape both consumption and production. Appadurai avoids this dialectic by stating, "This labor is not principally targeted at the production of commodities but is directed at producing the conditions of consciousness in which buying can occur" (1996, 83).

Yet, to seriously consider the social life of commodities, one must clearly attend to both sides of the equation — production and consumption — and identify the expropriation of labor from producers for the betterment of a privileged group of capitalists and consumers. The "work" of wanting to buy more things, or figuring out the means of financing to purchase items, is the goal of the finance and culture industries, and consumers must engage in this; too often those who produce the goods and services fall out of frame. Laborers are observed through a *camera obscura*[5] whereby production labor is either rendered invisible or callously disregarded. The self-centered focus on consumers and on the satisfying of one's own wants at the direct expense of others ignores the conditions of production and capital accumulation, the exploitation of laborers, and treatment of workers as disposable bodies. Unfortunately, Appadurai's approach to consumption lets consumers off the hook and does not critically challenge them to consider the social origins of the goods and services they consume.

We explore the social relations of production and consumption by examining how the largest consuming class in the world — US and Canadian citizens — shapes the conditions for labor migration and the exploitative/marginalized production by Mexican immigrants that make mass consumption possible in North America. From 1942 to the present, we present these relations as constituting a triad that includes capital accumulation, labor exploitation, and consumption practices in the making of Mexican labor for North American consumption.

As we document the relationship between production and consumption, we analyze a complex of social actors, including **transnational corporations** (TNCs), federal governments, nation-states, and consumers in the global North, that drives the service economy through advertising, marketing, and the TNC-led race to the bottom. As the owners of capital and corporate shareholders operate the motor of mass consumption for massive profits, the system of consumer-driven late capitalism fuels the concentration of wealth in the hands of big business. By getting people to consume more, the profit machine keeps rolling along.

Importantly, consumers also play a part in keeping the profit machine going, as their power to put pressure on changing production practices often goes unrealized. Too often, consumers are complicit in maintaining exploitation when they choose particular products or services with their pocketbook. If they do not collectively choose fair trade over exploitation, living wages over poverty wages, and socially responsible consumption over the satisfying of seemingly insatiable "needs," then capitalists march along unfettered by consumer power to alter production practices. In the case of Mexican immigrant labor, there are many examples of consumer-driven exploitation (e.g., day labor, lawn care, housekeeping, childcare, janitorial, home health care, etc.). In these cases, there are no big businesses directly benefiting from exploitation in the same way as in the oligopolistic industries of meat-packing and agribusiness.

For this reason, we discuss the exploitation of Mexican immigrant labor with the intent of finding alternatives to unjust production and consumption. Consumption is both an active and passive process, something consumers do willingly or unthinkingly, that can either positively or negatively impact those who provide the labor for services/products. Consumption is also shaped by capital's efforts to redefine consumer wants as "needs."

In our conclusion, we highlight several ways of approaching solutions to these unequal social relations. Following the lead of immigrant laborers who are seeking forms of **resistance** and building alternatives to end the exploitation to which they are subjected, consumers must become more cognizant of the impact of their purchasing practices. We can all follow the lead of immigrant workers' new forms of labor organizing that (re)build community, crossing racial and class lines to demand respect and dignity for all workers.

By examining the concentration of Latinos in the workforce (of which Mexicans constitute about 66 per cent), we find that they are overrepresented in the industries of restaurant and hospitality, manufacturing, agriculture, construction, and private household services (see Table 0.2). If we use occupation to identify their share, we find similarly that they are over-concentrated in farming, building/grounds cleaning/maintenance, construction, production, and food preparation (see Table 0.3). They are least likely to be found in high-status, high-income occupations such as architecture, engineering, law, sciences (computer, math, life, physical, and social), and health care. The concentration in low-wage, service-sector occupations and industries has a deep impact on the future life chances of Mexican immigrants.

The TNCs that are raking in all-time record revenues and profits as a result of US consumer practices and Mexican immigrant labor exploitation are companies quite familiar to most people (e.g., Walmart, Pepsi, General Motors, Ford, etc.). Some are less well recognized, but the brands at the end of the supply chain (e.g., Taco Bell, Kentucky Fried Chicken, and Marlboro) are the profit generators for corporations such as Yum! Brands and Philip Morris International (see Table 0.4). The industries of the agri-

Table 0.2: *Latino Share of Employment in Five Highest Industries, 2004*

	%
Private household services 31.0	
Construction	20.9
Agriculture, forestry, and fishing	20.1
Manufacturing—non-durable goods	20.0
Eating, drinking, and lodging services	18.9

Source: Pew Hispanic Center http://pewhispanic.org/files/reports/40.pdf.

Table 0.3: *Latino Share of Employment in Selected Occupations: Five Highest and Five Lowest, 2004*

	%
Farming, fishing, and forestry	40.0
Building/grounds cleaning/maintenance	30.2
Construction and extraction	24.2
Production	20.6
Food preparation and serving	18.4
Architecture and engineering	6.3
Legal	5.9
Computer and mathematical science	5.6
Health-care practitioner and technical	5.5
Life, physical and social sciences	4.8

Source: Pew Hispanic Center, http://pewhispanic.org/files/reports/40.pdf.

food complex rely completely upon Mexican farmworkers to cultivate their mixed berries in California (Dole), oranges for orange juice in Florida (PepsiCo), tobacco in North Carolina (Altria and Philip Morris), tomatoes in South Florida (Yum! Brands), and peanuts for peanut butter in Georgia (ConAgra). Those products can be purchased at the three major grocery chains (Walmart, Kroger, and Safeway) that have increasingly bought out or out-priced their competition.

Table 0.4: *Corporate Revenues and Profits*

Corporation	Fortune 500 Rank 2009	Fortune 500 Rank 2003	2009 Revenues ($US Millions)	2009 Profits	2003 Revenues	2003 Profits
Walmart	2	1	405,607.0	13,400.0	246,525.0	8,039.0
General Motor	6	2	148,979.0	-30,860.0	186,763.0	1,736.0
Ford	7	4	146,277.0	-14,672.0	163,630.0	-980.0
Kroger	22	18	76,000.0	1249.4	51,759.5	1,204.9
Home Depot	25	13	71,288.0	2,260.0	58,247.0	3,664.0
Lowe's	47	60	48,230.0	2,195.0	26,490.9	1,471.5
Safeway	50	41	44,104.0	965.3	32,399.2	-828.1
PepsiCo	52	62	43,251.0	5,142.0	25,112.0	3,313.0
Tyson	89	72	28,130.0	86.0	23,367.0	383.0
Altria Group	11	160	15,957.0	4,930.0	62,182.0	11,102.0
Philip Morris	93	–	25,705.0	6,890.0	–	–
Manpower	119	176	21,522.8	218.9	10,610.9	113.2
Smithfield Foods	183	255	14,264.1	128.9	7,356.1	196.9
ConAgra Foods	188	50	13,808.7	162.0	27,629.9	783.0
Yum! Brands	239	240	11,279.0	964.0	7,757.0	583.0
Dole Food	329	371	7,732.4	121.0	4,392.1	36.3

Source: http://money.cnn.com/magazines/fortune/fortune500/.

More and more, the construction industry is buying its products (from lumber to nails) at Home Depot and Lowes, and in many locales contractors or do-it-yourself-ers can pick up their cheap labor outside the parking lots of these businesses where Mexican day laborers station themselves, looking for any work that comes their way. The meat, pork, and poultry industries depend heavily on Mexican and Central American labor for their disassembly lines in Kansas, Nebraska, North Carolina, Arkansas, and Alberta. The oligopoly firms that control the industry (Tyson and Smithfield as publicly traded companies, Cargill as the second-largest private corpora-

Table 0.5: *US Average Annual Consumption Expenditures*

	2003	2006	% of 2006
Expenditures total	**$40,817**	**$48,398**	**100**
Food	5,340	6,111	12.6
Housing	13,432	16,366	33.8
Apparel	1,640	1,874	3.9
Transportation	7,781	8,508	17.6
Health care	2,416	2,766	5.7
Entertainment	2,060	2,376	4.9
Personal care and services	527	585	1.2
Tobacco products	290	327	0.7

Source: US Bureau of Labor Statistics 2003, 2006.

tion in the world) are constantly working to maximize market share and follow the lead of other TNCs by looking to Canada and Latin America for expanding market shares and supply chains.

Pepsi is the quintessential NAFTA corporation. It kept controlling interests in spin-off entities such as Yum! Brands and significantly diversified holdings in Mexico when it could not compete with former Mexican president Vicente Fox's Coca-Cola firm, currently the best-selling soft drink in Mexico. Pepsi's Sabritas brand in Mexico City corners about 80 per cent of the snack chip market, and its brand Gamesa in Monterrey is the nation's largest manufacture of cookies. As former Detroit automakers Ford and General Motors move more operations to *maquiladoras* on the Mexican border, they too follow the NAFTA race to the bottom of maximizing profits by minimizing labor costs and expanding their global market share.

The clothes we wear, the food we eat, the automobiles we drive, even the tobacco we smoke are increasingly the product of Mexican immigrant labor. US consumers spend nearly 80 per cent of their income on products and services in which Mexican immigrant labor is concentrated (see Table 0.5). Though housing is the largest expense and most profits go to companies that service home loan mortgages, the residential construction industry is increasingly dominated by Mexican laborers (depending on how it is measured, between 20 and 24 per cent of the labor market are Latino laborers). Food, nearly 12.6 per cent of average expenditures, is increasingly harvested by Mexican farmworkers, served by Mexican wait staff, and prepared by Mexican workers. Understanding this link between consumption and pro-duction is crucial if we seek to remedy the exploitative conditions that result in cheap goods and services provided by low-wage workers.

Mexican Labor for North American Consumption

The central thesis of *Consuming Mexican Labor* is that the current con-sumption level of the North American population rests squarely, though clearly not exclusively, on the backs of Mexican labor. In every region of the US (and increasingly in Canada and Mexico), the particular usurpa-tion of Mexican labor (and land) constructs relational forms of inequality that unjustly enrich and overcomfort North American capitalists and con-sumers. In this **post-Fordist era** of flexible specialization and consumer-driven capitalism, a great deal of work by capitalists goes into shaping con-sumer wants and tastes for the sole purpose of maximizing profits. At the same time, consumers often directly employ Mexican workers and exploit low-wage immigrant labor in order to improve their own quality of life. Appadurai's consumption analysis overlooks the role of the "serving classes" in the formation of commodities. He misses the central tenet by Marx that human labor is the ultimate source of commodities, and he ignores how commodities are turned into value by expropriating surplus value. This oversight mystifies how consumption is implicated in the process of recruiting labor for production (in the postwar era, the US con-sumption of Mexican labor and increasingly in the NAFTA era, Canadian consumption of Mexican labor).

In recognizing how Mexican immigrants are exploited for production and consumption, we seek to counter a more insidious and pervasive ide-ology that justifies capitalist accumulation by suggesting that exploitation is necessary and inevitable. Many responses to immigrant workers, from Right to Left, are based on the pervasive assumptions of the "culture of poverty" (Lewis and Lewis 1959), which suggest that immigrant workers themselves represent the "social problem." Following this logic, dominant social institutions, from social services to schools to churches, treat Mexican workers as individuals whose cultural pathologies require social interventions to assimilate or normalize them. The more violent form of this logic suggests that they should be excluded so that they do not "con-taminate the native population." Our study emphasizes that the "social problems" surrounding immigrant workers are not caused by pathologies of Mexican workers. On the contrary, we repeatedly identify how Mexican workers, as individuals and in collective formations, draw on rich cultural and individual strengths and resiliency. We demonstrate that the triad of exploitation of Mexican workers, capital accumulation, and overconsumption are systemic and ongoing problems.

We also demonstrate that the social movements and resistances of Mexican workers, often in collaboration with other community members and often across racial lines, reveal the possibilities for (re)building community and for imagining and constructing new forms of economic relations of production and consumption that are not based on the systematic physical and emotional violence of exploitation.[6] Not only are Mexican workers not "the problem" in North America, they are playing leading roles in creating innovative solutions.

Mexican labor migration has ebbed and flowed historically due to the dialectical processes of attraction and repulsion. As Mark Reisler (1979, 1976) pointed out, Mexican laborers are "always the laborer, never the citizen" from World War I to the present. We show how this central contradiction unfolded in patterns of Mexican labor recruitment and deportation. The first mass migration from Mexico was stimulated by the push of the Mexican Revolution, which displaced hundreds of thousands but was not fully codified into a well-defined and state-sanctioned process until World War I. On the US side, the demand for labor to fill the gaps left by men leaving to fight in the war effort led to the development of the first Bracero era. A unilateral decision by the US state allowed growers to recruit substantial numbers of Mexicans not only at border entry points such as El Paso but additionally in the interior of Mexico. Without the permission of or acceptance by the Mexican state, the first Bracero era built upon the pre-established *enganchadores* system (see below) to ensure adequate labor pools.

Development in Mexico, particularly of transportation systems, was financed by the US robber barons who made their fortunes in the railroad transportation system. Promoting the flow of goods was not the only important role of the railroad industry. US labor contractors, or *enganchadores*, rode the rails south into the interior of Mexico to recruit agricultural laborers and track workers. *Enganchadores* used the rail system to recruit and transport sugar beet workers (*betabaleros*) to the rural Midwest. Many workers continued on to the termination points and eventually found factory, steel mill, and stockyard jobs in Chicago, Gary, Indiana

Harbor, Kansas City, and Detroit. The mining industry of the rural Southwest found that the rail lines that shipped silver, gold, iron, copper, and coal to modernize the US also brought a steady supply of Mexican track workers who could easily be rehired as miners.

The US government, particularly as expressed by Herbert Hoover during the massive labor shortages occasioned by World War I, recognized the unique relationship between Mexico and the US that facilitated a northward labor migration. During the first Bracero era, Hoover was appointed to the cabinet as Food Administrator. He was one of the politicians who heavily encouraged a policy of recruiting Mexican immigrants to fill US labor shortages. In a letter he wrote to Felix Frankfurter (Assistant to the Secretary of Labor) dated June 4, 1918, Hoover states:

> … There are several restrictions in force which are handicapping the movement of Mexican labor north across the border. The first of these is the restriction which permits this labor to come in for agricultural purposes only. It is hardly necessary to say that these men are needed for various other kinds of work in Texas and New Mexico, and this restriction first of all should be disposed of. Next, there is a provision that twenty-five cents a day must be deposited (until fifty dollars is reached) as a guarantee that the laborer will return. This, too, is bad, as it is deducted from his wage and further, we do not want him to return. There also exists a clause providing that he must return in six months and, although this period is possible of extension, the restriction should be waived so that there is no limit on his stay in the states. A further objection is a provision to the effect that two photographs must be made of each immigrant. The Mexican has a primitive suspicion of the camera and besides has been given the idea that this proceeding is to net him into the Draft and this one feature, though apparently insignificant, has been a great deterrent to immigration. Yet another provision is that the farmers must meet and contract with the laborer at the border. We hope to overcome this by having special representatives make these contacts at Brownsville, Eagle Pass, Laredo, and El Paso. All these restrictions should be removed if possible in the immediate future. We need every bit of labor that we can get and we need it badly and Mr. Peden is authority for the statement that we will need it for years to come. (Quoted in Kiser and Kiser 1979, 13–14)

Hoover called for unrestricted migration from Mexico, even as "primitive" as he claimed Mexicans were, to work in all needed economic sectors. He felt the US government should lift restrictions that would inhibit long-term and sustained labor migration. However, all that changed with the onset of the Great Depression, which put an end to economic growth. The first scapegoat identified by US citizens and the Hoover administration was the so-called horde of unwanted Mexican laborers who were said to be taking jobs from "real" Americans. The US then embarked upon its largest repatriation campaign ever to be experienced by an immigrant group with little to no legal precedent and relative impunity. "Dismayed local welfare officials, faced with skyrocketing relief roles during the early years of the depression, hoped to alleviate their burden by deporting Mexican immigrants.... The Hoover administration obliged by initiating a campaign to rid the nation of illegal aliens. Secretary of Labor William Doak dispatched a special supervisor to Los Angeles to direct a deportation campaign aimed at Mexicans" (Reisler 1976, 230). Mexicans, regardless of their legal status, were rounded up in the major destination points such as Los Angeles, El Paso, Detroit, Chicago, Gary, and all points in between. The repatriation campaigns eventually led to the forced and voluntary removal of 1 to 2 million Mexicanos, and the nativist sentiment had found a new target: the Mexican population residing in the US.

The same migrants Hoover so actively encouraged to work in the US and to establish long-term residency were the exact same migrants who were forcibly encouraged to leave when economic times soured. Many returned on the same rail lines they helped build, and those same rails that brought the *enganchadores* to Mexico to recruit them were utilized to send them back after their labor was no longer of service.

Mexicans, regardless of citizenship status, were targeted as the first to go and were the first to be blamed for economic woes. The mass repatriation of Mexicans made it perfectly clear to all that their status and rights in the US would be tenuous during bust times, essential during boom times, and eminently politicized at all times. Nowhere is this dialectic more prominently on display than during the period of the Bracero Program, 1942–1964, and Operation Wetback, 1954—the subjects of Chapters 1 and 2.

Patterns of US consumption are centrally tied to a production system that disproportionately relies upon the full-scale exploitation of Mexican laborers. Historically, this production system created the American Southwest, but in the past 20 years similar patterns of production have spread to every region of the nation (Midwest, Pacific Northwest, Southern, and Eastern US), the US-Mexico border region, and most recently and vociferously in Mexico itself. The social forces of globalization and deindustrialization mean that local shoppers at the area Walmart will buy the majority, if not all, of their goods from commodity chains that originate in "lesser developed" (more accurately low-wage) nations such as Mexico, China, Indonesia, India, and the Dominican Republic. In global commodity chain analyses, scholars Phil McMichael (2003), Jane Collins (2003), and Gary Gereffi and Miguel Korzeniewicz (1994) find that the contemporary face of globalization is marked by labor regimes that increasingly exploit female, Third World, racialized workers in the low-wage world economy. In Part I: Establishing Connections, we place the postwar US state in its context as international labor broker by examining the central contradiction of the attraction/repulsion of Mexican immigrant labor.

Chapter 1: The Bracero Program, 1942–1964 uses the testimonies of ex-Braceros on their experiences and explains how the program officially sanctioned migrant labor streams to every region of the US. It also demonstrates how this 22-year guest-worker program shaped contemporary patterns of labor immigration. Chapter 2: Operation Wetback, 1954 introduces the central contradiction in US immigration policy by examining the events of this dubiously named repatriation program. It concludes with a discussion of how the 1965 Immigration and Nationality Act (INA) unintentionally opened migration from Latin America and Asia. Its family reunification provisions as well as the skills-based criteria for admittance into the US have drastically changed the face of migration. The INA is a crucial bridge between one partially closed chapter in Mexico-US relations (with the end of the Bracero Program) and an opening of a new one in the Mexican immigrant experience (the making of Mexican immigrants as undocumented and, by extension, criminalized as illegal).

But Mexican immigrants have not passively accepted their marginalization. A great deal of resistance has been mounted. Part II: Mounting Resistance details the efforts of Mexican immigrants to resist exploitative labor conditions, racialized hierarchies, and long-standing exclusions to citizenship and human rights. This is most fully evidenced by migrant farmworkers who were viewed to be the least organized and least likely to rebel. The United Farm Workers (UFW) landed in the national spotlight with their successfully organized boycott of grape producers and supermarket chains that carried their produce. Chapter 3 discusses the rise of the farmworker civil rights movement. We focus on the recent campaigns by the UFW, Farm Labor Organizing Committee, and Coalition of

Immokalee Workers and their strategies for effective labor organization and class struggle.

Chapter 4: Organized Labor and Mexican Labor Organization explores in much more detail the role and strategies of organized labor in recruiting Mexican immigrant members. Labor organizing efforts were preceded by *mutualistas*, or mutual aid societies, and followed the community unionism model during the Justice for Janitors (J4J) movement initiated by the Service Employees and Industrial Union (SEIU) and similar approaches deployed by United Food and Commercial Workers (UFCW), the Teamsters for Social Justice, the Union of Needletrades, Industrial, and Textiles Employees, and the Hotel Employees and Restaurant Employees Union (UNITE-HERE). Immigrant rights now figure prominently in each of the aforementioned unions, which affiliated in the Change to Win Coalition (CTW), so we also discuss the current immigrant rights movement and non–union based labor organizing in worker centers and hometown associations.

Chapter 5: Backlash and Retrenchment (1980s–1990s) critically interrogates the limited upward mobility of Mexican immigrants due to the resistance mounted by a conservative White majority to turn back the gains made during the Civil Rights era. It situates the politicization of Mexican immigrants as the "alien invader" in public discourse during the last decades of the twentieth century. The general mood of the US can be characterized in terms of the provisions of the 1986 Immigration Reform and Control Act and the California propositions that have led to Mexican immigrant bashing, such as ending bilingual education and public services for undocumented and illegal immigrants.

Part III: Regions examines these processes of labor exploitation, capital accumulation, consumption practices, and the resistance mounted to marginalization as they play out in different regions of the US, Canada, and Mexico. Chapter 6: Mexican Labor in *Aztlán* discusses the contemporary labor trends for Mexicanos living in the Southwestern US by analyzing the service (restaurant and hospitality) industry, day laborers, temporary economy workers, and other industries. We draw upon Mize's ten years of direct work experience as a janitor in office buildings, churches, warehouses, and assembly plants in this chapter.

Chapter 7: Mexican Labor in the Heartland looks at the agricultural, meat-packing, and rural factory production industries. Though one would think that Mexicans were unwanted newcomers to the Midwestern

US if one relied solely on local newspaper accounts, most of these migrant streams began either in the early 1900s or during the second Bracero Program. In fact, Mexican laborers have been doing the bulk of the arduous, low-paying, and dangerous work in the fields and factories of the Midwest for nearly 100 years. With case studies of meat-packing company towns, metropolitan cities (such as Detroit, Gary, and Chicago), and rural agricultural communities throughout the heartland, we examine the current fears of White citizens and the racialization and marginalization of Mexican immigrant workers.

Chapter 8: Mexican Labor in the Hinterlands addresses those regions of the US (predominately the Pacific Northwest, Northeast, and South) that are currently experiencing the largest percent increase of Mexican immigrant laborers. Although recent Mexican immigrants may experience these places as strange new worlds, we document how the second Bracero Program in particular generated most of the migrant streams that led to destinations such as Washington, Oregon, Arkansas, North Carolina, and Georgia. We focus on resistance to this in-migration in the form of rising White supremacist attacks on Mexican immigrants.

Chapter 9: Mexican Labor *en la Frontera* discusses the role of labor along the US-Mexico Border. We consider the role of NAFTA in developing the *maquiladora* system as well as *las maquilas del norte*, the sister distribution plants located on the US side of the border to avoid shipping tariffs, and the assembly plants along the Mexican side of *la linea*. The border represents a unique geographic and economic entity that reshapes relationships and definitions in ways distinct from any other part of the nation-state configuration. The largest land border between an underdeveloped and overdeveloped nation, the US-Mexico border serves as the vantage point where one can best see and feel how globalization is impacting the life chances of all global citizens. The idea of consuming Mexican labor cannot be underestimated along the border.

The final two chapters focus on the nations bound to the US by the passage of NAFTA. Chapter 10: Mexican Labor in Mexico: The Impact of NAFTA from *Chiapas* to *Turismo* focuses on how NAFTA has been used to end collective subsistence farming and to replace it with export agriculture. The impacts of trade liberalization stretch all the way from Mexico's industrial triangle to the tourist industry and the indigenous uprisings in Chiapas. Chapter 11: Mexican Labor in Canada: From Temporary Workers to Precarious Labor starts with the premise that Canada's recent flow of

Mexican labor migrants is experienced much differently than the US. We begin with the history of the migration of Mexican workers to Canada, considering how the NAFTA relationship to migration is in terms of the macrostructures that facilitate the flow of capital and integrated firms but also, increasingly, the flow of labor. Marked differences in Canadian and US immigration law require us to consider how Mexicans have been defined as seasonal laborers, family class, economic immigrants, and humanitarian cases or refugees. The safeguards and worker guarantees in the Mexican Seasonal Agricultural Workers Program identify an exceptional approach to utilizing temporary laborers that scholars such as Basok (2002) deftly contrast with US state-sanctioned programs. However, our aim is not to take the Canadian exceptionalism argument too far, and thus we compare the agricultural program to what Goldring, Berinstein, and Bernhard (2007) refer to as the "precarious status" of Mexican immigrants in relation to Canadian immigration law. Finally, we present regional analyses of emerging Mexican labor markets in Canada and of campaigns to publicize and protect the rights of Mexican immigrants in order to demonstrate how Canadian consumption patterns are increasingly defining Mexican labor migration in this NAFTA era. These chapters show that contemporary Mexican immigration cannot be understood without a hemispheric perspective. Politics in Canada and Mexico reveal that US policies in fact create the patterns of immigration that are subsequently framed as a "problem" by the Right.

In the Conclusion, we summarize each chapter's key findings and expand on contemporary issues in relation to historical injustices and current strategies for improving the life chances of Mexican laborers. We discuss proposals of liberal adjustments to reparations, social democratic forms of redress, and transformative politics originating in truth commissions for Mexican laborers. From liberal adjustments to the California Agricultural Labor Board to a return to the civil rights agenda with economic rights at the forefront, we discuss possibilities for expanding labor unions to Chicanos in the hinterlands and Midwest as well as cross-border labor networks in an age of increasing globalization and NAFTA. Solutions to the exploitation of undocumented labor will bring the role of the immigrant rights movement and network politics to the center of recent efforts at transforming the conditions of Mexicans residing in the US as well as addressing conditions in Mexico. To transform the North American consumption of Mexican labor, we will discuss movements that involve people across national, racial, and ethnic lines, and across borders, and that are guided by the acknowledgement that no one is free when anyone is oppressed.

Notes

1. See Yanz and Smith (1983), Piore (1979), and Mize (1996) for discussions of the limits of the industrial reserve army thesis as applied to contemporary migrant laborers.

2. In the recent focus on Mexican immigrant communities, the best exemplars draw from early Chicano historiography situated at the city or state level. Sanchez's (1993) analysis of Los Angeles, Mario T. García (1981) on El Paso, Matt Garcia (2001) on Orange County, CA, Foley (1997) on the Texas cotton belt, and Martinez's (1994, 1988, 1975a) studies of the border region exemplify the delimited spatial approach. At the state level, Acuña's (2010) seminal textbook follows a state-by-state focus while Montejano (1987) on Texas, Deutsch (1987) on Colorado and New Mexico, and Almaguer (1994) on California expand their respective analyses beyond bounded communities. From Chicano/a labor history, Zavella (1987), Ruiz (1987), Vargas (2007, 1999), Valdes (1991), and Weber (1996) detail the shared Chicano working-class experience and bring together the aforementioned topics, above and beyond their spatial limitations, into a coherent field of inquiry.

3. The research on consumption is extremely wide-ranging. Some scholars explicitly draw from the pioneering Thorsten Veblen (1994 [1899]), who introduced the world to "conspicuous consumption" in his *The Theory of the Leisure Class* (see Hochschild and Ehrenreich 2004; Schor 1999). Others are engaging, and most often rejecting, the "culture industries" that Adorno (2001) and Horkheimer and Adorno (2002) identified in their seminal essay on the manufacture of culture (see Ritzer 2004; Willis 1978; and du Gay 2009; du Gay et al., 1997). From studies of transnational migrants in a global era, the intimate connections between affluent consumers and immigrant service laborers is well-covered in the global movement of Filipina nurses and domestics (see Choy 2003; Tadiar 2009; and Salazar Parreñas 2001). Finally, the work on Mexican and Central American maids, nannies, and childcare providers in Los Angeles (Hondagneu-Sotelo 2007, 1994) and the post-NAFTA transnational employment options for the Mexican working class, as detailed in Alvarez (2005), are important precursors to our discussion of how the vital relations of consumption and production are lived out between affluent

Americans (both as consumers and owners of capital) and working-class Mexican immigrants in the postwar US.

4. The development of Appadurai's approach to cultural consumption as it relates to the emerging phenomena of globalization is foregrounded by his introduction to *The Social Life of Things* (1986). Beginning with another central dichotomy that has plagued the origins of modernity since the rise of the European Enlightenment is the distinction between gifts and commodities. The former are posited to be pre-modern, in the sense developed by Mauss (2000), and the latter defined as integral to the advent of capitalism (see Marx and Appadurai's preferred take by Simmel 1972). The distinction between the West and the Rest is often how a barter economy is defined as pre-modern in comparison to a modern capitalist economy based on exchange values and the circulation of money as the universal commodity. This misses the crucial point in Appadurai's critique of Marx (a criticism that more so applies to Mauss and the origins of anthropology), which is that the basis for all commodities is sensuous human labor. To speak of the consumption of commodities is to understand how consumption (or exchange) is inextricably bound to production and to speak of consumers is to speak of producers. In the third chapter of *Modernity at Large* (1996), Appadurai dissects the Veblen effect of viewing consumption practices solely through the lens of conspicuous consumption and argues that consumption becomes habituated over time by all social actors. His analysis avoids the damning critique of power that Veblen so strongly deploys in his *Theory of the Leisure Class*, but similar to his critique of Marx in his first book, Appadurai subjects Veblen to an immanent critique to create a more robust theory of consumption that is sensitive to time and space contexts. Appadurai speaks of the work of consumption-based time discipline as: "the equivalent of [E.P.] Thompson's time discipline now reigns not just in the realm of production but also in the realm of consumption. But tied as it is to uneven, complex, and often long periodicities, these temporal disciplines of consumption are more powerful because they are less transparent than the disciplines of production" (1996, 82).

5. We identify this simultaneous inversion and mystification in Marx's sense as he described in *The German Ideology*:

> Consciousness can never be anything else than conscious existence, and the existence of men is their actual life-process. If in all ideology men and their circumstances appear upside-down as in a *camera obscura*, this phenomenon arises just as much from their historical life-process as the inversion of objects on the retina does

from their physical life-process. In direct contrast to German philosophy which descends from heaven to earth, here we ascend from earth to heaven. That is to say, we do not set out from what men say, imagine, conceive, nor from men as narrated, thought of, imagined, conceived, in order to arrive at men in the flesh. We set out from real, active men, and on the basis of their real life-process we demonstrate the development of the ideological reflexes and echoes of this life-process. The phantoms formed in the human brain are also, necessarily, sublimates of their material life-process, which is empirically verifiable and bound to material premises. Morality, religion, metaphysics, all the rest of ideology and their corresponding forms of consciousness, thus no longer retain the semblance of independence. They have no history, no development; but men, developing their material production and their material intercourse, alter, along with this their real existence, their thinking and the products of their thinking. Life is not determined by consciousness, but consciousness by life. In the first method of approach the starting-point is consciousness taken as the living individual; in the second method, which conforms to real life, it is the real living individuals themselves, and consciousness is considered solely as their consciousness. (Marx 1845)

6. As we focus on the systematic exploitation of Mexican immigrants' labor, we recognize that neoliberal globalization is not actually good for anyone. African Americans are systematically imprisoned and unemployed. White rural poor people are systematically unemployed and underemployed. Workers face unemployment and foreclosures as companies downsize and outsource. Resources are extracted and toxics are dumped on Native American land. Even as they accumulate wealth, capitalists and consumers are alienated, bored, anxious, depressed, stressed out, and longing for fulfillment and community. We recognize the potential that all these forms of exploitation, exclusion, degradation, and alienation generate resistances as people organize collectively, realizing that our fate is interconnected. Grassroots organizing efforts reflect attempts to remake community and redefine ways of relating.

part I
Establishing Connections

Introduction

The Bracero Program was the first and largest formal guest-worker program initiated by the US government at the behest of the agribusiness and railroad sectors. It was clearly a message to the Mexican government and its people that Mexicans were wanted in the US to do the dirty and difficult work that US citizens abstained from doing themselves. At the very time the program was in full gear, the US government initiated a border enforcement and repatriation program, dubiously dubbed "Operation Wetback," which sent the contradictory message that the US in fact did not want Mexicans toiling on its soil. Chapters 1 and 2 explore this central contradiction, placing the Bracero Program and Operation Wetback within the larger framework that links US consumption, capital accumulation, and Mexican labor exploitation.

Social scientists study migration at its most basic level in terms of factors of attraction and repulsion or the push-pull model of migration. For Mexican immigrants recruited to work in the North, these push-pull factors are rooted within the contradictory dialectic of the US tendency to rest consumption practices squarely on the backs of Mexican laborers even as many disdain the Mexicans who reside there.

Table I.1: *Timeline of Establishing Connections*

Date	Event
August 4, 1942	US-Mexico Bracero Program begins in Stockton, California, as US government responds to wartime requests by Southwest growers to recruit foreign labor.
October 13–18, 1948	In what became known as the "El Paso Incident," Texas growers defy the terms of the binational Bracero Program and their state's blacklist by imploring the Border Patrol to open the border for the recruitment of 6,000 undocumented migrant workers.
1952	As part of the passage of the McCarran-Walter Immigration and Nationality Act, a little-known provision, the temporary visa (H-2) program, authorizes East Coast growers to employ Caribbean laborers.
1954	Operation Wetback begins a mass repatriation campaign.
1964	Bracero Program ends, but over its 22-year period of operation, more than 4.5 million work contracts were signed, representing approximately 2 million temporary workers from Mexico.
1965	Hart-Celler Immigration and Nationality Act is passed.
December 2007	Mexican government offers "cash assistance" payments of US$3,700 to former Braceros. The government accepts no culpability for past wrongs. On October 12, 2008, US judge Charles Breyer allows ex-Braceros residing in the US to file claims at Mexican consular offices between October 23, 2008, and January 5, 2009.

Chapter One

The Bracero Program, 1942–1964

The Bracero Program was extremely important in codifying existing migrant streams and constructing new streams to every region of the continental US. Its large scale meant that temporary workers — or Braceros — were often herded more like cattle than people through migration, recruitment, processing, transportation, housing, boarding, and work. Though certain guarantees were placed in individual work contracts, the testimony of former Braceros shows that contracts were rarely, if ever, enforced on behalf of workers' rights. The Bracero Program was highly successful in creating a readily exploitable workforce but rarely protected the paltry rights accorded to workers.

From 1942 to 1964, the federal governments of the US and Mexico arranged a set of accords that supplied US agricultural growers, and for a brief time the railroad industry, with a steady stream of Mexican labor. Initially intended to serve as a wartime relief measure, the temporary-worker arrangements were allowed to continue until 1964. The vast majority of workers were sent to three states (California, Arizona, and Texas), but altogether 30 states participated in the program (see Table 1.1).[1] A total of 4.5 million work contracts were signed over the 22-year period, representing approximately 2 million Braceros employed by agribusiness. The current almost total reliance by US large-scale agriculture on Mexican nationals (legal, undocumented, and contracted) can be traced back to its origins in the Bracero Program.

Deciding to migrate to the US was the first step on the road to becoming a Bracero. Don Andre de Guanajuato describes the conditions in Mexico that forced his departure: "Well, there was a lot of poverty, much poverty, and one had to leave out of necessity, not because of pleasure, for necessity so that one could progress a little, right. And because with family

Table 1.1: *Braceros Contracted by US Region and State, 1942–47, 1952*

	Workers Contracted (1942–47)	Workers Contracted (1952)	Workers Employed on December 31, 1952
Southwest	**146,744**	**173,371**	**66,467**
Arizona	5,975	19,618	12,491
California	124,305	63,197	18,031
Colorado	7,643	4,959	0
Nevada	2,577	45	0
New Mexico	151	23,307	9,211
Texas	0	60,432	26,710
Utah	3,361	355	24
Wyoming	2,732	1,458	0
Midwest	**31,625**	**9,409**	**111**
Illinois	1,083	302	0
Indiana	382	483	0
Iowa	3,033	149	0
Kansas	796	25	0
Michigan	7,516	3,972	3
Minnesota	5,288	19	0
Missouri	0	2,837	88
Nebraska	4,039	1,139	20
North Dakota	3,094	0	0
Ohio	0	19	0
South Dakota	1,577	147	0
Wisconsin	4,817	317	0
South	**410**	**30,247**	**517**
Arkansas	0	28,363	500
Georgia	0	596	0
Louisiana	0	822	17

	Workers Contracted (1942–47)	Workers Contracted (1952)	Workers Employed on December 31, 1952
Mississippi	0	60	0
North Carolina	410	0	0
Tennessee	0	406	0
Northwest	**51,891**	**4,951**	**93**
Idaho	11,088	326	1
Montana	12,767	1,841	0
Oregon	13,007	823	91
Washington	15,029	1,961	1
TOTAL	**230,670**	**217,978**	**67,188**

Sources: Adapted from Rasmussen 1951 and Lyon 1954, 225.

one had to help my mother and brothers, there were nine siblings in my family... well, that is why we would go over there as Braceros" (Interview 2005).[2] Potential Braceros had to obtain letters of support from local government officials, get their names on lists of potential contractees, and finance their transportation to the nearest recruitment center. Passage to the US was complicated by the Mexican government's habit of shifting the locations of recruitment centers. Processing centers in the US facilitated the batch handling of Braceros, including medical and prior work experience examinations. The men were humiliated throughout, demonstrating their marginalization in both Mexico and the US.

Once in labor camps, Braceros' lives were thoroughly managed and subject to intense surveillance. Mass transportation, housing, and boarding continued their batch handling. As we shall see below, scholars confirm that their living conditions were akin to military barracks and mess halls. But these men were not soldiers; they were guest-workers hired to do a job. Unlike other laborers in the US, Braceros were not allowed private lives. If they lodged a complaint about negative treatment, they risked reprisal in the form of deportation. They were not allowed to shift to another job because contracts stated that they could be deported for doing so. To answer why they chose this existence rather than life in Mexico requires closer attention to the hacienda system.

Deciding to Migrate

Why do people move? What can we learn from the Braceros' stories about their migration experiences? Life stories provide substantial insights into the conditions that Mexicans faced when considering migrating to the US. Señor Palmas, a vendor who supplied tortillas to Braceros in Colorado, stated:

> Why are those guys willing to leave their families, their culture, their language, everything that they've ever known? I can't imagine waking up in the morning and saying, "I'm tired of all this bullshit. I'm tired of the Spanish. I'm tired of my religion. I'm tired of my culture. I'm tired of my family. I'm going to the United States." I don't believe that that's the way it happens. OK. What happens is that his level of existence, the economic level, is somewhere in the neighborhood of flat-ass desperation. (Interview 1997)

Manuel Gamio was one of the first scholars to study Mexican migration to the US and, in *The Life Story of the Mexican Immigrant* (1931), found that "reasons for migrating" stories had three recurrent themes: the Mexican revolution, the good money to be made, and the friends and community members (who were former migrants) who coaxed others to migrate.[3] Don Jorge Colima notes that he

> ... started working when I was 11 years old, in the fields. Over in our country there's work for the children, cutting lemons, oranges ... there's a lot of work that children and women do. There they would plant cucumbers, cantaloupe, and watermelon. There was plenty of work there. But sometimes one would have to venture out to see if there was more, or better, work elsewhere. The money one earns is usually spent day to day. There's not an opportunity to save money, to buy a house, it is just to survive. (Interview 1997)

Friends and family who previously migrated influenced many Braceros to begin securing work contracts. Don Jorge continues: "I came to the United States because I had a lot of friends, who were older than me, and they were already coming to the United States. And they would tell me that it is pretty, and there's a lot of work and all. But I could not come because I was doing my military service." Stories of the relative wealth one could accrue in the US also contributed to the decision to leave. As Hector Coahuila said: "It's the money. Once you get used to having the money, it keeps you coming" (Interview 1997). Most heard about the Bracero Program from fellow community members, not from mass-media sources (Galarza 1964; Interview, Don Ramon Sinaloa 2005).

> **Interviewer:** How did you find out about the Bracero Program?
> **Don Crecencio:** Through Rosendo. He was a neighbor of ours.... He was the one that invited me. I did not know anything. I did not have experience in anything. He said, "Let's go North." I said "With what? There is no money." (Interview 2005)

In some cases, men decided for their families; in other cases, family members decided for them. Every state in Mexico participated in the program, but the majority of Braceros were sent from the agriculture-rich central valley states of Guanajuato, Michoacán, Jalisco, and Zacatecas, as well the northern border state of Chihuahua (see Table 1.2). During World War II, the only recruitment center was in the capital city, so many Braceros then were residents of the Federal District.

Braceros saw remittances as the key to a better life, allowing them to provide their families with small appliances (sewing machines, dry-cell battery radios, and small electronics) and savings (no matter how meager they might have been). A glimpse at US standards of living encouraged a large number of Braceros to settle in the US with their families.

The Recruitment Centers in Mexico

The Mexican government touted the recruitment process as "free," yet none of the Braceros interviewed were able to find these "free" contracts. There were fees associated with every step of the process of becoming eligible for work in the US. Some local government officials charged fees for providing a letter that stated there would not be a labor shortage if this person left his village or town.[4] Another informal arrangement circumvented this process by putting a person able to pay at least 500 pesos directly on the list. The majority of those interviewed took the latter route. The final means of securing paperwork consisted of buying papers from men who decided they could no longer wait outside the recruiting centers.

Braceros also paid for transportation to travel from their homes to the recruitment centers, which were moved three times during the program's

Table 1.2: *Braceros by Mexican State of Origin, 1942–46 and 1951–64*

	1942–August 1946 Total Number	% of Total	1951–64 Total Number	% of Total
Aguascalientes	8,137	2.52	80,970	1.89
Baja California	0	0.00	21,078	0.49
Campeche	723	0.22	1,256	0.03
Coahuila	3,466	1.07	191,074	4.47
Colima	0	0.00	12,190	0.28
Chiapas	330	0.10	1,473	0.03
Chihuahua	5,203	1.61	434,938	10.17
Durango	8,818	2.73	386,260	9.03
Federal District	144,401	44.67	44,431	1.04
Guanajuato	23,829	7.37	567,514	13.27
Guerrero	6,793	2.10	133,821	3.13
Hidalgo	5,544	1.72	33,712	0.79
Jalisco	7,258	2.25	465,396	10.88
México	3,235	1.00	79,288	1.85
Michoacán	32,082	9.93	463,811	10.84
Morelos	2,743	0.85	38,376	0.90
Nayarit	0	0.00	46,660	1.09
Nuevo León	0	0.00	185,311	4.33
Oaxaca	10,766	3.33	126,453	2.96
Puebla	3,382	1.05	63,381	1.48
Querétaro	3,598	1.11	50,853	1.19
Quintana Roo	0	0.00	75	0.00
San Luis Potosí	6,440	1.99	211,703	4.95
Sinaloa	0	0.00	42,546	0.99
Sonora	0	0.00	44,527	1.04
Tabasco	5,813	1.80	16,032	0.37
Tamaulipas	5,883	1.82	56,652	1.32
Tlaxcala	3,504	1.08	29,430	0.69

	1942–August 1946 Total Number	% of Total	1951–64 Total Number	% of Total
Veracruz	6,659	2.06	10,802	0.25
Yucatán	261	0.08	47,285	1.11
Zacatecas	24,364	7.54	390,061	9.12
TOTAL	323,232		4,277,359	

Sources: Secretaría 1946; Garcia 1980.

tenure. The Mexican government wanted the centers close to the major sending areas of central Mexico. The US government, to ease transportation costs for growers, pushed to have them along the border. A publication by the Mexican government's *Secretaría del Trabajo y Previsión Social* (Secretaría 1946) stated that the Mexican government wanted to use the program to alleviate unemployment in populous central Mexico, possibly even in urban areas with high unemployment. On the other hand, US growers wanted seasoned veterans (i.e., *campesinos*) because this minimized their training expenses.[5]

The changing locations shifted the economic burdens of travel expenses from the US government and growers to the Braceros themselves. Mexico's northern border states—Baja California, Sonora, Chihuahua, Coahuila, Nuevo León, and Tamaulipas—sent only 21.92 per cent of all Braceros contracted to work in the US from 1951 to 1964 (Garcia 1980). The remaining 78 per cent shouldered the increased cost of a bus ride or train ticket to Sonora, Chihuahua, or Nuevo León. Often, workers had to request loans from local elites. Don Jorge, who lived in Colima, traveled less than 200 miles to the recruitment center in Irapuato, Guanajuato. The cost of his bus ticket there was minimal compared to the hardships he endured once he was almost 700 miles from home:

> Then I returned again, April or May 1958. This time I went to Monterrey, Mexico. We were there three months in the streets. There were so many people there, we just had to wait and see who was chosen, and finally they contracted us. At that time there was money sent to me from home to get back because I could no longer afford to stay there. But when the money got there I was contracted. (Interview 1997)

Cities hosting recruitment centers became way-stations, their streets temporary homes for those waiting for their numbers to be called. This tended to be the most difficult period for would-be Braceros because they had to wait at great personal expense in an unfamiliar city, often without housing or jobs. If he was lucky enough to be contracted, a worker's experiences in the recruitment centers suddenly taught him he was to be mass-handled. The US counterparts of the Mexican recruitment centers reproduced the practices of batch handling, humiliation, and dehumanization.

US Border Processing Centers

A small number of processing centers were opened on the US side of the border to connect Braceros with growers. Eagle Pass, Texas, was the main center for grower associations that recruited workers in the East and Midwest. El Paso was the way station for the Rocky Mountain states and the Midwest. Calexico and El Centro, located in the Imperial Valley, processed workers headed for California and the Pacific Northwest. At these processing centers Braceros were deloused, given medical exams, and processed *en masse*: "Upon arrival at the US labor reception center, the worker and his luggage are thoroughly dusted with DDT powder as a sanitary measure and to prevent insects from being brought into the US. His [the Bracero's] next stop is for a chest X-ray, then for a photograph for passport purposes" (Colorado Agricultural Experiment Station 1958, 63).[6] As Don Ramon recalled, "They would take off our clothes and would throw powder on us and it had a small smell like DDT" (Interview 2005). What Don Andre best remembered also were the mass medical examination and delousing procedure:

> [W]hen we got there to the revisions where they would pass us they would disrobe us, disrobe us. And they would pull the penis like that [demonstrates using finger how foreskin was pulled back] to check to see if they had gonorrhea or some infection. En Empalme? [he asks the wife sitting across the room]. And then they would open your anus to see if you had hemorrhoids. And the doctor would stick a finger to those who had a hernia. If you had these, you would not go. All of that. All of that. They would disrobe you completely then they would fumigate you. All of us were healthy, the majority of us we were young. Only the older people ... would not go; it was mostly the young people. I was 23–24 years of age. But those were their requirements. (Interview 2005)

The experience of the ordeal was best captured by Don Crecencio's comment that it made him feel ugly. He said he changed after the exam. His word choice is crucial: what was changed was not only his clothes but also the man.

> **Don Crecencio:** I am not sure what I would feel. I felt ugly in those terms because what the Americans would do to us [laughs]. They would fumigate us, then one had to go take a shower. One then changed.
>
> **Interviewer:** Why have you never forgotten what they did to you?
>
> **Don Crecencio:** No, because we were all naked. We were all naked. They would fumigate us and all. It was really hard in that time. (Interview 2005)

The stated purpose of the selection process was to find the most experienced men who would not require training in the US fields. Don Jorge recalled, "The first time I came I was placed in Sonora.... They would check your hands, how they looked, and if some had calluses on their hands 'oh, come over here.' But if your hands were clean, they would say, 'no, you're a secretary.' And I, ever since I was young, I worked in the fields, I had huge balls of calluses" (Interview 1997). The processing centers were responsible for delivering a homogenous product. The Braceros were touted as disease-free, unattached, hard-working, experienced and, above all, subservient young men.

The Standard Work Contract and Recontracting

The Bracero contract was signed by the grower or growers' association, a Mexican government official, a US Department of Labor representative, and the worker. It specified the work tasks, duration of contract, and pay rate. Unfortunately, growers and their intermediaries systematically ignored all three provisions. The individual work contract specifically barred Braceros from engaging in non-agricultural work and operating farm machinery, but many stated that they operated tractors and installed irrigation pipe while under contract. A World War II–era Bracero claimed that he was contracted as a "janitor—someone to clean streetcars and trains transporting wounded soldiers from ports in Los Angeles" (Hanrahan 1999).[7]

Even though the pay rate was specified on every individual work contract, there was no guarantee that workers would be paid that amount. Deductions from paychecks included legitimate expenses such as boarding and non-occupational insurance but were at times supplemented with illegal deductions for room, board, transportation, and farm tools and supplies. Even if all of the rules were followed and deductions were legitimate, growers still held a comparative advantage over non-agricultural employers in the US because agriculture was specifically exempt from minimum-wage laws.

The work contract also specified whether pay was based on a piece or hourly rate. The Bracero arrangements guaranteed that the wages paid would be equal to those paid to American workers for similar jobs in the respective regions of the US (Secretaría 1946, 85). Some current research (i.e., Grove 1996; Calavita 1992) assumes that the wage guarantees were in fact a reality, since growers complained about them and the US government agreed to them in writing. The standard work contract did state how much the worker would be earning for each crop he was contracted to harvest, but direct testimonies by Braceros attest to the cunning of authority in remuneration practices. Workers never really knew how much they were making from week to week. The availability of work, number of hours worked per day, shifting wage schedule (piece or hourly), amount of deductions, and changing pay rate all allowed the growers to pay the wages they deemed appropriate, regardless of what had been contracted.

Wages varied a great deal, but the few who could earn what was guaranteed to them did so only by working extremely long hours. In 1946, Washington State pea farmers boasted that their workers averaged $90 per week, but to do so they had to work 15-hour days, seven days a week, at 85 cents per hour (Gamboa 1990, 88). Since the minimum wage for non-agricultural jobs in the US was 75 cents per hour and agricultural work was exempt from minimum-wage laws, the 85-cent hourly wage was, in fact, rarely paid. After deductions for non-occupational medical insurance, board, and transportation, wages were rarely enough to live on in either the US or Mexico. Since most Braceros sent upwards of 80 to 90 per cent of their paychecks back to Mexico, they barely subsisted on their meager earnings in the US.[8]

The standard work contract stated the amount that would be deducted for food. As Galarza (n.d., Box 3, Folder 1) notes, the $1.75 per week maximum deduction set by the government was translated into the minimum amount deducted by growers. This amount was intended to guarantee that Braceros would be charged at cost for the food prepared. Other deductions officially sanctioned by the agreement was a mandatory non-occupational health insurance policy that cost Braceros $3 per month ($3.50 at one camp that Galarza surveyed). "In conforming with the established international rules and contracts, of the amount paid to the Mexican braceros of their salary ten percent was deposited into a savings fund [in Mexican National Banks] for each worker" (Secretaría 1946, 88). This money would not be returned to the Bracero until he fulfilled the conditions of his contract and had returned to Mexico. Galarza (n.d., Box 18, Folder 6) also exposed the illegal deductions made by growers in the Salinas, California, area where some Braceros were charged for blankets and even for the twist ties used in banding carrots together.

Under the terms of the International Agreement signed on August 1, 1949, contracts for work in sugar beets could not be for less than six weeks; employment in cotton could not be less than three months; for all other employment, the contract period was no less than four months, and no contract could be for more than six months. However, with the consent of the Mexican consulate, the worker, the US Employment Service, and the INS, workers could be contracted for additional periods provided that he remained in the US no longer than one year (US President's Commission 1951, 46).

Most often, the Mexican Bracero was the sole signatory expected to fulfill his portion of the agreement. "If you violated the 45-day contract and didn't come home on time, they wouldn't renew your contract. They wouldn't let you go back," according to Don Liberio (Interview 1997). At their own discretion, growers could extend the worker's stay, regardless of whether they were violating the contract's maximum six-month period. While under contract, Don Francisco worked for the same association in Santa Clara, California, for three months, then re-contracted because he was *told* he had to stay (Interview 1997). Because of their limited bargaining power and the huge amount of effort and money required to gain the "free" contracts from the Mexican government, many Braceros decided it would be easier to stay in Mexico or come over illegally rather than subject themselves to harsh conditions that they could not alter.

The US government was charged with enforcing grower compliance. The Department of Labor was enlisted to check compliance with wage contracts, and housing conditions were supposed to be monitored by state housing authorities. A former housing commission officer, Mr. Allen, provides substantial insight into what happened to Mexican migrants after their contract ended:

> Well, a lot of places what they would do is tell these people that they would hold the money for them and give it to them when they left. And then call the Border Patrol themselves, and then Border Patrol comes and picks them up, and if they didn't do something the guy's gone and his money is still here. Some crew bosses did that and some growers did that. (Interview 1997)

The fact that the agencies in charge of monitoring compliance were severely understaffed made it difficult, if not impossible, to ensure that growers met the stipulations of the contract, both during and after the program. Mr. Allen was one of two housing inspectors for the entire rural region of Colorado.

Braceros and Mass Transportation

While Braceros had to save to pay their own way to the recruitment centers in Mexico, employers "would pay all transportation costs and guarantee the workers' return to their points of origin" (Scruggs 1960, 145). Yet the majority still had to cover transportation expenses after their work contract expired. Growers were expected to be responsible for transportation from the recruitment centers to processing centers, but the US government covered the expenses initially. No similar subsidy was made available to Braceros who had to find transportation to the recruitment centers in Mexico. Transportation from US processing centers to labor camps was the sole responsibility of growers or more often the associations that represented them. According to Señor Paulo, a bus driver for Braceros in Southern Colorado, "the bus ride was direct with one stop for food. It was the law that the men had to be fed one meal. They stopped at a diner or restaurant where the Braceros purchased their own meals. A ride on the 24-passenger bus lasted for 15 hours from the processing center in El Paso to the labor camps in the San Luis Valley" (Interview 1997). The law he mentions was intended for the safe steerage of livestock but was subsequently applied for worker protection.

Once the Braceros settled into the labor camps, they had to be transported to and from their various work sites. This transportation resulted in the largest number of accidents and safety violations they experienced, according to Ernesto Galarza (1977), who was commissioned to conduct a study of unsafe transportation practices during the Bracero Program. He found drivers who were overworked, mandatory rest stops that were ignored, and too many workers loaded onto flatbed trucks without any safety rails or harnesses. Many of the buses and trucks involved in accidents did not meet code, and drivers were not qualified to drive the vehicles they operated or had expired licenses. State regulation of the wanton disregard of safety measures was poor or non-existent.

Galarza investigated a bus accident in Chualar, California, that left 31 Braceros dead. A converted flatbed truck that formerly hauled vegetables had been equipped with a canopy to make it a "labor transporter" and collided with a moving train. In Visalia, California, an accident occurred during a driver's second trip in one night. While transporting re-contracted Braceros from El Centro to the San Joaquin Valley, after a trip to the Valley from the Coachella Valley, the driver fell asleep and the truck ran off the road, killing two and injuring 15 (Galarza n.d., Box 17, Folder 2). The driver's total mileage behind the wheel exceeded 800 miles within 24 hours. Galarza (1977, 86) notes other accidents occurring in September 1963 near Woodland, California, and in the Imperial Valley.

Transportation also served the purpose of controlling the workers. Since Braceros were required to get to the job sites or the local community by means of grower-provided transport, they were subject to the schedules of the buses and trucks: "Large concentrations of aliens in camp barracks call for mass transportation, quite different from the sort of transportation that domestic laborers, in family groups of neighborhood car pools, used in years past" (Galarza 1977, 87). Mass transportation, coupled with lax safety enforcement on the part of the state, put many Braceros directly in harm's way. Such accidents were one of the most unfortunate — yet easily preventable — aspects of the program.[9]

Workplace Resistance and Squashing Discontent

During the Bracero Program, the threat of returning a contractee to Mexico if he did not meet the demands of the job without complaint was usually enough for workers to conform to grower expectations. Growers were not compelled to respond to worker protests, and the stakes for resisting were particularly high. If a worker did not comply, he was deported. If he caused a ruckus or started making demands for better working conditions, he was deported. Growers could rely on fear rather than violence to keep workers in line because workers were made well aware of the history of state agents, usually local law officers, who were recruited to do the dirty work of punishment. Yet workers did resist, individually and collectively, even given the reprisals that further pushed them to the margins of subsistence. The power imbalance was often too great for the worker to begin seriously talking about leverage in negotiations. Asked about working conditions, one said:

> Three days ago our crew stopped work right in the field. There were 50 men in the group. It was explained by one of the men who could express himself that it was not our desire to make a strike but we wanted to have eight hours work or to have our board without charge if we worked only one or two hours. The foreman said that assuredly there would be plenty of work and we went back to cutting. The next day the bracero who had spoken for us was not in the camp. The foreman said he had been taken to the Association but he did not know the motive. In the field, the boss said there are plenty more where we came from if we were disgusted. I have read my contract, but it is not worth the pain to insist on the clauses. Here, the contract has no value. (Galarza 1956, 18)

If Braceros wanted to continue working, they had to accept a pay schedule that changed from day to day, cope with rancid food that was deducted from wages, and accept illegal deductions for blankets and work supplies. They had to live in whatever housing was provided, whether a tent or a "converted" barn or chicken coop. They risked personal safety riding in overcrowded flatbed trucks. They had to be willing to endure the loneliness and isolation of living in a country whose language they did not speak and in a labor camp where surveillance was the order of the day and outside contact was infrequent or non-existent. The central means for ensuring that they would suffer these deplorable conditions was the threat, implied or actual, that they would be replaced if they publicly voiced their grievances.

To control the workforce, outright intimidation was not often necessary because the expectation of powerlessness was drilled into workers even before they arrived in the US. Galarza (n.d., Box 3, Folder 1) noted how Braceros were indoctrinated by Mexican government officials at the contracting centers:

> You are going to be representatives of Mexico in the US. Be an example of honesty and show what good workmen you are. Do not spend your money there but send it home. Don't go on strikes or make trouble for your *patrones*. Remember, if you make good, you will be wanted again and again in the future.

Even if they were intimidated or threatened, most Braceros did not see reporting bad practices as a viable option. Deportation was the most common fate for agitators who attempted to convince others to strike or participate in work stoppages. Señor Palmas, the Colorado food vendor, recalls what Braceros failed to mention in their recollections:

> Any infraction by any one of those individuals would constitute immediate deportation in terms of conduct, insubordination, or this type of thing. They weren't mistreated or anything, they simply… you're gone. You violated the terms of the contract… and you were gone. It was as simple as that. At some point there was guys that were kind of chow-hall lawyers type of people, you know what I mean. And I got to see plenty of this. These guys says "You know these conditions aren't going to work," he says, "this, this and this." And I see him standing on the table… if you want to call it inciting these guys to go on strike and call for better conditions. Well, this guy would be immediately deported simply because he was upsetting the balance of the whole operation. Of course, there are always those people that would follow anything that pops up. But anybody like that would immediately be deported and that's the end of that. His contract, in other words, would be ended.
>
> **Interviewer:** Did this happen a lot?
>
> **Señor Palmas:** There's only two camps that I saw this actually happen. Now I heard about it in other camps.… Normally they were guys with a little bit of educational background, a little bit, well maybe a little bit, more ambitious than the run of the mill Bracero who was up here, who was up here simply to fulfill a contract to make enough money to maybe carry over the rest of the year in Mexico, and that's the end of that. (Interview 1997)

For those few Braceros fortunate enough to remain working after making a complaint, "forms of punishment [are] used by contractors on recalcitrant men who ask for improvements: deprivation of work for one or more days; scheduling the same crew to leave camp last in the morning; keeping men waiting entire day for their pay" (Galarza n.d., Box 3, Folder 1). Galarza also noted what happened to three active resisters: one "[s]poke up for [the] group and got ten days in jail," another died in a fall from a truck, and the third was deported (n.d., Box 18, Folder 1).

Whether the method of deterrence was deportation, punitive working conditions, jail time, or even death, what mattered was the symbolic value of consequences for those who questioned authority or demanded improved conditions. It is scarcely surprising that those with complaints — perhaps 20 to 33 per cent — simply left the program. Those who wanted to continue working under contract remained silent. Braceros were expected to tolerate conditions not of their own making. As they reported in their own interviews, they "endured." For one Bracero who voiced what most knew but were not saying, how workers were treated was of little concern; after all, "we were here to work" (Don Daniel, Interview 1997).

Bracero Labor Camps and Boarding

Bracero life was also subjected to control through the kinds of living conditions imposed upon them, often in compounds or camps that were designed to separate them physically from the rest of society. Conditions within the camps were designed to treat the workers homogeneously, as interchangeable and replaceable. There were three types of housing. First, former Japanese internment camps, in operation during World War II, and government work camps from New Deal programs for employing the Depression-era working poor were used by some associations, growers, and farm labor contractors who leased the grounds. Second, a much less frequent but very important type of housing consisted of houses, barns, tents, and converted chicken coops, most often on small-acreage operations. Finally, grower associations provided the majority of housing in the form of temporary barracks, such as an abandoned school in Blanca, Colorado, and a converted gym in Fort Garland, Colorado. Each camp housed from 35 to 300 Braceros. Placing workers in former Japanese internment camps and in tent colonies was justified by government officials and growers because they felt "Braceros deserved nothing better than their own homes in Mexico" (Gamboa 1990, 93). In California, Galarza noted that the quality of housing was directly related to its visibility to the general population (n.d., Box 3, Folder 1).

Looking at the enforcement of rights for workers reveals a consistent pattern of neglect. Every agency (state or federal, US or Mexican) that had the power to enforce workers' rights lacked not only state-appointed officials to oversee the program but staffing, resources, and at times commitment (Galarza 1956; Gamboa 1990). Housing conditions were rarely visited or questioned by government officials. The state of Colorado investigated labor camps only when a resident or concerned citizen filed a claim. As a result, labor camp conditions rarely came under the government scrutiny dictated by the contract. The camps placed Braceros in similar conditions, cut them off from US society, and dictated that their schedules would center around work. Military-style housing enabled mass handling by keeping workers in a centralized location and allowed for the efficient distribution of labor to meet the short-term needs of growers. The deplorable conditions attest to the lack of regulatory control by the US government. Quite likely, this control was intentionally lax because the logic of a program that would meet the needs of large-scale agribusiness did not coincide with the logic of instituting a strong system to ensure compliance with workers' rights.

The institutional preparation of food was a central component of Bracero life. Food represented the major source not only of deductions from their paychecks but also of discontent. According to the standard work contract, Braceros were to be given a choice whether to prepare their own food or have food prepared for them at cost. In reality, the choice was made for them. Growers were allowed to deduct at most $3.00 a day for food and were expected to give lower rates to those who prepared their own food. Since growers had to provide the necessary items to prepare food, they were allowed to deduct those expenses from wages as well. That maximum became the *de facto* minimum in assessing deductions from paychecks (Galarza 1956). None of those interviewed were able to recall the amount deducted from their pay for food.

In the large camps, food was institutionally prepared, usually by a professional commissary, but several Braceros recalled buying and preparing their own food. Companies, or commissaries that specialized in catering to institutional groups, often submitted bids to grower associations to provide food for the workers. In the San Luis Valley, commissaries handled all food preparation and distribution. The only food item subcontracted to a local business was corn tortillas.

Complaints about bad food abounded. Not only did it often taste bad, but there were many incidents of food poisoning due to rotten provisions. One interviewee mentioned the salty drinking water in a Texas camp where he picked cotton. Gamboa (1990) noted that wage strikes rarely resulted in change, but food strikes were more successful in the short term.

Reports of food illness continuous. Mostly individual reportd [sic]. Planada camp group reported that some 15 men were ill for several days. Some stayed in the hospital for three days until recovered. Cook changed from camp to another after too many men complained of stomach trouble. Men ask what the best laxative is when they discuss stomach troubles with interviewers. Observe kitchen practices closely and criticisms of these practices often leads to "trouble" in the camp when men protest to cook. Practices most common seem to be: use of food left over from previous meals; sour beans; smelly meat. Men report that they have seen no food inspectors in any of the camps. (Galarza n.d., Box 3, Folder 1)

When contracted to work in North Carolina, Don Liberio reported that the food served in the camp occasionally would be rancid. If the workers united and complained, the quality would improve temporarily, but within a couple of days, rancid food would be served again. It was a continuous cycle for the six weeks he spent there (Interview 1997).

Conclusion

The responses of Braceros interviewed in 1997 were shaped by the role expectations enforced during their time as contract workers. They stated in vague terms that times were tough, but they rarely were willing and/or able to give details.

Interviewer: Why not renew?
Don Antonio: Because it was kinda bad, bad, bad. Times got bad. Things were getting bad for them and us and it was time to leave.
Interviewer: Why didn't you apply the following year?
Don Antonio: Because one suffered much trying to get the same contract. It took a lot of effort and money to come over here again. It took a lot of effort to buy a contract to come. It's like today, we had coyotes. The government wouldn't give us a card. They would pocket the money.... The last time they gave me this card [he removes his Bracero identification card from his wallet]. Yeah, but the problem here is they put the wrong date.
Interviewer: Can we make a copy?
Don Antonio: Will this affect me in any way?

Overall, however, Don Antonio presented himself as one who endured, who was willing to sacrifice for the chance to work. His concern over sharing his 39-year-old expired identification card reminds us of his real and sustained fear of retribution, of being perceived as recalcitrant, and of paying a price for that. When asked about the food, housing, and other living conditions, another Bracero, Don Emilio, initially told me "*está bien*" (it was fine).

Interviewer: All the time? You never had problems? I've heard from others that everything was fine. Most of the time it was? What was it like when it wasn't fine?

Don Emilio: Well, they had no beds for us. We slept on the concrete floor. We were given one meal a day. There were no bathrooms. (Interview 1997)

Mize and Sergio Chavez conducted another set of interviews in 2005 with a group of ex-Braceros who were seeking redress for the mandatory savings deductions they never received. Although, as we saw above, the agreement stipulated that the money was to be held for them in a Mexican savings bank, many found upon returning home that it was not available at *Banco Nacional de Crédito Agrícola, Banco de México* (where their funds were transferred from Wells Fargo Bank), or any other designated Mexican federal bank or land trust. The struggle for redress was organized in the Coachella Valley of California with the assistance of labor organizer Ventura Gutiérrez. In Mexico, a march on the capital first brought the savings program issue to the attention of the Mexican public, who are much more cognizant as a whole of the abuse that Braceros endured than are US citizens. Like an earlier march to the soccer stadium where Braceros were processed during World War II, a pilgrimage followed the tracks north to the border recruitment centers. Though the number of protestors was small, the publicity it generated in the media focused the public eye on this historical wrong. The Braceros' deplorable experiences will be best rectified if the movement moves beyond its focus on the savings program to shed light on how all the Braceros' rights were systematically denied.

Alianza Braceroproa, the National Assembly of Ex-Braceros/*La Asamblea Nacional de Ex-Braceros*, and the Binational Union of Former Braceros are the most recognized social movement organizations placing pressure on the Mexican government for monetary redress. Their main means of organizing is to bring ex-Braceros together on a weekly basis to talk about their shared experiences. Most of their conversations have centered on the humiliating aspects of the Mexican processing centers, especially, and quite predictably, on the STD and hernia examinations and the delousing ordeal. By allowing the men to share some of the more unfavorable and humiliating aspects of the program, the redress movement has given them a basis for solidarity. Even though the Mexican government agreed in 2007 to a monetary settlement, referred to as a cash "assistance" payment of US$3,700, collective action has contributed to a shared recognition of past wrongs and to ways of remembering, thinking, speaking, and acting that counter the role expectations imposed on the men during the time they served in the Bracero Program.

Notes

1. One respondent Mize interviewed stated that her father worked in the agricultural fields of New York. Mize has found no official record of Mexican Braceros working in New York agriculture, although Driscoll (1999) finds Mexican railroad workers in New York state.

2. This chapter is based on oral history research conducted by Mize in 1997 and 2005 with former Braceros. The "I" refers to Mize. Those interviewed are identified by pseudonyms to protect their anonymity.

3. The Revolution shaped the stories of later Mexican American generations whose parents, grandparents, and great-grandparents migrated around that time (1910–17). Since then, it was the money to be made, difficult living conditions in Mexico, and friends' encouragement that structured the story of why one migrated.

4. For the elite who had access to Mexican government channels, registering laborers for contracts became their main source of wealth. Like the current day *coyotes* that transport undocumented workers across the border for an exorbitant fee, men with inside connections to local governments sold contracts. Before he could qualify, a potential Bracero had to obtain a letter from the local official stating that there was no labor shortage in the community and he could be spared. This "complimentary" letter actually cost the potential Bracero on average 200 pesos.

5. In 1942, the sole center was in Mexico City. This remained unchanged until 1944 when it closed and operations were relocated to Irapuato and Guadalajara. In 1947, centers were moved to Zacatecas, Chihuahua, Tampico, and Aguascalientes. In 1955, centers were again moved to Monterrey and Hermosillo with the Chihuahua location remaining open. These were all located in northern border states and continued operations until the end of the program in 1964 (Durand 1994, 130).

6. The use of DDT, a pesticide banned for use in the US since the 1970s due to its carcinogenic effect, is documented by the Colorado State Agricultural Bulletin, a credible source of evidence of the "supposed" delousing practice. The article exhibits an explicit Great Western Sugar Company/grower bias, so the identification of the delousing chemical comes from a source that was not

promoting a "pro-labor" agenda. According to the article, the advantages of using Bracero labor are the following: "1. Workers could be moved easily to the beet area at the time they were needed and in numbers which were needed, 2. Workers could be shifted from farm to farm and from area to area as needed, 3. as all people handled were [unattached male] workers, there were no problems of moving and housing women and children, and 4. workers were moved out of the area as soon as the work was done" (Colorado Agricultural Experiment Station 1958, 60–61). During that time, DDT was an extremely popular pesticide and used extensively.

7. There are no US government documents that document Braceros used in any industry other than railroad construction and agricultural work. It is likely that the person interviewed for the story was contracted to work in railroad construction but used for janitorial purposes.

8. Another source for documenting wages, other than self-reports and contract stipulations, is the pay stubs Braceros received with their paychecks. Labor organizer Ernesto Galarza collected hundreds of such pay stubs, which revealed that after deductions and time off due to inclement weather, they were consistently making just enough for themselves and their families in Mexico to subsist. Of the 181 workers that Galarza interviewed in the Salinas area, 160 reported earning less than $40 (net) in a one-week period. The highest weekly net earnings never exceeded $75 for 171 of the 181 interviewed (Galarza n.d., Box 18, Folder 6). The factor that tended to account for the differences in earnings, whether the pay was based on a piece or hourly rate, was the number of hours worked. The more hours in a week worked, and the less the Bracero spent in the US, the more he could send back to Mexico.

9. The statistics on deaths and injuries sustained by Braceros in vehicle accidents are difficult to ascertain. Galarza (1977, 86–87) notes: "The number of accidents of this kind [involving farm laborers] have been reduced steadily from 140 in 1952 to 50 in 1962. But the fatal number of injuries was 13 in the former and 13 in the latter of those years.... In those 11 years, 1953 claimed the record of men killed—28—and 1958 was second with 18. In the month of September 1963, both records were broken with 34 dead, all braceros."

Chapter Two

Operation Wetback, 1954

At the height of the Bracero Program, when over 309,000 contracts were issued, the US government instituted a forced repatriation program that shared many of the insidious aspects of an earlier Depression-era repatriation. As fewer contracts were issued, the number of undocumented migrants from Mexico increased. In 1954, the INS began repatriating these undocumented workers under a program with the name "Operation Wetback."

Undocumented migration followed earlier recruitment patterns by labor contractors and stemmed from the regions of Mexico that sent the largest number of Braceros to the US. Although the US did not take an active stance against undocumented migration until 1986, Operation Wetback led to the eventual mass deportation of, according to the INS, 1.3 million Mexicans, who were mostly undocumented but also legal temporary migrants and US citizens of Mexican descent.

This chapter discusses the rise and role of undocumented labor, particularly in Texas, as a direct result of the phases, or bureaucratic shape-shifting, of a Bracero Program developed to serve the interests of US growers and looks at the operations and methods of repatriation and the impact of Operation Wetback on subsequent INS border enforcement policies. The Mexican government initially restricted Braceros from entering states known for racial or wage discrimination as evidenced in the blacklisting of Texas and its state government's response by forming the "Good Neighbor Commission." The El Paso Incident occurred when Texas growers demanded that the federal government meet their labor demands lest they take matters into their own hands. These actions laid the groundwork for Operation Wetback.

The Blacklisting of Texas: A Case in Confronting Racism
One of the provisions of the Bracero Program arrangement was the Mexican government's insistence that workers not be subject to discriminatory

Table 2.1: *Timeline of Operation Wetback*

Date	Event
August 1953	Attorney General Henry Brownell tours Southern California and decides illegal immigration is a "shocking and unsettling" issue.
May 1954	Brownell hires retired Lieutenant General Joseph Swing to head Immigration Service. His task is to plan and implement Operation Wetback; he hires two generals, Frank Partridge and Edwin Howard, as consultants.
May 11	At a dinner with international labor leaders, *Laredo Times* publisher William Allen is told that Brownell suggested "shooting illegals" as a method of deterrence.
June	Plans are unveiled to punish illegal immigrants, make them subject to mass deportation, and discourage employers from "knowingly" hiring illegal migrants.
June 9	California roundup and deportation begins.
June 10	*Phase One of AZ-CA Operation: Buslift* First Greyhound bus leaves El Centro, California for Nogales, Arizona, with detainees from the San Francisco regional detention center and roadblock inspection captures. A total of 28 buses with 1,008 migrants are shipped to Arizona for rail transport to Mexican interior.
June 17	*Phase Two of AZ-CA Operation: Sweeps* Agricultural regions of Arizona and Southern California are targets of sweeps. INS authorities find a great deal of grower willingness to help identify those without papers.
June 17–July 26	Special detail dispatched in Los Angeles, with assistance of local police, nets 4,403 people, 64 per cent of whom are located in non-agricultural jobs.
June 20	Sweeps continue in same fashion in Central Valley of California by setting up bases in Fresno and Sacramento.
June 24	Bills 3660 and 3661 are introduced in both houses of Congress to deter employers and smugglers from the illegal immigration racket. Neither bill passes.
July 3	First mobile task force deployed in McAllen, Texas, to set up roadblock inspections, inspect trains, and deter migrants from moving northward.
July 15	First day of full operations in Texas. Focus on Lower Rio Grande Valley.

September 3   First deportation via sea. *SS Emancipation* and *SS Vera Cruz* eventually sail the 2,000-mile voyage from Port Isabel, Texas, to Veracruz, Mexico, 26 times, both ships carrying a total of 800 deportees per trip.

September 18   First airlift from Midwest begins. Deportees from Chicago are sent to Brownsville, Texas, followed by airlifts from Saint Louis, Kansas City, Memphis, and Dallas. After flight, most are shipped by sea to Veracruz.

---

treatment. Yet interpersonal and structural racism reached such a fevered pitch in Texas that the Mexican government refused to allow Braceros to go to work there from 1942 to 1947. Texan-style Jim Crow segregation was visibly apparent in public establishments where signs declared "No Dogs Negroes Mexicans" and "We Serve White's [sic] Only, No Spanish or Mexicans" (see Foley 1997). The US railroad industry quickly attempted to circumvent the Texas blacklisting by contracting Braceros outside of the state and then transferring them to work on the tracks in the Texan towns of Monahans and Midland (McCain 1981, 58). The discrimination against these workers was detailed to a representative of the Mexican Foreign Office in September 1943. The Braceros in question contended that they were denied entrance to public places of entertainment, were not permitted to sit at tables in refreshment parlors or to purchase items there except by using the service entrance, and could not patronize barbershops or other places of service except in areas almost inaccessible to them. On the matter of unequal treatment, they complained that they were given straw mattresses while Americans had cotton ones; they had no first-aid kits; they had inadequate bathing facilities and sanitation, as well as overcrowded conditions; and they were charged $1.00 every two weeks for lodgings, a fee that the employer refused to show on payroll slips (McCain 1981, 59). As a result of these complaints, the Mexican government used an expansive definition of racial discrimination to bar the use of contracted workers in Texas by both the railroad and agricultural industries:

> The Mexican government also tended to view discrimination in economic as well as social terms, as connected with jobs and wages as well as schools, restaurants, and barbershops. In other words, its definition included the treatment of Mexicans as farm laborers. Because of the proximity of cheap labor in Mexico, discriminatory hiring practices of American labor and industry that

restricted Mexicans to field work, and the workers' lack of non-agricultural skills, parts of Texas had long remained among the lowest farm wage areas in the country. (Scruggs 1962, 124)

Texan growers began to formally request contract labor from the Mexican government as early as 1943, although they strenuously objected to US and Mexican government interference and wanted a program similar to the first Bracero Program that operated during World War I. When the blacklisting continued beyond 1943, growers encouraged undocumented laborers to migrate to Texas through the same type of direct recruitment strategies that were implemented during that war.

Aware of the need to take action to improve a situation made more acute by acts of discrimination against Mexican Americans in uniform and visiting Mexican dignitaries, Texan Governor Coke Stevenson induced the state legislature to pass the so-called Caucasian Race resolution, which he approved on May 6, 1943. The resolution affirmed the right of all Caucasians within the state to equal treatment in public places of business and amusement and denounced racial discrimination as "violating the good neighbor policy of our state." Doubtless, this manifesto of good intentions added to the surprise that greeted the Mexican announcement that Braceros would still not be allowed to go to Texas (Scruggs 1979, 88). As University of Texas historian Neil Foley notes, "This clever resolution was intended to convince Mexico that discrimination against Caucasians would not be tolerated in Texas, the assumption being that Mexicans were, of course, members of the Caucasian race, which they were only in some legal, pseudo-scientific, and ethnographical sense; but practically no Texans regarded Mexicans, particularly Bracero farmworkers, as white" (Foley 1997, 206). The resolution kept the system of racial discrimination against Blacks intact. Its intentions were not to promote racial equality of treatment and the eradication of racist beliefs. Rather, it was meant to ensure that Anglo[1] growers in Texas would have access to the labor they desired. The resolution stated:

Our neighbors to the South were cooperating to stamp out Nazism and preserve democracy and to assist the national policy of hemispherical solidarity, the state of Texas resolves that all persons of the Caucasian Race ... are entitled to the full and equal accommodations, advantages, facilities, and privileges of all public places or business or amusement. Whoever denied to any person these privileges shall be considered as violating the good neighbor policy of our State. (Texas Caucasian Race Resolution 1943, as paraphrased in Foley 1997, 206)

How ironic that in the effort to link the common agendas of Texas and Mexico in the eradication of the Nazi threat, the state promoted an agenda of equality for *Caucasians only* in terms of access to public space. The law disregarded economic inequalities among racial groups, as well as the continued intolerance toward Blacks.

Throughout World War II, Stevenson beseeched Mexican Foreign Labor Minister Ezequiel Padilla to permit the flow of recruited labor to his state. Drawing upon President Franklin D. Roosevelt's 1933 inaugural address, which stated the US intention to pursue a policy of the "Good Neighbor" toward the citizens of Latin America, he created a Texas Good Neighbor Commission in September 1943 and promised that state law officials would deal severely with Texans who discriminated against Mexicans (Kirstein 1977, 54). The Commission would investigate charges of racial discrimination brought to its attention and promote a gradual education program for Anglo Texans about Latin America (Gutierrez 1995, 140–41). Texas became the focal point of the Good Neighbor policy "… due to the high percentage of Mexicans in its population, the correspondingly greater number of 'incidents,' and the application to Mexicans of many of the formal restrictions against Negroes throughout the state" (Scruggs 1962, 120). Mexican Foreign Minister Padilla stated that the Texas blacklist would continue because of the state's inability to solve its racist practices:

In many parts of Texas … Mexicans cannot attend public gatherings without being subject to vexations, complaints and protests. There are towns where my fellow countrymen are forced to live in separate districts. Just a week ago the daughter of a Mexican consul was refused service in a public establishment. The ban would not be lifted … until Texas had passed a law prohibiting such practices. A bill to this effect was introduced into the 1945 session of the Texas legislature but, needless to say, it did not pass. (McWilliams 1990 [1948], 242)

In response to the Good Neighbor policy, the Texas Good Neighbor Commission, and the Caucasian Race Resolution, people in Mexico developed their own organization, *Comité Mexicano Contra el Racismo* (Mexican

Committee Against Racism) to document racial discrimination practices in the United States in the areas of education, labor, and consumer establishments. The Committee's publication, *Fraternidad*, included a column entitled "Texas, ¿*Buen Vecino?*" ("Texas, Good Neighbor?"), which detailed incidents of discrimination against Mexicans in nearly 150 Texan communities. The Committee pressured US and Mexican state officials to deal with these racist practices.

In addition to *Fraternidad*, the Mexican popular press also documented the mistreatment of Mexicans residing in the US: "Hardly a day passed, [US] Ambassador Messersmith informed Washington in March 1944, that some bitter article about discrimination against Mexicans in the United States did not appear in the press of Mexico City" (Scruggs 1962, 121). In addition, the headlines of major newspapers in Mexico during 1942–47 consistently referred to the continuing significance and persistence of racism in Texas (Galarza 1956; McCain 1981).

The Texas situation clarifies how race was deployed in a power struggle to define the subordinate in ways that justified Mexicans' unequal and limited access to resources and social institutions. Anglo growers used race as a line of division within class blocs to ensure themselves a steady and cheap supply of Mexican immigrant labor. Hostile acts at the interpersonal level, documented by various sources, were bolstered by structural barriers to equality based on the demarcation of racial categories. The Caucasian Race Resolution and the Texas Good Neighbor Commission failed in their stated goals because their framers did not intend to promote social justice and anti-racist agendas. Quite simply, they represented attempts by the Texas state government to serve the interests of the most powerful in securing a cheap and controllable source of labor whose rights would always be in question and whose status could be easily amended to suit the needs of the employer. Texan and other Southwestern growers circumvented the safeguards put in place by the Mexican government by not contracting workers through the Bracero Program, with its rules and regulations, but by directly recruiting undocumented workers from Mexico. US state responses to these grower recruitment efforts are detailed below.

By 1948, a series of assurances by the Texas state government were secured before growers were finally allowed to import labor from Mexico. The Mexican government also blacklisted the states of Colorado, Illinois, Indiana, Michigan, Montana, Minnesota, Wisconsin, and Wyoming until the 1950s due to discriminatory practices there. The majority of documented cases were wage discrimination cases where Mexican sugar-beet workers were paid a lower rate than non-Mexican workers due to their racial identity.

Los Braceros y Los Indocumentados: Negotiating Legal Status to Fill the Labor Pool

The Bracero Program was not administered continuously, nor did it follow the same course of action throughout its 22-year history. Garcia y Griego (1983) notes three main phases, which corresponded to the level of regulation to which growers would commit in order to ensure a labor pool to their liking. Labor demands by growers were met by a number of specific actions taken by the state or growers themselves.

The first phase, 1942–46, was marked by significant Mexican government input into the operations of the program and a true bargaining position between the national governments in the bilateral labor arrangement. As we saw above, Texas and some other states were banned from the program because of discriminatory practices. Garcia y Griego (1983) estimates that only 4 to 7 per cent of all Bracero contracts were signed during this time of wartime labor relief. Its greatest flaw was the automatic deduction of 10 per cent of the Braceros' wages for deposit in Mexican banks. Class action lawsuits have brought to light a persistent pattern. Growers appeared to be diligent in collecting the automatic paycheck deductions, which were then to be deposited into an account managed by Wells Fargo Bank. From there, monies were wired to the Mexican National Bank and *Banco Agricultura*, among others. However, many Braceros claimed that upon returning to Mexico to request their savings, local bank officials told them there was no money for them. Scruggs (1960, 149) says that the original intent of the savings deduction was that the money would "… be used to purchase for [the worker] agricultural implements which the [US] Farm Security Administration pledged the Mexican government it would try to obtain in the United States." Jones (1945) provides an account of the large sums of money involved but does not track the extent to which claims were made by Braceros and the eventual payout rate. The Mexican banks all filed for bankruptcy and were closed in the 1980s, so recent attempts to claim the funds that were automatically deducted from workers' wages have fallen on deaf ears. This era was certainly marked by a higher degree of cooperation between the federal governments of Mexico and the US, but the savings debacle sheds light on how the workers experienced the program.

The second phase, 1947–54, constituted a shift in policy from mass legalization to mass repatriation. The events that dramatized these coupled approaches were the El Paso Incident and Operation Wetback, which are discussed in more detail below. They represented a serious breakdown in bilateral relations and the extent to which the US government committed itself to both securing a workforce for US growers and dealing with the "illegal invasion." Rather than putting a stop to illegal migration, INS agents who found undocumented workers were authorized to contract or legalize them as Braceros at the US work sites where they were already working. The bureaucratic regulations of the Bracero Program were applied *ex post facto* to legalize illegal workers. Legalization was the process by which deportable Mexicans who had been in the US for a certain number of weeks were given Bracero contracts, usually to work for the same employer, without the laborer having to return to Mexico and undergo the screening process in the interior or the employer having to pay transportation to the US (Garcia y Griego 1983, 57).

Overall, it became obvious that South Texas growers were going to secure a Mexican labor force either through the Bracero Program's formal mechanisms or through informal recruitment of undocumented labor. In many ways, the US government and agribusiness created the illegal immigration "problem" as a way to undercut the Mexican government's bargaining power. The Mexican government's aim of protecting its citizens from Anglo discrimination was consistently eroded by an employment sector that directly recruited labor from Mexico through extra-legal means while the US government turned a blind eye. As the number of contracted Braceros increased during this period, the accompanying number of undocumented immigrants similarly rose. Because of this derisively dubbed "wetback invasion," the INS instituted a practice of forced mass repatriation that deported a total of 1.3 million Mexicans, most but not all undocumented, according to US estimates.

The final phase of the Bracero Program from 1955–64 represented both the program's mass scale as well as the contradictions that eventually led to its termination. The principal contradiction was between the desire for immigrants as a source of labor and the abhorrence of immigrants by the Anglo population. Though Public Law 78 was passed in 1951, at the behest of the Mexican government, to formalize the program through a US federal law, its provisions effectively favored US growers. It was designed to end the informal recruitment and *ex post facto* legalization process but ended the restrictions on Texas and other blacklisted states. The overall number of Bracero contracts remained at 1954 levels and represented truly a mass recruitment. "Of the total 4.6 million contracts issued during the life of the program, about 72 per cent occurred between 1955 and 1964," according to Garcia y Griego (1983, 57–59).

The El Paso Incident

In October 1948, the Texas-Mexico border was opened by immigration officials to allow several thousand undocumented workers across the border and into the agricultural fields of Texas. In open defiance of bilateral agreements, what came to be known as the "El Paso Incident" created a political morass for the two governments while appeasing Texan growers by lifting the moratorium on allowing Braceros to receive contracts for work in the state. Most workers went directly to work in the cotton fields and were processed and often escorted by Border Patrol agents. This event formalized the informal practice of using undocumented Mexican labor to till Texan fields while the blacklist was in place. What made this particular incident problematic was the direct US state involvement in managing and controlling the migrant stream.

The most egregious aspect of the El Paso Incident was the direct role played by cabinet-level officials in the decision to open up the border in direct betrayal of the agreement with Mexico. The main source of contention was the prevailing wage standard as determined by the Texan cotton growers and Mexican federal government representatives. Agricultural wages in Texas were by far the lowest in the nation, and growers set the prevailing wage (the hourly rate that domestic laborers would supposedly accept as the lowest tolerable wage) at $2.50 per 100 pounds of harvested cotton. This practice of growers setting their own wage rate was fully allowed by the US Department of Labor, and the growers' figures were neither verified nor examined by Labor officials. When Mexican officials set the prevailing wage at $3.00, the growers were infuriated. The El Paso Growers' Association fought the challenge to their wage rate by the Mexican government's drafted contract (similar to the World War II Bracero contract), so "on Oct. 15, 1947 [Mexico] abrogated the Texas agreement" (Scruggs 1979, 95). The growers turned to the Border Patrol to open the border to illegal immigrants, and they did so under the direct supervision of Department of Labor officials.

Between October 13 and 18, 1947, some 6,000 Mexicans entered the

US. They glutted the Texas labor market so that, according to press reports, wages dropped to $1.50. G.J. McBee, chief patrol inspector at El Paso, stated that 6,000 men had been arrested for illegal entry and had been paroled to the growers because the Border Patrol had been "unable to cope with the situation" (Galarza 1964, 49–50).

> The director of the United States Employment Service (housed in the Department of Labor) took direct responsibility for opening the border and for the subsequent release of undocumented Mexican workers directly into the hands of Texas cotton growers. "[Director] Robert Goodwin claimed at hearings before the Bureau of the Budget that the 'El Paso Incident' was created by him on the allegation that the present treaty is not working in that we are not getting needed farm labor from Mexico." (Kirstein 1977, 69)

"Go Back!" The Repatriation Campaigns of Operation "Wetback"

The unending demand for labor, the US government support for growers to secure workers by legal or illegal means, and the lack of Mexican government bargaining power created a significant backlash against Mexican immigrants working and residing in the US. At the same time that the US government encouraged illegal immigration, government officials voiced mounting pressure to deal with the "wetback problem." Some were truly talking out of both sides of their mouths, but this contradiction also represented a bureaucratic struggle between the Departments of Labor, Agriculture, State, and INS (Calavita 1992; Cohen 2001; Garcia 1980; Kirstein 1977; Ngai 2004).

US Attorney General Howard Brownell was a vehement opponent of undocumented Mexican laborers, and he went to great lengths to formulate and seek congressional approval to use the US military to repatriate the undocumented. It was rumored that he sought support from organized labor to eliminate undocumented workers by any means. He was cited as saying that "one method of discouraging wetbacks would be to allow the border patrol to shoot some of them" (Garcia 1980, 172). He eventually hired former lieutenant general Joseph Swing, who had served in the punitive expedition against Pancho Villa in 1916, to carry out the repatriation campaign. Using a mobile task force deployed along strategic points on the border where illegal entry prevailed, his forces proceeded from west to east, then encircled and forced Mexicans, assumedly but not necessarily undocumented, over the border (see Table 2.1).

In 1954, Commissioner Swing mounted a mass repatriation campaign of illegal Mexican workers, dubbed "Operation Wetback," which resulted in what the INS estimated as a return of 1.3 million workers to Mexico.[2] The means of repatriation varied—some migrants were forced to return; some left voluntarily—but the effect was the same: "Operation Wetback did not bring an end to illegal immigration from Mexico. It did slow the influx for a short time, but it brought no permanent solution to the problem. It was a stop-gap measure" (Garcia 1980, 232). It sent a strong message not only to the Mexican people about their rights to live and work in the US but to Anglo growers as well: they would not be held responsible for the mass migration that they initiated and perpetuated by actively recruiting and employing undocumented labor. This mass repatriation occurred at the same time the Bracero Program was running at its peak. The contradiction was made manifest: Mexican immigrants were not wanted in the US if they came on their own, yet their labor would be remunerated and rights protected if they had a Bracero contract.

In what might have been possibly the first military-style public relations operation, Swing and his agents controlled media coverage, created press releases to tout the success of deportations, and crafted media relations in a manner conducive to INS interests. In contrast to the strongly controlled media campaign in the US, there was no INS attempt at coverage or commentary on Operation Wetback in Mexico. What the Mexican media covered were the deplorable working conditions that Braceros endured; the slow descent of a binational program into one decided unilaterally by the US; and events that epitomized the callousness of the operation, such as forced bus, train, and ship deportations.

Bus lifts often resulted in flooding Mexico's border cities with thousands of unemployed, displaced men who knew full well that jobs were waiting for them over the border. "Some 88 Braceros died of sunstroke as a result of a round-up that had taken place in 112-degree heat, and [labor official Milton Plumb] argued that more would have died had Red Cross not intervened" (Ngai 2004, 156). Train and air deportations were modeled after the Depression-era repatriation program. The main goal was to deposit men hundreds of miles south of the border to impede re-entry. "More than 25 per cent were removed on hired cargo ships that ran from Port Isabel, Texas, to Vera Cruz, on the Mexican Gulf Coast; a congressional investigation likened one vessel (where a riot took place on board) to an 'eighteenth-century slave ship' and a 'penal hell ship'" (Ngai 2004, 156).

Repatriation serves as a persistent reminder of the second-class citizenship status of Mexicans in the US. Xavier Castañeda, a Mexican public health officer, addressed a group of undocumented workers who were being returned to Mexico via the Rio Grande Valley International Airport with the following:

I am charged to tell you that you have committed a great sin in coming to this country without being asked for, without being needed here. The Government of Mexico is disgusted, fed up with this clandestine business of you, its citizens, going to the United States for the mirage of the dollar. But now it is all finished.... Now I beg you, in the name of our country, in the name of Mexico, I beg you not to return in this clandestine manner. In the name of Mexican Immigration, in the name of these American officers, I am charged with speaking to you in clear and simple Spanish, that you abstain. Your hands are needed in Mexico, and only the man who is worth nothing there, comes here in this manner. Do not continue to make yourselves warehouses full of cheap Indians.

You should be ashamed of yourselves, abandoning your homes, traitors to your Mexico. Mexico is esteemed and loved in the world, you are making a bad example with this situation.... So I, a Mexican among the rest of you, with all my soul, as the shield of the University of Mexico says, "My spirit speaks for my race," I am speaking for my race.... So I want you to tell me, boys, are you going to come back illegally? (All answer "No, no.") Louder, are you going to come back? ("No.") May God help you and the Fatherland reward you. Above all, Mexico is our country. Later, if they start contracting, everyone of you who comes here legally contracted will be received with open arms. You will bear the name of a true Mexican citizen, rather than as a wet-back, as you are now designated, a very sad thing for Mexico.... Finally, in the name of Mexico, I am going to repeat once more, are you going to come back without permits? (Answer: No.) We hope to God you don't. Go on back to your country. Your mothers, your daughters, the most precious treasures are awaiting you there. Viva Mexico! (Castañeda [1951] in Kiser and Kiser 1979, 164–66)

Castañeda's message was clear and unequivocal. First, undocumented immigrants were to blame for their situation. Second, he presented a clear racial demarcation between his fellow Mexicans who were acceptable and to be honored and the "Indian" wetback who was a source of embarrassment, easily exploitable by greedy Americans. Third, all forms of social control would be utilized to deter further undocumented immigration—forced repatriation, calls to Mexican patriotism, a sense of pride in self, invocations of God and sin, the law of the land in both Mexico and the US, intimidation, and a mix of guilt and patriarchy in the form of "precious treasures." Finally, the Bracero Program was the only viable means of migrating to the US. Even though the reasons for migration were the same (chasing the "mirage of the dollar") and the results were the same (abandoning homes, losing hands needed in Mexico, leaving families behind, etc.), somehow that would all be acceptable as long as the would-be migrant subjected himself to the US and Mexico state-sanctioned contracting process. Thus, this Mexican public health officer denigrated the deported in ways that fit both Mexican-based racializations of poor, indigenous, rural Mexicans and US racializations of Mexican immigrants as "wetbacks." In one speech, these two differing racialized definitions are closely articulated into a unified means for denigration, intimidation, and social control.

The specific principles that informed how Operation Wetback was conducted are now recognized as Low Intensity Conflict (LIC) doctrine. LIC is a military science concept developed in response to guerrilla tactics deployed by first Korean, then Vietnamese soldiers in response to US military aggression. Its general contours include: "(1) an emphasis on internal (rather than external) defense of a nation, (2) an emphasis on controlling targeted civilian populations rather than territory, and (3) the assumption by the military of police-like and other unconventional, typically non-military roles, along with the adoption by the police of military characteristics" (Dunn 1996, 21).

The US government deemed the border out of control, and Attorney General Brownell intentionally sought out a career military man to bring military knowledge and expertise to the issue of illegal immigration. Swing employed techniques with which he was most familiar to effectively militarize the US-Mexico border region. His mobile task force of agents were deployed in pre-specified positions along the border and in major cities that had a large undocumented Mexican labor force in order to round-up Mexicans and force them south. Quite literally, communities were encircled by several hundred border patrol agents. "Sweeps" and "operations" were used to contain the population and force them over the border by bus, boat, train, and air lifts. "Perhaps the most important principle evident in the Border Patrol's leading role in

Operation Wetback is that undocumented immigrants were treated in terms analogous to that of an 'enemy' to be repulsed and driven out" (Dunn 1996, 16).

Many of the physical markers that currently define the militarization of the US-Mexico border were either used or suggested during Operation Wetback. Swing urged the building of a chain-link fence at the major illegal crossing points, but this was not immediately constructed. Dunn (1996, 15) notes the use of aircraft to survey the region in subsequent "mop-up operations"; the use of military vehicles to hunt down and capture suspected illegal immigrants; and joint Border Patrol and local police "round-ups," which have been documented and critically analyzed by Romero and Serag (2005).

1965 Immigration and Nationality Act

In response to the Bracero Program and Operation Wetback, US legislators became much more aware of the need to address the immigration laws that determined who could legally enter the US and become permanent residents. The 1952 McCarren-Warren Act was basically an extension of the 1924 Quota Acts that severely restricted immigrants from Southern and Eastern Europe, barred Asian immigration, and left Western Hemispheric migration mostly unregulated except for establishing the Border Patrol. Due to the paternalistic character of the US state, quotas were never applied to nations of the Western Hemisphere, but the flat rate of admittance based on national origin was applied to Western Hemisphere nations in the new 1965 law.

There are currently two competing views on this readjustment of immigration law. On the one hand, the Immigration and Nationality Act (INA) is considered to be an advance in civil rights because it struck down the discriminatory quota system. Thus, it can be seen as part of the larger civil rights legislation that sought to remove *de jure* discrimination from the laws governing US society. On the other hand, the law continued the legacy of marginalizing temporary workers by extending the ability of agricultural firms to employ immigrant labor on a temporary contract basis. In some ways, the INA was a continuation of the Bracero Program that had officially expired a year earlier. What is not in dispute is that the emphasis on family reunification and skills-based criteria irrevocably changed the face of immigration, and Latin Americans and Asians were by far the major, yet unintended, benefactors of the shifting criteria for admission and citizenship.

Early support for the 1965 Immigration and Nationality Act was voiced during the Kennedy Administration. US Attorney General, Robert Kennedy testified in 1964 before Congress that the 1952 extension of the 1924 Quota Acts is a standing affront to many Americans and to many countries. It implies what we in the United States know from our own experience is false: that regardless of individual qualifications, a man or woman born in Italy, or Greece, or Poland, or Portugal, or Czechoslovakia, or the Ukraine, is not as good as someone born in Ireland, or England, or Germany, or Sweden. Everywhere else in our national life, we have eliminated discrimination based on national origins. Yet, this system is still the foundation of our immigration law. (Cited in Reimers 1985, 69)

Johnson's Secretary of State Dean Rusk argued that immigration law was discriminatory (Reimers 1985, 69), and the final version of the new law included a preference system that contained seven ranked criteria for admission: the first five operationalized the family reunification criteria, the sixth "skilled and unskilled workers in occupations for which labor is in short supply," and the seventh "refugees" defined as "conditional entrants." Of the seven preferences, four privileged family reunification as the basis for admission, two were based on employee skills and labor shortages, and one was designated for refugees. With the intention of ending racially discriminatory quotas, the major unintended consequence of the 1965 INA was that subsequent applicants for admission would be overwhelmingly non-European and predominately Latin American and Asian.

One little-known provision within the 1965 INA was an extension of a temporary visa program that brought farmworkers from the Caribbean to Florida and along the East Coast migrant stream. The H-2 Program was in many ways the East Coast equivalent of the Bracero Program but, instead of Mexican laborers, the vast majority of temporary contract workers were Haitian, Jamaican, Puerto Rican, and West Indian. On the books, growers were still accorded access to a temporary, foreign labor pool whenever domestic supply was deemed inadequate. The H-2 Program was expanded in the 1986 Immigration Reform and Control Act and in recent years has become a crucial aspect of labor recruitment for the dirty, dangerous, underpaid, and undesirable jobs that US citizens refuse to do.

Conclusion

The blacklisting of Texas from receiving Braceros between 1942 and 1947 demonstrates the deep-seated racism that prevailed in the state and included growers, local community members, and Texas state government managers themselves. The formation of the Texas Good Neighbor Commission and the passage of the Caucasian Race Resolution did little to change racist attitudes and practices toward the Mexican population. These government initiatives were designed to ensure that Anglo growers had full access to Mexican immigrant labor. Also indicative of the racial climate were the repatriation campaigns that sent an estimated 1.3 million people of Mexican origin back to Mexico. This campaign, dubbed Operation Wetback, along with the 1948 El Paso Incident, served to solidify symbolically the definitions of citizenship, racial groups, and economic classes. The contradictory message that Mexicans received was that their labor was wanted but they were in no way welcome as citizens in the US.

One of the main results of the program was a steady increase in the number of Mexican undocumented workers. This influx was dealt with in three ways. The most common was to ignore them and allow them to seek work in the US. They were usually directly recruited in Mexico by farm labor contractors or other intermediaries on behalf of growers. In particular, growers near the border were able to recruit Mexican laborers directly and avoid the bureaucratic channels of the Bracero Program. The illegal status of undocumented farmworkers was an advantage to growers since the rights guaranteed to Braceros did not have to be met. At no time were growers held responsible for directly recruiting "illegal" labor. It was not until 1986 that growers could be held legally responsible for hiring undocumented workers.

The second effect was the increasing militarization of the border and the utilization of military-style roundups and LIC doctrine that in many ways set the stage for the current morass along the border. As much as the 1965 INA sought to rectify the discriminatory elements in immigration law, it also reproduced the marginal status of low-wage immigrant workers by including the H-2 temporary visa provisions so that growers would be assured that the US government would continue to guarantee their access to cheap, temporary, foreign labor.

The third result was the development of organized resistance by Mexican immigrant laborers to contest exploitation and racialization, even in later eras of backlash and retrenchment. We shall turn to these now in Part II.

Notes

1. In the Southwest and particularly along the border, Anglo is a non-pejorative identification of Euro-Americans and a term that Mexicans use with great frequency. White is really a term (there are Spanish equivalents like *guero, gabacho, gringo*) that is limited to refer to White racists or specifically those who intentionally marginalize Mexicans.
2. Garcia (1980, 227–28) notes that this number was greatly exaggerated by the INS. The campaign in Texas and California resulted in the repatriation of 80,127 and 84,278 undocumented immigrants, respectively. The INS claimed that the remainder of the 1.3 million left voluntarily before they were forcibly deported. Garcia finds little evidence of that number voluntarily returning to Mexico, but voluntary leave counts or even estimates seem to be non-existent, so we cite the INS number throughout.

part II
Mounting Resistance

Introduction

The consumption patterns of North American consumers and the inter-ests of an oligopoly of agricultural firms are driving the agri-food system that increasingly relies upon migrant temporary labor to harvest the crops designed by large-scale agribusiness firms. The vertical integration of the food industry means that agribusiness owns everything from seed to plate. In post-Fordist agricultural production, consumer preferences deeply shape industry practices. This means that supply chains are particularly vulnerable to consumer boycotts, negative public relations, and other forms of social protest that hold big businesses culpable for worker exploitation. A brand, label, or chain tainted with negative associations is the worst nightmare for consumer-conscious companies, such as Yum! Brands, McDonald's, Mount Olive Pickle, and Washington apple growers. In Chapter 3, we examine the resistance movements of the United Farm Workers (UFW), the Farm Labor Organizing Committee (FLOC), and the Coalition of Immokalee Workers (CIW), which reveal how strategies to resist exploitation, including boycotts, truth tours, and worker organizing are effective means of shifting industry practices in favor of workers' rights.

Table II.1: *Timeline of Mounting Resistance*

1955	American Federation of Labor (AFL) and Congress of Industrial Organizations (CIO) merge into the AFL-CIO after the more radical CIO (representing the majority of Mexican and immigrant union members) is purged of its "communist element."
September 1965	Filipino American members of the Agricultural Workers Organizing Committee (AWOC) strike against Delano-area grape growers on September 8. César Chávez's National Farm Workers Association (NFWA) joins the walkouts on September 16, Mexican Independence Day, thus beginning the five-year Delano Grape Strike.
Spring-Summer 1966	A strike and boycott of the DiGiorgio Fruit Corporation results in UFW representation for workers.
July 29, 1970	Delano-area table grape growers sign their first contracts at the UFW's Forty Acres union hall.
June 1975	Agricultural Labor Relations Act of California is passed in response to UFW strikes and boycotts as well as mounting pressure from the supermarket industry; growers agree to a state law guaranteeing California farm workers the right to organize, vote in state-supervised secret-ballot elections, and bargain with their employers.
1986	Farm Labor Organizing Committee (FLOC) signs innovative three-way contracts with Campbell Soup and its growers in Ohio and Michigan, setting labor history. Union recognition is won, along with wage increases and benefits. The contract ends a nine-year battle with Campbell.
October 5, 1991	*Frente Indígena de Organizaciones Binacionales*/Binational Front of Indigenous Organizations (FIOB) founded in Los Angeles.
March 2001	Mexico's president Fox signs into law the 3x1 remittance program, modeled after the Federation of Zacatecan Clubs of Southern California and available to all 31 states; every remitted dollar through a hometown association is now matched by state and federal governments.
September 15, 2004	FLOC signs a contract with North Carolina Growers' Association to represent the Mexican H-2A visa holders working in the state.
2005	Calling for more grassroots organizing, SEIU, UFCW, UNITE-HERE, Teamsters, Laborers' International Union, and the UFW form the Change to Win Federation (CTW), which splits from the AFL-CIO over disagreements about the future of the labor movement. In 2009, UNITE-HERE returned to the AFL-CIO after organizing jurisdictional battles with SEIU.

2005	The Zapatistas issue the Sixth Declaration of the Lacandon Jungle and initiate the "Other Campaign," articulating a more directly anti-capitalist position and calling for sympathizers to join them in working for political and economic transformation.
March 8, 2006	Coalition of Immokalee Workers (CIW) reaches agreement with Yum! Brands subsidiary Taco Bell to adopt the penny per pound pass-through program to increase wages of tomato harvesters in South Florida.
March 30, 2006	UFW reaches agreement with Global Horizons farm labor contractors to represent H-2A temporary visa workers. The agreement between Global Horizons and UFW stems from labor contractors' violations of Washington State labor laws.

Chapter 4 focuses on three recent strategies of organizing among Mexican workers — labor unions, new *mutualistas*, and the immigrant rights movement. Over the past 25 years the successes of labor unions serving Mexican immigrant workers has stemmed from the two surprisingly effective campaigns by Los Angeles Drywallers and Justice for Janitors (J4J). We examine how these campaigns ran counter to the AFL-CIO business-as-usual strategy of ignoring Mexican immigrant workers. The recent labor split that resulted in the Change to Win Federation (CTW) focuses on immigrant organizing and democratic reforms as a burgeoning source for a renewed labor activism. Mexican immigrants are not waiting for the AFL-CIO leadership structure to recognize their needs but rather are organizing in a new *mutualista* tradition by creating non-affiliated labor organizing strategies, day labor and worker centers, and hometown associations. This immigrant rights movement was thrust on the national stage in 2006 when popular protests in Los Angeles, Chicago, Denver, New York, El Paso, San Diego, and many other US cities demonstrated the emergence of undocumented workers from the shadows to demand recognition for the hard labor they provide. These popular mobilizations reject the criminalization, racialization, and marginalization that often shape the lives of Mexicans in contemporary US society.

In Chapter 5, we chart the effects of backlash and retrenchment on the Mexican immigrant community residing in the US and consider the changes that came with the implementation of the 1986 IRCA and the expansion of the H-2 program into three new temporary worker visa classes — H-2A, H-2B, and H-1B (see Chapter 5, p. 94–96). Neoliberals have orchestrated what Hall (1988) calls the "great moving right show" toward laissez-faire economics, minimal government, and social conservatism. The ascendancy of the Radical Right in the US was ushered in by the 1980 presidential election of Ronald Reagan, who earlier prided himself on consuming table grapes in press conferences at the height of the labor battles between California growers and the UFW. Reagan's transformation from well-intentioned Hollywood liberal and labor leader (as former president of the Screen Actors Guild) to ultraconservative big business champion and subtle hate-monger of minorities set the stage for the political scene in California and nationwide. As a result of Reaganism—a specific political expression of US neoliberalism—the limited gains of the civil rights era have been under constant threat of rollback. The last 25 years of political backlash and retrenchment are strongly felt by low-income minority communities.

Chapter Three

Farmworker Civil Rights Movement / *El Movimiento Campesino*

The struggle in the fields for farmworker civil rights invokes images familiar to many: the black eagle flag of the United Farm Workers (UFW), its charismatic leaders César Chávez and Dolores Huerta, and its philosophy of non-violent resistance. During the civil rights era, the UFW became the symbol for Mexican Americans who collectively struggled to relinquish their second-class citizenship. The UFW trade journal, *El Malcriado* describes the vision of the labor/civil rights movement as follows:

> The only way that poor farmworkers can ever beat the rich growers, and to make the rich ranchers pay good wages, is if all farmworkers get together in one big union. That is why the National Farm Workers Association...and AWOC [Agricultural Workers Organizing Committee] joined together into one big union. We are now stronger than ever. The union now has thousands of members in California, Texas, Florida, Arkansas, Michigan, Oregon, and other states. And we are a union for all farmworkers, for Whites and Negroes, for Mexicans, and Puerto Ricans, and Filipinos. The growers have already tried to play off one group against another, to keep us divided and weak. But now we are gaining unity through our union, a union just for farmworkers, where farmworkers elect their leaders, where the leaders are also farmworkers. (UFW 1966, 12–13)

Designed from its inception as an interracial coalition of agricultural workers, the UFW viewed growers as the target for their ire, rather than racial groups that it claimed growers pitted against them. Yet, in the same issue of *El Malcriado* as the quote above, a full-page advertisement entitled

"Rotten Deals in Tomatoes: Government Gives Away Our Jobs" noticeably restricts the expansive definition of who was welcomed by the UFW:

> Over 6,000 Mexican Braceros will start work in California's labor harvest this week. That means more people competing for fewer jobs. It means lower wages for all. And it is possible that this crime against the farmworkers will get bigger. Growers want 13,000 more braceros for tomato[e]s and 25,000 for other crops.
>
> The Bracero Program was ENDED by Congress two years ago.... The growers pay lousy wages, refuse to sign a contract, and turn local workers away. THEN they scream for Braceros. They know they can pay Braceros less, since $1 in US money equals $12 in Mexican money. The Bracero Program is just one more weapon which the growers use to beat us down and keep us poor. (UFW 1966, 18)

The ad goes on to explain that the competing labor union for farmworkers, the Teamsters, supports a temporary worker program because of its sweetheart dealings with growers.

Clearly the UFW did not consider Braceros as "workers"—or at the very least not "our workers"; they are characterized in the ad as simply a weapon in the growers' arsenal. The organized labor divide between Mexican Americans and Mexican immigrants, as Chicano historian David Gutierrez (1995) aptly notes, highlights that common ancestry is a tenuous link when labor, border, citizenship, and assimilation pressures are all operating. The UFW's actions represent some of the most positive successes for Mexicans residing in the US and some of the worst ways in which the Mexican-origin population is divided by excluding immigrant workers. As the UFW came to seriously consider the challenges offered by fellow Mexican American organizations, its organizing strategy eventually shifted to an organizing *sin fronteras* (without borders) approach.

Agricultural labor organization and strikes for recognition and protection of rights can be seen as early victories of Mexicans residing in the US.[1] Mexican migrant workers organized in spite of countless attempts at marginalization and at relegating those of Mexican ancestry to the dustbins of, at best, second-class citizenship if not total exclusion. Early, persistent attempts at organizing for better wages and working conditions, coalition building with other racialized groups, and overcoming frequent rebukes from organized labor and Wobblies (Industrial Workers of the World communist organizers) stand as a testament to the tenacity of those most often viewed as "unorganizable."

If the UFW organized at the most distant margins of organized labor, it is more than a little ironic that the AFL-CIO (American Federation of Labor and Congress of Industrial Organizations) today most often uses "immigrant rights = labor rights = civil rights" as their rallying cry since it historically viewed labor rights as belonging only to White male citizens, even during the time of the initial UFW successes. The UFW itself was not immune from exclusionary practices in the beginning. We will discuss the 180-degree turn of the UFW and its willingness to organize and represent the Braceros of today as symbolized by the Global Horizons contract, which allows it to provide a grievance procedure and collective bargaining agent for temporary H-2A workers (primarily Thai immigrants; Global Horizons brings workers to the US from all over the globe, including Mexico).

In the Midwest, the Farm Labor Organizing Committee (FLOC) was initially inspired by the UFW but has moved beyond the union's shadow to register landmark contracts and organizing that most often goes unnoticed or underappreciated. FLOC's negotiation of a third-party contract with Campbell Soup and Midwest tomato growers is in many ways novel as a collective bargaining strategy. Its recent boycott of Mount Olive Pickle Company in North Carolina (subsequently expanding to the North Carolina Growers' Association) and the resultant multi-party contract that represents H-2A temporary visa workers established the precedent for the UFW's contract with Global Horizons.

In the swamps of South Florida's Everglades, some of the most important organizing efforts are not union-affiliated but grassroots in origin and global in reception. Applying the lessons learned from the power of consumer boycotts, grassroots organizing, and building a broad base of church and student support, the recent campaigns and truth tours against Taco Bell and McDonald's by the Coalition of Immokalee Workers (CIW) are testaments to the power of resistance movements as the motors of progressive social change.

UFW, Global Horizons, and H-2A Workers

Against seemingly insurmountable odds, the UFW has come to represent the larger struggle of the racialized and economically marginalized Mexican American population. Nowhere were Mexican Americans more marginalized than in the fields as migrant workers. Every time the UFW registered a win against wealthy White growers, the "*sí se puede*" or "yes we can" rally cry, or *grito*, was a call to all Mexican American activists who saw their struggles as intertwined with the farmworker struggle. The institutional legacies of the UFW's struggle in the fields and a recent campaign represent a major attempt at addressing the previous limitations of the union in the contemporary era of global capital, transnational temporary workforces, and Global Horizons. The UFW's role in this turnaround is represented in a little-known contract engineered in 2006 with Global Horizons, a labor contractor that works with growers and other companies to bring in a pool of laborers under the various temporary visa work programs administered by the US government.

In 2004 Global Horizons brought agricultural workers from Thailand to Washington State under the H-2A program (see Chapter 5, p. 94–96) to harvest the apple crop. According to the UFW, work conditions the following year were terrible:

> According to the WA Dept of Health, these [167 Thai] workers were forced to live in outrageously crowded, unsanitary conditions—with only 21 beds for 45 people at one location, no cooking facilities at multiple locations, and workers were forced to wash their clothes in trash cans. Additionally, some of the Thai workers were told by officials that they weren't receiving pay stubs and that money deducted from their paychecks to be sent back home never arrived.[2]

The UFW had been committed to organizing apple workers in Washington for over 20 years but had had little success. When growers began to use a third-party labor contractor, Global Horizons, the UFW monitored its actions, using as precedent FLOC's negotiation for union representation of H-2A workers employed by the North Carolina Growers' Association. FLOC's initial focus was on the Mount Olive Pickle Company and its exploitative treatment of H-2A workers from Mexico, but the campaign spread when it became clear that a third-party contract with Mount Olive—which was not the direct employer of labor because its pickles are grown by contracted growers—would not follow the earlier pattern the union had established with Campbell Soup in Ohio. Therefore, the focus spread to the North Carolina Growers' Association, allowing for a much more expansive representation system across particular crops or industries. According to the UFW's website, "The United Farm Workers of America and Global Horizons signed the first nationwide union contract protecting agricultural guest workers. Global Horizons is one of America's largest suppliers of imported foreign farmworkers, operating in dozens of states" (UFW 2006). Rather than securing a contract with a grower associ-ation, the UFW targeted the labor contractor and was successful due to the clearly horrendous conditions that Global Horizons created in the employment of H-2A workers.

The plight of farmworkers today is much the same as it was during the Bracero Program. The undocumented status of a large number of farm-workers leaves them at an extreme disadvantage *vis-à-vis* growers, since the threat of deportation is very real and is at times carried out. Capitalist-labor relations can best be described as coercive, and the state's role has been particularly one-sided. As much as growers bemoan state interven-tionism in the form of portable toilets and clean drinking water in the fields, the contemporary reality is that state intrusion into agricultural class relations most often results in favor of growers. The abolition of *el cortito* (short-handled hoe) due to legal action (Murray 1982), the require-ment of employer verification of citizenship status, explicit rules regulat-ing pesticide application procedures, and the short-lived successes of the Agricultural Labor Relations Board (ALRB) of California are often cited as examples of worker victories.

In spite of these gains, the arduous nature of manual labor and meager pay for Mexican migratory workers has not been significantly altered by legal protections. Due to lack of state enforcement, growers disregard many laws that are intended to protect workers. The California ALRB is now firmly in the hands of those pursuing growers' interests, thanks to Republican governors Deukmejian, Wilson, and Schwarzenegger. Piecemeal gains in the interests of workers have had very little impact on

---

United Farm Workers (UFW)

The farmworkers' movement was more than simply a collective bargaining agent. The union's formation and its activities became part of a larger civil rights movement for Chicanos,[4] but it probably had its largest impact on subsequent movements. It was not until the rise of the UFW that farm-workers were able to call a union their own and see tangible results from organizing, boycotting, and strike efforts. In terms of public conscious-ness, the UFW succeeded by bringing the plight of migrant farmworkers into the everyday lives and conversations of the US citizenry. With their boycott of California table grape growers and supermarket chains, the march to Sacramento, and Chávez's hunger strike, the UFW became part of a much larger movement for social justice.

---

the capitalist agricultural labor process, so picking grapes, strawberries, and oranges in 1948 is not so different from picking those same crops in 2008. The labor struggles beyond factory farms will be discussed in the next chapter with an eye to how those efforts are improving the quality of work and life for Mexican laborers.[3]

Against All Odds: FLOC[5]

When the Farm Labor Organizing Committee (FLOC) was formed in 1967, it appeared that founder Baldemar Velásquez would ride the tide of farmworker organizing that was sweeping the nation and create in effect a sister union to the California-based UFW for Midwestern farm laborers. Conditions for farmworkers in the Midwest were markedly difficult from the very onset, but FLOC always seemed to secure the most innovative labor contracts under some of the most seemingly impossible circumstances. The first weapon at FLOC's disposal was the strike. In Northwest Ohio, migrant farmworkers are recruited primarily to pick tomatoes and cucumbers (for pickles). The first wave of strikes in 1968 quickly led to contracts with 33 growers who worried that their perishable tomato crop would wither on the vines without the labor to pick it. But those contracts were fleeting as growers switched to less labor-intensive crops and mounted a successful anti-FLOC media campaign in the ensuing years. Some of their criticisms reflected the very real contradictory position into which growers were forced between the food processors they supplied and the workers calling for better wages. Growers "claimed that their own ability to provide wages, housing, and other benefits were governed by the prices paid by the large food-processing corporations" (Barger and Reza 1994, 58).

Not deterred but definitely delayed by supplier and processor tactics, FLOC reorganized efforts and eventually mounted their second tactic, a consumer boycott against the beneficiaries of the area's cheap tomatoes and pickles: Campbell Soup (who owned Vlasic Pickles), Libby, Heinz, and Dean Foods. The food processors quickly passed the buck on labor relations to growers. Because they did not directly employ the migrants, the standard corporate line was that they could not interfere in collective bargaining agreements. Skillfully, FLOC pointed to the mechanization of the tomato harvest, the requirement that growers who supplied tomatoes must use the company-owned seedlings, and the contract arrangement at the beginning of each growing cycle that predetermined costs and crop yield returns as evidence that food processor decisions had a direct impact on labor relations between growers and migrants. As a result, the first third-party contract in labor history (including growers, workers, and Campbell Soup) was signed in 1985. This occurred at a time when agricultural labor was exempt from National Labor Relations Board (NLRB) and minimum wage protections. The third-party contract states that a mutually recognized commission would arbitrate labor-relations matters and that Campbell recognized the freedom of association of tomato and cucumber growers in Ohio and Michigan that would "specifically participate in representation proceedings and collective bargaining" with FLOC (Barger and Reza 1994, 79).

The boycott of Campbell Soup, the main beneficiary of tomatoes grown by Midwest growers, began in 1979 and included informational pickets, strikes that closed down production, church group vigils, a well-coordinated consumer boycott, and a hunger strike led by Velásquez. The first major boycott waged by FLOC, Campbell Soup (tomatoes) eventually involved over 1 million consumers and support for picketing workers primarily from local church groups and some of American Federation of State, County, and Municipal Employees (AFSCME) and Communication Workers of America (CWA) locals.

One of the main reasons for including cucumber workers was the further debasing of workers' rights. Many pickle growers employed sharecropping as the main mode of cucumber picking to skirt income tax, child labor laws, minimum wage requirements, and any employee benefits. In addition, the risks were displaced to the sharecropper whose eventual pay depended on the particular yield. What do tomatoes and pickles have to do with each other? The answer is related both to the horizontal integration of large food-processing conglomerates and the migrant stream that brings Mexican farmworkers to Indiana, Ohio, Michigan, and Illinois. Companies that rely on tomatoes for soup, juice, and catsup are the same companies, or subsidiaries of these companies, that control the pickle market. Additionally, the Midwest migrant stream is usually sequenced so that workers move north in the spring or early summer to pick cucumbers when they are still small and fresh and then move on to the tomato harvest. Aware of both factors, FLOC's organizing base started with tomato workers, but on any given week a tomato worker may also be a cucumber picker, or truck crop harvester, or blueberry picker.

A consumer boycott and strike of H.J. Heinz resulted in a three-year, third-party contract signed in June 1987. In November 1991, after a successful organizing campaign in the migrants' home bases of Texas and Florida, FLOC represented workers entered into a contract with Dean Foods, and thus the vast majority of the Midwest pickle market was producing union-harvested pickles. But there is a major drawback to the third-party contracts. "The ad hoc and voluntary understanding depends primarily on the parties' good will and acceptance of the document as a binding contract. Workers have no legal protection when they organize or seek to bargain collectively, nor are there any mechanisms for government protection or enforcement of contract terms except for the possibility of civil litigation for breach of contract" (Edid 1994, 59).

Interestingly, the national AFL-CIO has provided absolutely no financial support to FLOC even though FLOC is affiliated to it and did not break ranks when the Change To Win (CTW) left (see below). For its most recent organizing campaign of North Carolina's temporary visa holders or H-2A workers, FLOC was on its own. The Mount Olive pickle boycott began as an extension of strategies deployed by FLOC in Ohio and Michigan. A right-to-work state, North Carolina has a very long history of squelching labor discontent and busting unions. Undeterred, FLOC utilized the previous strategies of consumer boycotts, picket lines, and church group support to force the Mount Olive Pickle Company into negotiations. The local, community-friendly image that Mount Olive portrayed was recast by FLOC as a crisis within the family farm — not growers vs. workers per se, but growers and workers vs. agribusiness. What was different in the North Carolina organizing attempt was the temporary status of the migrant farmworkers. Mount Olive was following a trend of other North Carolina agricultural producers by increasingly employing temporary visa holders under the auspices of the H-2A program, thus hiring Mexican migrants for short-term contracts.

In the early 1990s, Florida's US Sugar, Montana sheepherders, and the New England Apple Council were the main employers of H-2A temporary agricultural workers. Most growers complained that the program was too cumbersome, due to the several requirements they must adhere to when employing H-2A workers, that is, respecting prevailing wages and providing code-compliant housing, at-cost meals, and worker's compensation insurance. Most agricultural employers preferred the less bureaucratic option — employing undocumented workers. But in North Carolina, the H-2A program was the most recent attempt at solving a perennial labor shortage problem as first African American sharecroppers then Caribbean immigrants left the fields for better options. Currently, though no data are published or publicly available, FLOC reports that the vast majority of North Carolina's H-2A workers are Mexican migrants. It was this immigration law context that further complicated FLOC negotiations with the Mount Olive Pickle Company.

There are no legal provisions protecting temporary visa holders' right to organize. Yet the shared status as temporary workers proved to be a major bonus to FLOC as the H-2A workers' shared social situations meant that FLOC could spread its net more widely to encompass all employers of H-2A labor in North Carolina. The breakthrough happened on September 16, 2004. The third-party contract includes Mount Olive Pickle Company (processor), FLOC (union), and the North Carolina Growers' Association (growers), which is used by a plethora of growers to minimize expenses and jointly apply to the US Department of Labor for workers. The FLOC agreement includes tobacco workers, pickle workers, and all other industries whose growers are affiliated with the North Carolina Growers' Association. FLOC's most important duties are to register grievances in the recruitment center in Monterrey, Mexico, and maintain seniority lists for returnees. FLOC has successfully documented worker abuses, recouped lost wages, and provided a collective voice for North Carolina's more than 10,000 H-2A workers. All of FLOC's activities have been performed by an extremely small, dedicated, and chronically underpaid or voluntary staff. The dangers associated with challenging the *enganchadores* system were made apparent when FLOC organizer and compliance officer, Santiago Rafael Cruz, was murdered in the Monterrey office on April 9, 2007. FLOC workers' activities and sacrifices are a testament to the power of the few to take on the most powerful.

Fighting Goliath with Pennies, Students, and Faith: The Coalition of Immokalee Workers[6]

In the heart of South Florida's Everglades, a small farming community has taken on international significance in demonstrating the power of a small and determined group of farmworkers to force concessions from one of the giants of the fast-food industry—the less recognized Yum! Brands. The Coalition of Immokalee Workers (CIW) was founded in 1993 when workers began to meet to discuss the shared labor conditions in the tomato fields that surround the largest farmworker community in Florida. The

US Census calculates that 71 per cent of Immokalee's nearly 20,000 residents are Latino. Almost 60 per cent self-identify as Mexican, but the CIW calculates the breakdown as 50 per cent Mexican, 30 per cent Guatemalan, 10 per cent Haitian, and 10 per cent other ethnicities.[7] The discrepancy is related to the undocumented status of many of the farmworkers and the fear of deportation. The Guatemalan population has learned what many Central American and South American immigrants have realized: it's better to say to government officials that one is from Mexico as the deportation and return trip distance is reduced and significantly less complicated.

The Census 2000 data on Immokalee reveal an abysmal situation. The rate of housing rentals (62.2 per cent), educational attainment (76 per cent have not earned a high-school diploma and only 2.5 per cent have a college education), per capita median income ($8,576), and individuals below the poverty line (39.8 per cent) all point to a community with seemingly few resources to take on a multinational corporation like Taco Bell's parent Yum! Brands, but that is exactly what the residents of Immokalee have done. "Immokalee, Fla., is home to the Six L's Packing Company, Inc., where predominately immigrant farmworkers are paid from 35 to 45 cents for every 32-pound bucket of tomatoes they pick. They are paid about $7,500 annually. They don't have health insurance, sick leave, paid holidays or vacations, or a pension" (Critzon 2004, 618).

The initial campaign was very small and had no intention of solving every social problem in Immokalee. Rather, the demand was for one penny per pound of tomatoes picked. The logic was that a wealthy corporation could easily afford one cent per pound more to bring workers out of dire poverty to at least a minimum, though not a living, wage. "The workers wish for Taco Bell to pay 1 cent more for each pound of tomatoes they buy from the Six L's. This would nearly double the farmworkers' annual pay to about $14,000 and would cost the consumer about one-fourth of a penny more for a Chulupa" (Critzon 2004, 619). CIW's campaign involved church congregations, students, truth tours, skillful use of Internet communications, a hunger strike on the steps of the corporate headquarters, and the framing of workers' demands in human rights terms. On March 8, 2005, Yum! Brands agreed to the penny per pound proposal, and the Immokalee area growers (Six L's, Pacific, Collier, Nobles, and Gargiulo) agreed to pass that along to workers' wages.

Of course, this success is limited as it means that Immokalee workers are now making poverty-level wages and still have no benefits. However, the incremental improvement from farmworker wages and living conditions to working-poor wages and conditions is a step in the right direction. Further, the victory in the Taco Bell campaign is precedent-setting because the corporation has taken responsibility for the wages of subcontracted workers down its supply chain. The CIW has reorganized its efforts and energies by taking on McDonald's, Burger King, Whole Foods grocery stores, and the Bon Appétit foodservice company. In cooperation with the Presbyterian Church (USA), Robert F. Kennedy Memorial Center for Human Rights, National Economic and Social Rights Initiative, and Student/Farmworker Alliance Interfaith Action, the CIW founded the Alliance for Fair Food,[8] a broad-based coalition of food advocates, religious organizations, unions, faith-based organizations, community groups, student/youth groups, and human rights organizations (e.g., Food First, Pax Cristi, AFL-CIO, CTW, United Students Against Sweatshops, and Amnesty International).

One of the CIW's tools is the truth tour, first used to challenge Taco Bell and now McDonald's and Burger King. Building on coalitions with congregations and university student activists, truth tours are designed to personalize the working and living conditions in Immokalee while juxtaposing the farmworkers' poverty status to the opulent displays of wealth by owners of the fast-food industry. The one penny per pound campaign is designed as a first stage in making visible the obscured supply chain that links fast-food consumers to the exploitation of farmworkers.

The CIW has a particular flare for the dramatic, first by targeting the fast-food chain that supplies US citizens with Mexican fast food, highlighting the fact that the Mexican workers who provided the tomatoes for Taco Bell's tacos were not paid enough to order from the 99-cent menu. They have also targeted a brand that is part of a much larger conglomerate, the largest restaurant corporation in the world, which includes Pizza Hut, Long John Silvers, KFC, and A&W. Consolidated and owned by the Pepsi Corporation, PepsiCo spun off its fast-food industries under the Yum! Brands but still has the controlling interest in the publicly traded corporation. The food purchaser, Unified Foodservice Purchasing Co-op (UFPC), while portraying itself as an independent cooperative, supplies all of the Yum! restaurant lines. "Taco Bell currently purchases all the fresh tomatoes for its corporate-owned and franchise restaurants (about 40 million pounds annually) through UFPC. In Florida, UFPC obtains its fresh tomatoes through a single broker who purchases directly from five or six different growers" (Oxfam 2004, 29).

Different from other labor campaigns, the boycott of Taco Bell was most prominently organized and carried out by university students at their college campuses and surrounding communities. The most successful boycott occurred on the University of California Los Angeles campus where students forced the termination of Taco Bell's contract at the student union. Boycotts were less directly organized by CIW staffers as their outreach was often limited to the truth tours that galvanized support for the cause. A multi-pronged, diffuse set of tactics led to the eventual pressure on Taco Bell to take corporate responsibility for enacting the penny per pound pass-through. Negotiations were aided by visible support from various individuals such as Ethel Kennedy, United Nations High Commissioner on Human Rights; former president of Ireland Mary Robinson and former US president Jimmy Carter; members of the music group Rage Against the Machine; actor Martin Sheen; *Fast Food Nation* author Eric Schlosser; and the Progressive and Hispanic Congressional Caucuses.

Another unique aspect of the CIW campaign is their framing the plight of Immokalee's farmworkers as first and foremost a human rights issue. Growers in Florida have a very long legacy of harsh mistreatment of workers. At their most extreme, they rely on labor conditions that meet both the common sense and legal definitions of slavery. The sugar industry in Florida was notorious for trapping foreign workers into debt peonage where any wages earned were retained by companies such as US Sugar to cover housing, boarding, or transportation costs. Well into the twenty-first century, slavery is still alive and well in Florida, according to the CIW website:

> In 2002, three Florida-based agricultural employers convicted in federal court on slavery, extortion, and weapons charges were sentenced to a total of nearly 35 years in prison and the forfeiture of $3 million in assets. The men, who employed over 700 farmworkers, threatened workers with death if they were to try to leave, and pistol-whipped and assaulted—at gunpoint—passenger van service drivers who gave rides to farmworkers leaving the area.[9]

The CIW anti-slavery campaign consists of a legal arm, which investigates cases and provides legal assistance to the enslaved, and a human rights arm called the "Freedom Network Training Institute on Human Trafficking," which trains state and federal law enforcement and social service personnel in the Southeastern US to recognize and assist enslaved people. It also includes a public information arm that holds corporations like Taco Bell publicly accountable for unjustly profiting from suppliers that utilize slave labor.

The CIW operates with other Mexican immigrant-led organizations such as Centro Comunitario Juan Diego (Chicago), Centro de Trabajadores Agricolas (El Paso), La Mujer Obrera (El Paso), and the North Carolina Farmworkers Project and is affiliated with the Poverty Scholars Program of the Poverty Initiative at Union Theological Seminary (New York). They join in the effort to re-ignite Dr. Martin Luther King's Poor People's Campaign to raise up generations of religious and community leaders dedicated to building a movement to end poverty led by the poor, as a social force united and organized across color lines. In the process, they work with poor people's organizations across the country that use the Universal Declaration of Human Rights to demand rights to food, housing, health, education, communication, and a living-wage job. In contrast to organizations that advocate for poor people, that work to ameliorate conditions of poverty, or that organize only among one racial or ethnic group, this is an emerging effort to unite the poor of every race, religion, community, and occupation so as to build and lead a broader and more powerful movement to end poverty altogether.

Conclusion

One cannot underestimate the inspirational effect of the UFW and FLOC in making another world both conceivable and achievable. The CIW's campaign against Taco Bell, its annual truth tours, and the significant church and university student support for the cause have resulted in a major labor victory for an organization that is not union-affiliated. FLOC's utilization of third-party contracts similarly relied upon church groups for publicizing workplace conditions and leading boycotts to publicize the supply chains that rely upon exploited Mexican immigrant labor to turn tomatoes into Campbell's soup and cucumbers into Mount Olive pickles. In Washington, the deleterious working conditions facing Thai immigrants allowed the UFW, in collaboration with state agencies, to end the exploitative working conditions fostered by labor contractor Global Horizons. After years of unsuccessful organizing in the Washington apple industry, the result was UFW representation of the state's H-2A temporary visa workers.

As agribusiness develops "factories in the field" in every region of the US (and increasingly in Canada and Southern Mexico), the large-scale demand for short-term labor leads to a rise in the usage of the H-2A temporary visa program as well as a larger proportion of immigrant workers without papers filling the bottom rungs of the agricultural ladder. Rather than moving up the ladder, most Mexican immigrants find employment options beyond agriculture as their sole means of economic mobility. As capitalist firms vertically integrate their supply chains, the agri-food system is defined by increased monopolization, increased labor exploitation, and minimal safeguards for workers. Since they work as temporary visa holders in a continuation of the Bracero Program, workers face many of the same restrictions (their bonding to particular employers, lack of voice in working and living conditions, and lack of enforcement of worker rights) in the H-2A program.

The allies of organized labor and grassroots organizations are fighting along with immigrant workers for their rights along several dimensions. Seniority hiring lists, worker grievance procedures, enforcement of wage and working conditions, and increased wages are central outcomes of a broader community organizing model that links workers to one another and puts them in charge of their union and/or organization. The most successful campaign to increase workers' wages with the penny-pass-through agreement was organized by a non–union affiliated organization by and for immigrants. These trends toward grassroots organizing and non–union affiliated labor organizing by Mexican immigrants are the topics of the next chapter.

Notes

1. The history of both farm labor organizing and Saul Alinsky's Community Service Organizations are two important precursors to the UFW that merit attention beyond the scope of this chapter. The history of Mexican farm labor organizing includes impressive gains, including the 1903 victory of the Japanese-Mexican Labor Association in Oxnard, the El Monte Berry strike of 1933 that led to the first collectively bargained wage gains, the union win of better wages and working conditions against the cantaloupe growers of California's Imperial Valley, and the organizing of the pecan shellers' union in Texas. It also includes repression—the treatment of the Wobblies (International Workers of the World) as subversives, repression of the Wheatland riot by the National Guard, and various local police efforts at ending strikes. The 1938 pecan shellers' strike with the United Cannery, Agricultural, Packing, and Allied Workers of America (UCAPAWA) was crucial but led to the disintegration of UCAPAWA and an important lesson in labor history as it coincided

with the red-baiting practices of the McCarthy era, the consolidation of the AFL and CIO, the presence of the Communist Party in US labor politics, and the difficulty of sustaining a multi-racial union in Jim Crow segregationist times.

The drive for union representation of migrant farmworkers was always ancillary to the industrial labor movement. Fringe unions, such as the Southern Tenant Farmers' Union, attempted to organize in the fields under the leadership of Ernesto Galarza and the National Farm Labor Union (NFLU). Recruitment was limited strictly to US citizens and was based on US labor laws, so many immigrant workers were automatically excluded from joining the ranks. In 1959, the AFL-CIO finally took an active interest in organizing farm workers and funded the Agricultural Workers Organizing Committee (AWOC). Unfortunately, AWOC seemed to be designed, according to Ernesto Galarza (1970), to replace the NFLU, and the union infighting assured its eventual failure in recruiting workers and improving conditions.

Several factors contributed to the failure of Mexican agricultural worker unionization before the mid-twentieth century. Besides the prevalent racism of organized labor and American society at the time, a lack of commitment by the labor movement, unjust labor laws that excluded farmworkers from protections, and a vicious state/corporate agricultural industry alliance all thwarted the unionization of Mexican farmworkers (Sanchez 1993; Gutierrez 1995; Mooney and Majka 1995; Guerin-Gonzales 1996). On top of the latter obstacles, key to the lack of success was the un-organic nature of these organizing drives (Ganz 2000; Mooney and Majka 1995, 130).

2. See UFW's Global Horizons-UFW Chronology, http://www.ufw.org/_page .php?menu=organizing&inc=keycampaign/globalhorizons/GHchron.htm.

3. Mize sought employment in the agricultural fields of Fresno County in 1997 that allowed him to understand contemporary working conditions first-hand.

4. Chicano is a term of group identification that was adopted during the Mexican American civil rights movement of the 1960s.

5. This section on FLOC benefited greatly from Mize's supervision of an undergraduate student's paper written for Cornell's Latino Studies Program Farmworkers course taught by Professor Ray Craib. Thanks to Erin ImHof for her efforts in documenting FLOC's experiences with H-2A worker organizing.

6. This section benefited greatly from Mize's supervision of an exemplary American Studies honors thesis written by Kristyn Walker.

7. See http://www.ciw-online.org.

8. See http://www.allianceforfairfood.org.

9. See http://www.ciw-online.org.

Chapter Four

Organized Labor and Mexican Labor Organization

The UFW has taken the position that "union rights = civil rights = human rights." In this chapter, we elaborate on how a constellation of Mexican immigrant movements are embodying that mantra. In the previous chapter, we also discussed the UFW's recent shift to temporary worker organizing, but a longer look at its history notes several missteps between the successful 1960s strikes and boycotts and the recent signing of the Global Horizons contract. The purge of key organizers and leadership in the late 1970s and early 1980s is rarely discussed in public but points to the singular power and vision of César Chávez and the fear of internal dissent. Yet these internal struggles have had some positive, albeit unintended, results. Some of the most talented leaders in the UFW shone on their own once they left Chávez's shadow. Most prominent is Eliseo Medina, currently the international executive vice-president of the Service Employees International Union (SEIU). Medina was the son of a Mexican Bracero and left Mexico for California at age ten. He first heard about the NFLU as a teenager and became one of its first organizers. During the Delano grape strike, Chávez asked Medina to organize the boycott in Chicago. Having never seen a large city, Medina learned the hard way how to survive in a metropolis and to seek outside support. His organizing skills also brought him to Florida to unionize farmworkers in the sugar industry. But Medina's departure from the UFW Executive Council after the great purge of many of its original organizers and staff created an opportunity that now defines labor unions in the current service economy.

Medina joined the SEIU and quickly moved his way up the leadership structure until he oversaw the Justice for Janitors (J4J) movement in the late 1990s. As a key leader in today's fastest growing labor union in the nation, with 1.8 million members, he has used tactics and techniques

developed during the UFW's rise to prominence and created new strategies that have given the labor movement a needed boost. Unquestionably,
Medina learned from his UFW days to reorient the labor union movement
toward viewing immigrants as an asset to be organized. Today, SEIU currently leads the way in promoting pathways to legalization and progressive
immigration law reform and serves as the main catalyst for organizing
immigrant workers in California, Texas, Florida, and New York. The
Change to Win Federation (CTW) of labor unions (SEIU, UFCW, Teamsters,
Laborers International Union, United Brotherhood of Carpenters and
Joiners of America, and until recently UNITE-HERE and UFW) is at the
forefront of labor organizing in an era when big labor is losing its grip.
Creative approaches to organizing, particularly organizing immigrants,
are key to this latest round of labor resurgence.

Organized Labor and Unionizing Mexican Workers

In his *tour de force* on the history of Mexican labor organizing, Zaragosa
Vargas documents the range of direct action and organizing strategies of
Colorado sugar beet workers, Tejano cotton pickers, Los Angeles garment
workers, Tejana cigar and domestic workers, New Mexico and Arizona
miners, California cannery workers, and El Paso smelter workers. He
argues, "[In] the period encompassing the 1930s and the World War II
years, Mexican Americans initiated a labor and civil rights movement that
was the precursor of the early civil rights movement of the postwar years,
which formed the foundation of the modern Chicano movement" (2007, 6).
These gains registered despite the actions of the Knights of Labor:

> As an organization devoted to closing skilled trades to any new competition,
> the craft union's reflex was to oppose outsiders. In this sense, most of the AFL
> unions were "exclusionary by definition" and marshaled economic, and to a
> lesser extent, political, arguments to exclude women, Chinese, Japanese,
> African Americans, the illiterate, the noncitizen, and the new immigrants from
> organized workplaces, and whenever possible, from the shores of the United
> States. (Roediger 2005, 79)

This double exclusion, based on race and immigrant status, relegated
most Mexican labor organizing actions to the mutual aid society model of
community self-help. As a result, the most successful labor unions targeting Mexican workers have sought to overcome this exclusion through

community unionism best evidenced by the actions of the UFW. When the UFW purged organizers and pursued bureaucratic gains with their insti- tutionalization of the California ALRB, other unions like SEIU and UNITE-HERE benefited directly by hiring those organizers. In this section we will discuss the successful J4J campaign that built upon earlier UFW successes and community organizing models, as well as the current CTW and its varied immigrant organizing efforts.

Justicia! *Justice for Janitors*

The SEIU was formed primarily as an African American union when Blacks were barred from White unions in cities like San Diego. Committed to representing those on the fringes, the SEIU organized in postwar times when manufacturing was at the core of the economy to represent the nation's janitors, health care workers, and other service workers. As the post-industrial economy of the 1970s led the way to a service-based econ- omy, the SEIU was strategically poised for growth in ways that most indus- trial labor unions were handicapped.

Until recently, scholars held that as long as immigrants were vulnerable to deportation and other forms of workplace exploitation, they would be "impossible to organize into viable unions" (Jenkins 1978, 529–30). Nonetheless, despite a plethora of strikes against them—their grim prospects for unionization, vulnerability to discrimination, the surplus of immigrant labor, INS/ICE raids of workplaces, increasing difficulties of crossing the border, and the possibility of deportation—Mexican immi- grants *have* continuously demonstrated their ability to organize them- selves into "viable unions." The best example of such organizing is the Los Angeles J4J campaign (Fisk, Mitchell, and Erickson 2000). Over the last 20 years, it has registered major organizing successes, deployed unique and creative strategies (such as targeting high-profile companies that rented office space to pressure seemingly untouchable building owners), and redefined how organized labor views Mexican immigrant laborers.

Los Angeles was unequivocally committed to janitorial unionism from the postwar economic boom through the 1970s. "By the mid-1970s, nearly all the downtown buildings were under union contract, as well as most of the large buildings in Hollywood, Pasadena, and Santa Monica" (Waldinger *et al.* 1997, 37). When the SEIU operated at its peak of 5,000 members, the majority of its members were African American. Contracts were signed between the building owners or a handful of the largest contractors, who controlled the vast majority of the market share, and primarily SEIU Local 399. Seeing a vulnerability in high wages and very little non-labor overhead costs, a group of ascendant mid-size, vehemently anti-union companies entered the contracting business by employing large numbers of Central American (non-state recognized) refugees and undocumented Mexican immigrants to work for minimum wage and no fringe benefits. Unexpectedly, it was the new labor force that returned often to their radical political roots and began the process of reorganizing the Southern California janitorial industry under the auspices of an understaffed and resource-poor SEIU.

After "modest success in smaller cities" such as Pittsburgh and Denver, the J4J campaign came to Los Angeles in 1988 (Milkman and Wong 2000, 107). Under the leadership of its then head (and recent president of the AFL-CIO) John Sweeney, SEIU demonstrated a new commitment to organizing. Consequently, despite its grassroots appearance, Milkman and Wong contend that the J4J campaign was "leadership initiated." Regardless of its top-down origins, it was a "comprehensive campaign" that included "determined and skillful organizing, backed up with adequate financial and legal resources" that ultimately led to its historic victory (Milkman and Wong 2000, 103, 108).

Centralization of the campaign allowed the national union to bypass the local union's bureaucracy and lack of enthusiasm for the organizing drive. In fact, most of the financial resources and leadership came from SEIU's national headquarters (Milkman and Wong 2000, 107). One of the key top-down decisions was to bypass traditional NLRB elections by opting for the more worker-centered approach of "card checking." This involves a majority sign-up process whereby authorization forms are public (as opposed to NLRB secret ballots) and more often result in successful votes for union representation.

The comprehensive campaign included legal challenges filed in the courts against building owners and cleaning contracting companies for a variety of wage and worker safety violations. But the more visible tactics of SEIU rank-and-file members drew the bulk of media attention. J4J's repertoires of contention ranged from UFW-like street theater to protesting at golf courses where corporate heads played. Eventually, the janitors escalated their tactics to various forms of civil disobedience such as "sitting down in the lobbies of buildings and refusing to budge, or barging into sensitive business meetings, chanting loudly, and tossing bags of trash," and even "parading along the highway and tying up traffic" (Fantasia and Voss 2004, 142–43). Conjuring up images of racist White police beating up peaceful demonstrators during the civil rights movements of the 1960s, during one of the J4J rallies and right in front of TV cameras "police attacked demonstrators at a peaceful march," causing harm not only to children in the crowd but also causing a pregnant woman to lose her unborn child. This beating caused a "public outrage" that increased both public and political support for the organizing campaign (Waldinger *et al.* 1997; Milkman and Wong 2000, 110).

Though some scholars (Waldinger *et al.* 1997, 42) caution against overemphasizing "community involvement" in the organizing drive, at least one J4J organizer contends that it was crucial to the union's victory. Rocio Saenz, an immigrant from Mexico and a "key leader of the janitors' movement," recalls: "One of the major things for the campaign was community. [J4J] started contacting organizations that have been fighting for many different things: housing, immigration, student organizations, and religious organizations, and we started having a response. People are eager to do something militant" (Saenz, in Milkman and Wong 2000, 25–26). In addition, Fantasia and Voss (2004, 145) observed:

> Immigrant workers relied heavily on ethnic networks for social support and for the necessities of everyday life like jobs and housing. Whereas these networks had been used in the past by contractors to recruit compliant immigrant janitors, the J for J campaign demonstrated that these same social connections could also serve as resources for building solidarity.

Thus, not only was coalition building with local community organizations and local politicians vital to the campaign's successes, but so was tapping into the informal social networks of these immigrant workers.

Coupled with later successes in organizing Silicon Valley and Sacramento high-rise janitors, the California janitorial organizing model is currently being replicated at the University of Miami and in downtown Houston.[1] Both Florida and Texas are right-to-work states, and both pose particular challenges to organizing campaigns, but the SEIU has followed the leadership of its executive vice-president, Eliseo Medina, and forged ahead into one of the most ambitious organizing strategies to date.

At the University of Miami, the SEIU has taken on Boston-based contractor UNICCO Services by targeting the absentee company and University of Miami president Donna Shalala (a former Clinton cabinet member) through a series of civil disobedience acts including a hunger strike, sit-ins, and marches, and by building coalitions with and support from student and community groups to place the plight of the poverty-waged janitors onto the national media stage. Vice-president Medina joined the janitors in a hunger strike that resulted in the hospitalization of several strikers. The organizing campaign broadened the Latino base of janitors to include primarily Cuban refugee women among the ranks of the SEIU. "Maritza Paz, who was admitted to the United States 13 years ago as a political refugee from Cuba, hired on at the university 11 years ago at $4.35 an hour. When the strike began, she had worked her way up to a sumptuous $6.70 hourly wage with no benefits, for which she cleaned 17 bathrooms and 20 offices every day" (Meyerson 2006, A23). The university relented on May 1, 2006, when it agreed to require its contractor UNICCO to allow majority union elections and thus bargain with the SEIU. "The contract, which runs from Sept. 1, 2006 through Aug. 31, 2010, provides janitors with raises each year, and guarantees that their health care will remain affordable."[2]

The campaign to organize Houston janitors has taken on a similar cast. Large public theater performances (including a well-financed national advertising campaign) holding oil conglomerates like Chevron responsible for employing janitors at poverty-level wages were coupled with direct action tactics on the ground that featured the lives of hard-working, poorly remunerated Latina immigrants as the rallying point. "The janitors who organized in Houston represented four of the five largest cleaning companies in the city and the companies agreed to allow the union to try to organize their employees. That agreement [representing 5,300 workers] came after the union organized a 10-day strike by Houston janitors" (Gamboa 2006). An estimated 80 protestors engaged in acts of civil disobedience even though firings and arrests were constantly threatened. On November 16, 2006, mounted policemen charged 50 Houston janitors and supporters during a non-violent protest, and this action seemed to turn public support squarely in their favor. As Medina (quoted in Gamboa 2006) has described the SEIU J4J strategy:

"I think we've shown that workers in the campaign in the South and Southwest want to be organized and need to be organized and if unions come forth with a plan and a vision, workers will answer the call," said Medina who spoke to a group of reporters. All but two of the 17 states, New Mexico and Colorado, are right-to-work states, meaning workers in those states always have the right to decide whether to join a union. Union membership in all the states, except Nevada, is between 2 per cent and 4 per cent, Medina said. Nevada's is about 14 per cent, largely because of the gaming industry there, he said.

The union is attempting to add to its 1.8 million member base with its immigrant organizing attempts in the Southwest and Southern US. It all began in Los Angeles and Century City with the highly recognizable J4J campaign, but the SEIU has the potential to change the low-pay, no-benefits service sector nationwide.

Organizing Immigrants in the "New" Economy: TDU, CTW, and UNITE-HERE

The campaigns in Houston and Miami were won after the SEIU joined other unions committed to popular organizing by splitting from the lobby-heavy, minimal organizing AFL-CIO to create the Change to Win Federation (CTW). CTW took AFL-CIO president Sweeney to task for his slippage into business unionism as its members combined into a new labor organization more devoted to grassroots organizing, serving new constituencies, and mass recruitment techniques. In the 1980s, the anti-union Reagan administration and its adherence to neoliberalism forced organized labor to rethink its strategies, abandon any sense of complacency in existing contracts, and re-prioritize their lobbying and organizing efforts.[3] For example, the AFL-CIO took a reactionary position in the hearings leading up to the Immigration Reform and Control Act of 1986 by adopting the line that illegal immigrants were competing for union jobs and their presence was depressing wage scales, undercutting union demands for wage hikes, allowing themselves to be used as strikebreakers, etc. This put the AFL-CIO in league with not only conservative xenophobic groups such as Zero Population Growth and the Federation for American Immigration Reform (FAIR) but also the National Association for the Advancement of Colored People (NAACP), which viewed immigrants as unwelcome job competition for poor working Blacks.

Clearly, strategies had to change if the AFL-CIO was going to adapt to the changes in the new economy and labor-market composition. The International Brotherhood of Teamsters (IBT or Teamsters), one of the most regressive groups in labor history, led the way in reversing the decline in labor organizing partly by innovating transnational labor and immigrant/

racially inclusive organizing. Within the larger organization, a dissident group, Teamsters for a Democratic Union (TDU), sought to recover the Teamsters from its legacy of cronyism, organized crime, sweetheart deals, and violent suppression of opposition. When it was becoming clear that international free trade agreements, deregulation of the trucking industry, and industry consolidation would hamstring organizing efforts, the TDU initiated a bottom-up organizing strategy with key locals taking on the Teamster leadership bureaucracy and pushing for democratic reforms.

One of the most fruitful sources of organizing support came from Mexican-origin truckers. "TDU became an active presence in Watsonville, California-based Local 912 in the early 1980s, when it campaigned for bilingual union meetings. While the TDU chapter was always small, it was able to provide a vision of what a union could be and to help organize the victorious 1986–87 strike at Watsonville Canning" (Moody 1988, 234). Fantasia and Voss (2004, 103) see direct linkages between the internal battles waged by the TDU, the election of Teamsters reformer Ron Carey, and the elevation of SEIU president John Sweeney into the presidency of the AFL-CIO in 1995. But by then the Teamsters were operating on very different terrain because of Reagan's attack on labor unions. The deregulation of the trucking industry was undercutting the organizing base of rank-and-file truckers as the industry was shifting heavily away from large trucking companies and more toward a model of independent contractors on a work-for-hire basis.

The Teamsters' internal contradictions are most clearly evidenced today in its responses to NAFTA. In one of the most important shifts in US organized labor at the international level, the Teamsters from Canada and the US partnered with Mexican reformist trade unions, such as *Frente Auténtico del Trabajo* (FAT), to create a united front against the agreement. Cross-border rallies were sponsored by the Teamsters and FAT union members who stood on both sides of the border with placards stating "NAFTA: bad for workers on both sides of the border" and "*Alto*/Stop" signs with the Mexican and US flags flying in both camps.

On March 13, 1996, the Teamsters' NAFTA Truckers' Summit brought together US and Canadian Teamster leaders with Mexican labor union leaders to create a united front against NAFTA.[4] Proclamations by Teamsters' US president Ron Carey and Canadian president Louis Lacroix illustrated the transnational philosophy of labor organizing against globalization. As Carey stated, "NAFTA threatens jobs and highway safety in all three countries. It's time for truckers to unite. Our fight is not with each other. Our fight is against corporate greed that is destroying jobs and wages on both sides of the border." Lacroix elaborated, "Canadian Teamsters are committed to working with their brothers and sisters in the US and Mexico to defeat the corporate agenda. International solidarity is the most powerful weapon that working people have to resist attacks by transnational employers."[5] The leaders espoused a commitment to a transnational organized labor response to transnational capital. The possibilities implicit in such proclamations have put the international in the IBT for the first time in labor history and allow global labor movements to contend with the overwhelming power of TNCs.

Conversely, with James Hoffa Jr. at the helm of the Teamsters, the union has taken to the Mexican-bashing and fear-mongering that made his father's union infamous. His most recent campaign is to continue the restriction of Mexican truckers into US border states along the proposed NAFTA superhighways. Hoffa has been quoted as characterizing Mexican truckers as drug mules and unsafe drivers who harbor terrorists, threaten homeland security, and terrorize US highways. A crucial Teamsters election in November 2006 pitted him against TDU-candidate Tom Leedham, who was narrowly defeated by Hoffa in a previous election but was soundly defeated in this one.

The Teamsters are emblematic of the organized labor dilemma: to connect with Mexican constituents in solidarity or to continue along the long path of immigrant bashing and divisive tactics that further splinter the workers of the world in response to globalization and neoliberalism. At the same time, when not pursuing the course of exclusion and divisive politics, the Teamsters may still easily slide into a model in which the labor elite seems ready to exploit Mexican labor as rank-and-file members but are resistant to viewing them as worthy of labor leadership. Top-down hierarchies reproduce the racialization of class relationships regardless of whether the culprits are growers, capitalists, or labor elites.

The Teamsters were one of the major players in the CTW, which split from the AFL-CIO in 2005. Joined by the SEIU, UNITE-HERE, UFW, Laborers' Union, Carpenters' Union, and UFCW, the coalition represents 6 million workers and devotes three-quarters of its overall budget to organizing. Convinced that John Sweeney's past successes as an SEIU organizer in Las Vegas are the future of the labor movement, the CTW also feared that he had become the face of big bureaucratic labor, which fills the coffers of politicians by becoming essentially a large lobby, sacrificing its rank-and-file members for political gain. The CTW is comprised of the unions at the forefront of today's organizing efforts that increasingly focus on Mexican immigrant workers. They draw from a long history of organizing garment workers, cashiers, and workers in transportation, trades and construction, and hospitality, which are cornerstone occupations in a post-industrial, service economy. Lessons can certainly be learned from "labor's biggest numerical gain in more than fifty years, bringing in seventy-four thousand workers" (Clawson 2003, 127). In 2006, the major CTW campaigns included a renegotiation of hotel worker contracts in six major cities, a concerted public relations campaign against Walmart and corporate CEOs, port worker organizing, a UFCW-led campaign targeting the Smithfield meat-packing corporation, and SEIU-led drives to unionize homecare workers and hospitality workers.

A wildcat strike of undocumented Latino workers in the Tar Heel, North Carolina, Smithfield plant was organized on November 17, 2006. The UFCW had been working diligently and publicly to organize what was the largest pork-slaughter plant in the world that "employs 5,500 people and slaughters 32,000 hogs a day" (Greenhouse 2006). Company officials estimated 550 workers walked out, while workers registered the number at 1,200 strikers. Both groups agree that all of them were Latino immigrants. Workers were protesting a new policy that dismissed 50 workers whose social security numbers did not match with the Department of Homeland Security (DHS) federal immigration database. "Smithfield Foods recently lost a case in the US Court of Appeals, which upheld National Labor Relations Board findings that managers at the Tar Heel facility had threatened, harassed, and fired workers trying to organize. In another case, Smithfield was found to have used its security forces to threaten workers with arrest by immigration authorities" (Gaouette 2006).

The SEIU homecare workers' campaign was aimed at the minimum-wage–earning, home-based medical attendants that are employed by the state government but are hired and fired by the elderly, infirmed, or disabled care recipient. There is no central worksite to organize, as workers are contracted to individual homes. The SEIU formed the California Home Care Council to begin a door-to-door and phone campaign to raise awareness among homecare workers of their rights and the benefits of union membership. With 75 per cent of the providers being women, and mostly immigrant, the SEIU trained organizers from among the ranks and established personal connections with Spanish-, Farsi-, Tagalog-, and Cantonese-speaking organizers. In 1999, when the workers voted for the SEIU as their bargaining agent, their numerical presence as new union members came with wage gains that doubled their minimum wage salary and health benefits that they historically had forsaken to serve the infirm.

1999 Congressional Testimony

My name is Maria Elena Durazo, V.P. at large of the HERE International Union and I am also the elected President of HERE Local 11 in Los Angeles, California. My parents are immigrants from Mexico and our family of 10 children worked in the fields of California as migrant farmworkers until I was in high school. I started in the labor movement as an organizer in the garment sweatshops with the then ILGWU.... The leadership of that Local had a policy of exclusion. 70% of the members are immigrants from Mexico and Central America. The meetings were held in English only; the publications were sent out in English only and members rarely attended meetings.... As a result of their exclusion, the members had no voice in their Union and on the job.... One thing was sure: I was unwilling to give up on our goals—that our members participate in the decisions of the Union because those decisions impact their lives and that Employers treat the members with Respect, whether they are dishwashers or front desk clerks, or housekeepers. As it turned out, the International assigned some of their best staff, former organizers with [the UFW].... We won historic collective bargaining agreements, the best wage increases in decades; we won a prepaid legal plan with a panel of attorneys to provide free legal services to members, and we protected free family health insurance.... In 1996 I am proud to have been elected the first Latina to the National Executive Board of HERE. Today Local 11 is a strong, financially viable Union presence in Los Angeles; specifically we are known for standing up for issues of concern to the Latino community.... Cooks, dishwashers, and house-keepers participate in negotiating their own contracts and their co-workers vote on whether or not to accept those contracts. Our monthly meetings have grown in numbers because we work hard to make sure the members participate in our Union's daily activities and because our meetings are held in both Spanish and English. The overwhelming majority of our new hires for positions as Organizers and Union representatives come from the membership.... We depend on the participation of our members to make decisions about what is important to them and their families. (Durazo 1999)

SEIU has also organized in the hospitality industry, which led to a major CTW rift that resulted in UNITE-HERE returning to the AFL-CIO in late 2008. The future of organized labor is in a constant state of flux, and internal competition, consolidation, and rifts too often define it. Nowhere is this on display more than in the long and storied history of UNITE-HERE. The testimony of then-HERE organizer and at-large vice-president Maria Elena Durazo, who currently serves as the president of the LA County Federation of Labor, was entered into the Congressional Record at a 1999 Subcommittee on Employer-Employee Relations hearing and represents that crucial Latino presence in organizing efforts (see box).

Durazo's experience is emblematic of the separate journeys of the International Ladies' Garment Workers' Union (ILGWU), Amalgamated Clothing and Textile Workers' Union (ACTWU), and Hotel Employees and Restaurant Employees (HERE) and how they all came together to form the Union of Needletrades, Industrial, and Textile Employees-Hotel Employees and Restaurant Employees (UNITE-HERE). However, it is important to note that, as a Latina, she is truly rare in the upper echelons of organized labor leadership.

When Durazo began as an ILGWU organizer, she faced a garment industry in Los Angeles that increasingly employed sweatshop labor processes that relied on the undocumented status of their female immigrant laborers to maximize exploitation. As the ILGWU was losing membership with the offshoring of garment production to low-wage, Pacific Rim nations, large cities like Los Angeles and New York City were rebuilding their garment industries on the cheap — and primarily on the backs of marginalized immigrant women.

The garment industry has a strong concentration of Latinos and Asian workers, including undocumented workers. Much of this production is organized on a sweatshop (or even homework) basis by employers who feel free to push around workers who can't speak English and who may be undocumented. Thus, the ACTWU and ILGWU have had a strong stake in organizing these workers. Additionally, local unions with large Latino memberships often seek to protect them even if their international supports AFL-CIO policy. They have opposed INS raids and attempted to provide arrested workers with legal and other forms of help. (Moody 1988, 283)

Yet the most serious opposition to organizing efforts was mounted by the apparel industry, and the various tactics at the disposal of corporations were evident during the organizing campaign of Guess jeans. The Guess campaign was aimed at the jeans producer who touted its products as "Made in LA" and "Made in the USA." At the higher end of the designer jean market, Guess's Los Angeles sweatshop practices were an easy target for public shaming. The ILGWU conceived of both a media blitz on corporate irresponsibility coupled with grassroots organizing and planned strikes. Most of the city's garment workers were Mexican immigrant women, joined by a significant number of Central American and Asian immigrants, which collectively provided the fertile soil for grassroots organizing. Milkman (2006, 163) notes that "[a]s early as the mid-1970s, the union's western organizing director had targeted immigrant workers for recruitment and hired some ten young, progressive Latino organizers for this purpose." The ILGWU organized workers in a variety of fabrication industries (a muffler factory, furniture shop, pillow-making plant, and tombstone producer), but the most skilled organizers could not counter the trend of a garment industry that was increasingly employing informal, piece-rate labor through an underground network of sweatshop contractors that exploited undocumented women (Milkman 2006). ILGWU organizer Cristina Vasquez stated, "We were building a union of immigrant workers more than a garment workers' union" (quoted in Milkman 2006, 115).

They thought they had an inroad into organizing the Los Angeles garment district by targeting its most profitable tenant, Guess jeans. When the ILGWU and ACTWU merged in 1995 to create UNITE, the Guess campaign was still in its planning stages. "Unfortunately, Guess retaliated in the predictable manner, by moving work away from contracting shops where strong workers' committees had formed and by moving a substantial proportion of its production work [approximately 40 per cent] to Mexico" (Bonacich and Applebaum 2000, 146). The newly formed UNITE stepped away from grassroots organizing and was particularly hurt by a group of Guess anti-union workers who were sponsored by the corporation to counter the sweatshop accusations. In the end, the Guess campaign faded into irrelevancy as the corporation employed every legal, off-shoring, media counter-campaign, and outsourcing tool at their disposal. While UNITE struggled in vain to establish a base in the new garment capital of the US (not New York but Los Angeles), its future partner would find greater success in the San Francisco, Los Angeles, and Las Vegas hotel industry.

HERE Local 2 is a consolidated representative of all types of workers in San Francisco's hotel industry. One of the few remaining bastions of high union membership, the San Francisco service sector was represented by so many locals that coordinated efforts were often sacrificed to craft protectionism. "[I]n 1975 the HERE International consolidated its five prior craft locals in the San Francisco hotel industry (cooks, bartenders, food servers, bellmen and room cleaners, and kitchen help) into Local 2" (Wells 2000, 110). HERE was at the forefront of creating a united labor front to challenge hotel chain oligarchies.

Like the rest of California, the immigrant population in San Francisco was on the rise as existing Asian American and Latino communities attracted new immigrants from Southeast Asia and Central America. This immigrant labor force increasingly cooked the meals, made the beds, checked the luggage, and served the food in San Francisco's hotel industry. Explaining why immigrant hotel workers were comparatively easy to organize, a HERE organizer stated:

> The fact is, most [immigrants] are situated in the lowest-paid, hardest, highest-turnover jobs. This means they can find another position easy. It also means that a union contract is their only protection. We point this out. They don't have the protection of citizenship or a job with seniority. I'd rather try to organize immigrant room cleaners any day than a food server who is a citizen, who gets tips, and a good wage and is paying off a mortgage. That sort of person is not so willing to risk. (Quoted in Wells 2000, 120)

HERE Local 2 went to great pains both to get to know its rank-and-file members and to cultivate leaders among them to ensure representation of the heterogeneous workforce at all levels. It was the first local to rescind the rule stating that leaders had to be citizens to hold office. As a result, it has several Central American, Filipino, and Vietnamese members in leadership positions. To resonate culturally with the immigrant hotel workers, the union holds celebrations ranging from Mexican Independence Day to Chinese New Year and ensures that its staff (from organizers to executive board members) are bilingual and bicultural in workers' own languages.

HERE registered similar organizing successes among hotel service workers in Los Angeles and Las Vegas. The Los Angeles area Local 11, under the leadership of Maria Elena Durazo, has embodied the best aspects of community unionism by establishing a base of support well beyond the immigrant hotel workers they have so successfully organized. In Las Vegas, a union town is emerging out of the ashes of political corruption and organized crime syndicates. The casino industry is now almost fully unionized thanks to the efforts of HERE Local 226 (Culinary Workers' Union) and Local 165.

In 2004, UNITE and HERE merged for purposes that have not been fully disclosed. "The unions will have a combined membership of more than 440,000 workers and 400,000 retirees, a staff that surpasses 1,000, an operating budget exceeding $60 million a year and assets that include the $3.6 billion Amalgamated Bank, the only union-owned bank in the country" (Malone 2004, 5). The *Wall Street Journal* speculated that the merger was due to HERE's financial woes. According to UNITE-HERE president Bruce Raynor, in the April 19, 2004, issue of *The Nation*, "Neither of these unions has to merge.... We're both unions with solid organizing problems, both well respected and secure. The question is: Are we bigger, better, stronger together? The answer is yes." However, the merger points to a conundrum: the leadership of UNITE and HERE is based on the East Coast, while some of the most vibrant campaigns and greatest organizing successes are taking place on the West Coast.

Mutualistas of Today: Worker Centers and Hometown Associations

The *mutualista* movement is crucial to understanding how independent Mexican labor organizing happens and how work was never viewed in isolation but as part and parcel of all the quality-of-life concerns of Mexican communities. These Mexican mutual aid societies promoted Mexican culture and provided loans, death benefits, financial assistance, bilingual schools, and insurance for the poor (Acuña 2010, 78, 196; Hernandez 1983). These self-help groups were the roots of the type of community unionism adopted later by Chávez and the UFW, as discussed in Chapter 3, and furthered in the J4J and other recent organizing struggles and unionization campaigns. As early as 1951, Mexican labor organizers Phil and Albert Usquiano in San Diego and their *La Hermandad Mexicana Nacional* were challenging INS deportations of Mexican workers who were given visas and permanent residency status to work in the US during World War II, but who, due to housing shortages, lived in Tijuana. When the INS attempted to revoke the work visas and deport them, *La*

Hermandad provided representation and successfully filed suit in many cases. Bert Corona's Centers for Autonomous Social Action/*Centros de Acción Social Autónomo* (CASA) in Los Angeles grew out of the structure of *La Hermandad* and were instrumental in providing housing, economic, legal, and medical assistance for undocumented workers from Mexico and Central America.

Today, union-supported worker centers, non-affiliated worker and day labor centers, and immigrant hometown associations have inherited the commitment of the Mexican mutual aid societies to address concerns beyond collective bargaining rights. The non-affiliated drywallers' strike in Southern California demonstrated that the *mutualista* spirit was alive and well in Latino immigrant communities and that labor struggles could address quality-of-life concerns. The number of worker centers has mushroomed over the past 15 years and, though they vary greatly in terms of their organizational purpose and overall mission, they all commonly work in the interests of immigrant laborers who are mostly left out of either the formal labor market or formal unions due to their undocumented status.

Hometown associations are Mexican immigrant remittance and development clubs or organizations that build infrastructure in Mexico, such as churches or schools, funded by "migradollars"—money sent home by Mexican workers who reside in the US—and Mexican government matching programs. With the immigrant rights movement, hometown associations are keys to understanding the future of immigrant organizing. Many of these non–union affiliated and CTW-affiliated groups came together in 2006 to mount the largest public protest marches since the Vietnam War in opposition to nativist and racist politicians such as US Representatives Tom Tancredo (R-CO) and James Sensenbrenner (R-WI) and Colorado governor Bill Owens.

Southern California Drywallers' Strike

Labor militancy and violent class warfare are often relegated to the dustbin of 1930s Depression-era American unionism (Zinn 1995). Descriptions of fights for union representation and better wages being met by superintendents "on the jobsite [who] carried guns" that they would shoot in the air "to try to scare" striking workers may sound like they come from a distant past, but these are the words of drywall organizer Jesus Gomez, circa 1992 (Gomez 2000, 41). Gomez and his family received "threatening letters" at home and even had shots fired at their house (Gomez 2000, 43).

Hundreds were arrested and key organizers were often tailed by police (Milkman and Wong 2000; Gomez 2000). The extreme levels of persecution against immigrant organizers should not be so shocking, given the constantly violent nature of labor conflicts during the early 1900s. But being subjected to deportation, followed by helicopters, and chased onto freeways were just some of the labor repression tactics aimed at the predominately Mexican drywall workers of Southern California during their famous 1992 strike.

Unlike the "leadership-initiated" origins of the J4J campaign, the grassroots nature of this strike is undisputed. After witnessing the profession become de-unionized and seeing his wages fall by almost 50 per cent in less than 20 years, Jesus Gomez proclaimed *Ya Basta!* — Enough was Enough (Milkman and Wong 2000; Gomez 2000). Gomez tapped into the social networks he had developed as both a worker and foreman and began to visit job sites to discuss with workers the unjust labor practices they were forced to endure. About 300 of the drywall workers were from his home state in Mexico, which helped foster the sense of community and trust that gutsy organizing drives demand (Gomez 2000, 40). After organizing for only a few months, demanding higher wages and union recognition, the immigrant drywallers' work stoppage managed to successfully "shutdown residential housing construction" from north of Los Angeles to the US-Mexico border (Milkman and Wong 2000, 169).

Family and community were key to the victory. After the struggle became public and received major media attention, "Local Latino community groups," such as *Hermandad Mexicana*, "rallied to the workers' defense" and "strikers' wives and other family members participated in various support activities." As worker incomes began to run low, organized labor decided to help. The AFL-CIO set up a "Dry Waller Strike Fund" that raised over $2 million from more than 20 unions to help pay for the rents and other expenses of the striking workers. While church and community groups helped with food and necessities, the California Immigrant Workers Association assisted with legal help (Milkman and Wong 2000, 170, 119, 171).

Because the drywallers were not affiliated with any official union, they were "not subject to the 30-day legal limit on picketing for union recognition." Similar to the J4J campaign, a combination of both a legal and media campaign with a militant grassroots movement eventually led to the dramatic drywaller victory. These "unorganizable" Mexican immigrants won not only union recognition, but also a two-year contract with "higher wages and medical benefits" (Milkman and Wong 2000, 118, 121).

Worker Centers

Immigrant workers are particularly vulnerable to labor exploitation as US labor law offers few, if any, protections for workers who are legal immigrants, much less those with irregular citizenship status. As Chapter 3 attests, Mexican immigrant workers were often ignored by organized labor as a result. One of the unique strategies that arose in the late 1980s to 1990s was the development of worker centers to serve basic needs as well as offer legal representation for enforcing the limited labor protections that are on the books. Fine (2006, 9) describes three waves of worker centers that originated "in response to changes in manufacturing that resulted in worsened conditions, factory closings, and the rise of lower paying service sector jobs." The first wave, arising in the late 1970s, included the Carolina Alliance for Fair Employment (CAFÉ in North and South Carolina), Black Workers for Justice (North Carolina), *La Mujer Obrera* (LMO in El Paso), and the Chinese Staff and Workers Association (New York City). The second wave was focused more directly on immigrant workers in major US cities and represented the largest growth from less than five to more than 35 worker centers by the end of the 1990s. From 2000, the latest wave focuses still on immigrants but more often on Mexican and Central American immigrants who are settling in suburban and rural areas. Only 14 per cent of worker centers are union-affiliated, yet of the remaining 86 per cent, "23 per cent of worker centers were founded by ethnic NGOs; 22 per cent by churches, Catholic Charities, or other faith-based community organizing projects; and 27 per cent by a combination of legal service organization, social service organization, and community-based organizations" (Fine 2006, 14–15).

The most prominent union-based attempts at creating immigrant-serving worker centers are the UNITE Garment Workers Justice Centers operating in New York, Miami, Los Angeles, and San Francisco (Ness 1998, 93).[6] Their overall goal is to organize workers into the union, but they continue to attract associate members, even when unionizing attempts fail, as they provide industrial job-skills training, English as a Second Language instruction, social networking, classes on human and workplace rights, and access to the Union Privilege Benefit Program (Ness 1998, 92; Shostak 1991, 63–64).

More anti-immigrant opposition has been directed at day labor centers that have arisen across the nation but are most heavily concentrated in the Washington, DC, suburbs, Los Angeles metropolitan area, Denver, and the quintessential suburb—Long Island, New York. The Workplace Project, or *El Centro de Derechos Laborales*, featured in the documentary *Farming-ville* (Sandoval and Tambini 2003) and in *Suburban Sweatshops* (Gordon 2006), has created a day-labor center in response to vehement local com-munity opposition to Latino immigrants standing on street corners seek-ing informal employment. Based in Hempstead, New York, with a satellite in Farmingville, the Workplace Project has been in operation since 1992 and has cultivated relationships with local government officials, church groups, Latino rights organizations, and local businesses to create two Long Island day-labor centers. It represents Mexican and Central American immigrants, who are subject to the daily whims of casual employers' needs and are paid informally on the sidewalks of busy thoroughfares, exit/entrance ramps to highways, or in front of home improvement cen-ters such as Home Depot. The Workplace Project aims to take the workers off the streets and to regularize employment relationships by serving as both the wage-rate arbitrator and enforcer of wage and hour infractions. In 2005, it recuperated more than $200,000 in unpaid or overtime wages (Workplace Project 2006, 11). It also intervened on behalf of more than 100 day laborers whose wages earned were never paid by the employers.

Locally and nationally, one-half of all complaints filed at day-labor cen-ters are to recoup unpaid wages. Recent negotiations with the Nassau County District Attorney have resulted in a more diligently enforced law and arrests of contractors for non-payment of wages. "Centers know that to win an equitable solution for day laborers in a given community, they must identify the interests of a range of stakeholders, including local police, area businesses, and neighborhood associations" (Fine 2006, 239–40). In addition to serving day laborers, the Workplace Project also organizes and offers services to Long Island's predominately Latino/Latina janitorial and domestic workers.

The more dangerous aspect of day labor is the racism to which these workers are subjected by some politicians and members of local commu-nities. Workplace Project has had much less success in Suffolk County due to a district attorney who operates as if he is a federal immigration enforcement officer. His efforts are strongly supported by anti–day labor groups such as Sachem (see the box below), who are in turn funded

---

Nativism on Long Island

Recently featured in a 2004 PBS documentary, Farmingville hosts a particularly vehement opposition group who call themselves the Sachem Quality of Life. As Gordon (2006, 19) notes, "Their methods [are] not subtle. In 1999, as a day laborer tried to give testimony at a public hearing, dozens of members of the group stood, put their hands on their hearts, and began to shout the Pledge of Allegiance to drown him out." The group has made national headlines by harassing day laborers on street corners and photographing potential employers to intimidate them from hiring Latino day laborers. Racial overtones and undertones are often at work in Sachem, though they deny their intentions as racist—even though they espouse principles that most would consider a call for ethnic cleansing to restore the lily-white, suburban definition of quality of life—i.e., a world without poor Brown people living in one's vicinity, yet somehow non-visibly present to cater to childcare, cleaning, lawn care, and food service.

---

by nationally prominent anti-immigrant groups. As Workplace Project director Nadia Marin-Molina states, "no-notice evictions have made hundreds instantly homeless and may eventually impact thousands more. It is clear that County Executive Steve Levy is using both policy and the podium against the newest members of the Long Island community. Rather than uniting the community, these attacks polarize it, turning neighbor against neighbor" (cited in Workplace Project 2006, 11).

Thinly veiled racist rhetoric and hand-wringing has had dire consequences for day laborers. In addition to the no-notice evictions that have displaced hundreds of poor Latinos, the xenophobia and racist discourse in Farmingville has led to death threats, gun shots fired at day laborers, firebombing of a house rented by day laborers in 2003, and a brutal beating that took place in 2000. "[T]wo young members of a neo-Nazi group picked up two Latino day laborers in Farmingville on the pretense of offering work. They brought them to an abandoned basement and attacked them with a knife and post-hole digger, intending to kill them" (Gordon 2006, 19). Luckily, the two men survived the attack, but the event demonstrated how a community that allows public xenophobia creates a context for physically violent manifestations of the constant haranguing and verbal abuse.

Even if Farmingville is an extreme case, most worker centers operate in a politicized context where the protection of immigrant worker rights is constantly questioned. Challenging the commonly held belief that labor competition is between US minorities and newly arrived immigrants, worker centers often cross racial boundaries to highlight the shared fates of minorities and immigrants *vis-à-vis* the employers who benefit from their marginalization and exploitation. The Black Workers for Justice joined forces with FLOC to create North Carolina's first African American Latino Alliance. CAFÉ also builds alliances with Latino immigrants and often references civil rights struggles as being both a Black *and* Brown struggle. Worker centers seem to be one space where multiracial understanding and mutual support are actualized.[7] As of 2005, there were 139 worker centers operating in 30 states and the District of Columbia (see Fine 2006, 8). Most worker centers operate in California (29) and New York (24), but they are found in most major metropolitan areas, select suburban communities, and a few agricultural and meat-packing rural areas.

Hometown Associations

The transnational mutual aid societies of today are the hometown associations that have proliferated among Mexican immigrant communities. Most hometown associations (HTA), or *clubes de oriundos*, are connected to urban and rural Mexican communities and tend to operate on a small scale primarily for social activities, networks of mutual support, collective yet voluntary remittances, and, on a larger scale, public works projects. "There are eleven statewide umbrella organizations in Los Angeles and Chicago representing the following states: Michoacán, Jalisco, San Luis Potosí, Oaxaca, Zacatecas, Guerrero, Nayarit, Sinaloa, Tlaxcala, Durango, and Guanajuato" (Bada 2005, 311).

Seeing it as a viable development strategy even among neoliberals, the Fox administration increased Mexican governmental support for the remittance practice of infrastructure development with a three-for-one matching program: for every peso sent in remittances, the local, state, and federal government commits three. "President Vicente Fox converted the Two-for-One program into a national-level program called the *Iniciativa Cuidadana-Tres por Uno* (Citizen Initiative-Three-for-One Program), which is administered by the *Secretaría de Desarrollo Social* (Ministry of Social Development or SEDESOL)" (García Zamora 2005, 21). The three states that benefit most substantially from this program are those that have sent migrants to the US for well over 100 years. Jalisco, Michoacán, and Zacatecas accounted for 48 per cent of the three-for-one projects in 2002 and 64 per cent in 2003 (Burgess 2005, 121). Zacatecas alone accounted for the same percentage of projects (36 per cent) as all other Mexican states combined (excluding Jalisco and Michoacán). García Zamora's 2004 survey of Jerez, Zacatecas, residents found that 60 per cent of remittances went to basic living expenses, which left very little for infrastructure development projects.

Notwithstanding, Jerez has become the poster child for HTA-led development strategies, primarily because of its thoroughly transnational character as a dual-citizen community. As one of the first communities to collectively participate in the Mexican government's loosening of citizenship restrictions to allow for dual citizenship, Jerez residents living in the US could actively pursue routes toward US citizenship while retaining their Mexican citizenship. Part of this development strategy is democratic in intent and part is very much a patronage system that socially coerces "voluntary" remittances and elite-led decision-making. The case of *El Rey de Tomate*, the Tomato King, points to this contradictory democratic-patronage relationship of Jerezanos to the Federation of Zacatecan Clubs of Southern California hometown association. "Andrés Bermudez, a US citizen known as the 'Tomato King,' was elected mayor of the large city of Jerez, Zacatecas, in 2001. Although he was stripped of his post by Mexican electoral authorities, this action was taken because he had failed to fulfill the requisite period of residence in Zacatecas; his US citizenship was not the issue" (Smith 2006b, 285). A constitutional amendment was passed the following year allowing non-residents to hold local political office, and Bermudez was again elected as *alcalde* or mayor. He is not alone, as the mayor of Apulco and two Zacatecan assembly seats are held by migrants (García Zamora 2005, 29). Jerez has also set up an Internet site so that residents in Mexico and the US can access the daily events of the local government, view progress on HTA-funded projects, and engage in daily conversation at the companion MSN group site through *Jerez Cuidad Virtual.*[8]

Depending on social networks and migrant flows, US and Mexican local communities are financially interconnected. For instance, "the states of Guerrero, Jalisco, Zacatecas, and Guanajuato account for nearly 70 per cent of the membership of all Mexican HTA's in greater Chicago" (Orozco 2002, 88). The Mixtec residents of "Ticuani,"[9] Puebla, living in Brooklyn,

New York, have funded more than two-thirds of the cost of major public works projects in their hometown, exceeding the contributions of federal, state, and local government (Smith 2006b, 3). Since 1970, the Puebla community has benefited from migrant remittances by repaving the *zócalo* or public square, installing night lights, constructing schools, refurbishing the church, making potable drinking water, and incorporating the Ticuani Solidarity Committee as a New York state–recognized non-profit organization (Smith 2006b, 56). Local politics have dramatically shifted to a transnational context where local Mexican electoral races are funded, run, and decided in New York City. Hometown associations have dramatically shifted the terrain that Mexican immigrants navigate.

Immigrant Rights Movement: From Amnesty to Popular Mobilization

The movement to regularize the status of undocumented immigrants has brought together various immigrant groups across the US. It not only brings the undocumented "out of the shadows of the law" but also publicly identifies the major contributions they make to contemporary US economy and society. With the call for blanket (or total) amnesty, current movement leaders are following the lead of the previous generation whose goals were partially realized in the 1986 Immigration Reform and Control Act (IRCA). The 2006 May Day rallies and March 25 "Gran Marcha" immigrant rights rallies in Los Angeles, New York, Chicago, Denver, Houston, El Paso, Washington, DC, and San Diego have inspired great optimism about the achievement of immigrant rights.

The first calls for total or blanket amnesty (a legalization of status for all undocumented immigrants, regardless of their date of entry) were voiced during the debate leading up to the passage of the IRCA. Groups such as the UFW for the first time identified with the struggle for securing immigrant rights and called for total amnesty. This represented a marked shift from earlier UFW positions that characterized undocumented and temporary immigrant laborers as detrimental to labor organizing. Other groups, like *La Hermandad* and CASA, kept to their previously held view that legalization would only be viable if total amnesty was coupled with the unequivocal right to US citizenship.

In the even more repressive post-9/11 era, with reduced civil liberties and restricted rights for immigrants, tireless activists have continued the movement for amnesty and broadened it across the entire US. Shared opposition to the Patriot Act has united Latino advocacy organizations, refugee and immigrant service providers, labor unions, socially conscious church groups, and members of all racialized communities, whether they be Black, Latino, Arab, Middle Eastern, Asian, or Native American.

Life-long Latina activist Emma Lozano in Chicago exemplifies contemporary organizing for amnesty and sanctuary for undocumented immigrants. A former staffer in the Harold Washington administration,[10] Lozano has worked tirelessly to develop organizations working toward amnesty and immigrant rights. She is founder and president of the community-based membership organization *Pueblo Sin Fronteras* and two related non-profits, *Centro Sin Fronteras* and *Sin Fronteras*. As a national leader in the amnesty movement, she was recently recognized by the Cook County Board of Commissioners for her work on educational reform, legal advocacy for undocumented immigrants, and union representation regardless of citizenship status. She has worked with Middle Eastern and African American leaders to push the Chicago City Council to urge the federal administration to repeal the Patriot Act and to challenge the increased racial profiling that results from the act.

Lozano's spouse, Reverend Walter Coleman, is the pastor at Adalberto United Methodist Church in Chicago. In August 2006, the church offered sanctuary to Elvira Arellano, who was scheduled to be deported as undocumented though her seven-year-old son Saul was born in the US and is thus a US citizen. Arellano is the president of *La Familia Latina Unida* and is representative of mixed-status Latino families. Saul himself wrote to former president G.W. Bush to describe his situation: "I want to tell President George W. Bush why I believe my mother should be allowed to stay with me in my country. I want to tell him also that there are more than 3 million children like me. We are US citizens but the government is taking away our mothers and fathers."[11] When Arellano left the church and toured the West Coast on behalf of immigrant rights, she was detained by ICE agents in Los Angeles and deported on August 19, 2007.

The struggle for immigrant rights harkens back to the sanctuary movement of Central American refugees in the 1980s. Because the focus now is on undocumented immigrants, the unjust laws targeted are US immigration laws that criminalize this current generation of immigrants while making it increasingly difficult for them to regularize their status and completely ignoring the transnational processes of migration that have been interrupted by a hypermilitarized border and backlogged naturalization applications.

In Providence, Rhode Island, Guatemalan-born activist Juan Garcia is waging a similarly broad-based campaign for amnesty. Employed as a community organizer with Saint Teresa's Catholic Church, he organized "Immigrants in Action/*Comité de Inmigrantes en Acción*" to secure amnesty for the undocumented. The efforts of the committee were stalled by the overall nativist reaction to 9/11. Earlier, Garcia employed models of self-education reminiscent of Brazilian popular educator Paulo Freire to help undocumented workers educate themselves about their rights and mobilize for amnesty. Since then, he has coordinated his efforts with local Middle Eastern activists to challenge racial profiling. He has worked with immigrant workers and labor organizers who lost their fish-processing jobs after organizing and detailing abuses and careless workplace practices that led to the death of an undocumented worker. Calls for amnesty become clearer within this context.

Garcia's committee is part of a nationwide network of amnesty advocates that organized the Immigrant Worker Freedom Ride of 2003. The National Coalition for Dignity and Amnesty includes labor unions, church organizations, civil rights organizations, immigrant rights organizations, community-based organizations, and elected officials. Together, they coordinated their Freedom Rides to connect undocumented immigrants' struggles with the struggle against racial segregation of Blacks in the Southern US during the civil rights movement. Along with original Freedom Ride organizers and national immigrant advocacy organizations, the most prominent labor unions (SEIU, UNITE-HERE, FLOC, UFW, and UFCW) sponsored nine buses in their cross-country journey to Queens, New York to rally for a blanket amnesty program. The 2003 Freedom Riders were successful in publicizing the plight of the undocumented in local newspapers but did not generate the strong national television coverage they had hoped for.

This lack of coverage all changed in spring 2006. On Thursday, March 23, more than 10,000 marchers voiced their support in Milwaukee, while on Friday, 20,000 protested in Phoenix, the largest march in the city's history. Two weeks earlier, an estimated 500,000 immigrants and their supporters marched in downtown Chicago to rally support for immigrant rights and comprehensive immigration law reform. On Saturday, March 25, the immigrant rights movement garnered national headlines when immigrants and their supporters took to the streets in cities across the nation. Nearly 1 million people marched in Los Angeles against the Sensenbrenner

Bill, HR 4437, which would have made it a felony to reside in the US without legal documentation. On the same day, over 50,000 people gathered in downtown Denver to stand up for immigrant rights. "But the monster protests in Los Angeles—which drew about 500,000 people to the city center March 25—hyper-charged activists everywhere, spawning hastily organized plans for protests April 9 and 10 and the actions planned today" (Althaus and Garza 2006). Though the journalists used the conservative city police estimate for this march, which, based on our experience with such reporting, most likely cut the number of protestors at least in half, they did report on the three waves of protest that characterized spring 2006. The April 10–11 rallies brought out 50,000 people in Atlanta, 500,000 in Dallas, 50,000 in San Diego, and 20,000 in Salt Lake City, while college towns such as Champaign and Madison turned out thousands of protestors, and meat-packing towns also turned out protestors at high rates compared to their population. For instance, Garden City, Kansas had 3,000 protestors in a city of 30,000, and the protests shut down meat-packing plants in Dodge City and Schuler.

These events culminated in the less spontaneous, more organized "A Day Without an Immigrant" rallies on May 1, 2006. The terminology is important as the first iteration was based on the mock documentary and motion picture *A Day Without a Mexican* and progressed to the more inclusive "Day Without a Latino" rally. The final "A Day Without an Immigrant" took immigrant rights to their most inclusive form and facilitated coalitions that labor unions and *mutualistas* can build upon in the future. The May Day rallies were also coined "The Great American Boycott" as organizers urged immigrants and their supporters to neither show up for work nor buy any goods. Many immigrant-serving companies closed in solidarity. The meat-packing plants were most affected, but the consumer boycott was not as large as anticipated. Chicano students walked out to join immigrant supporters in a daytime rally in Los Angeles and an evening rally that together drew 2 million people, according to a *Univision* estimate. Rallies exceeding 10,000 participants were held in Seattle, Salem (OR), San José, Santa Ana, Philadelphia, Providence (RI), Orlando, Portland (OR), New York City, Chicago, Milwaukee, Denver, Atlanta, and Las Vegas. All totaled, rallies brought out close to 5 million protestors across the nation.

This collective response to proposed legislation by anti-immigrant politicians was clear and unequivocal. In reaction to the immigration rallies, Colorado's Republican governor Bill Owens called for a special session to enact legislation similar to California's Proposition 187 (see Chapter 5), which would prohibit undocumented immigrants from using social services, health care, and public education and ordered that all Colorado cities that offered sanctuary would lose state funding. Most of the Colorado members of the Congressional Immigration Reform Caucus were summarily swept out of office in the 2006 midterm elections that saw the balance of power shift decidedly in favor of the Democratic Party. "Republicans lost at least 9 House seats held by members of Tom Tancredo's hateful 104-member "'House Immigration Reform Caucus.'"[12] Bob Beauprez, the former state chairman of the Republican Party, was slated to continue the vitriolic immigrant bashing that made Owens a two-term governor but lost the election to Democratic candidate Bill Ritter, who is enacting his own form of nativist state policy. Yet, nationwide, the voters resoundingly rejected the most vehement anti-immigrant rhetoric-spewers.

The 2006 May Day and pro-immigrant rallies coincided with the University of Miami settlement that allowed for a union vote in support of its janitorial workers joining the SEIU. It also dovetailed with the Houston janitors' campaign. The mantra of immigrant rights = labor rights = civil rights is at the forefront of the mass protests of 2006 and forms the core of UFCW organizing and worker-led walkouts at Smithfield's Tar Heel hog plant. At the forefront of both the organized labor and grassroots movements for social change, Mexican laborers are taking on leadership roles in rallying for their own fates. But these mobilizations have also raised the ire of anti-immigrant groups, politicians, and conservative talk-show hosts. The backlash against immigrant rights is articulated within a larger reassertion of White supremacist ideologies and a call for the rolling back of the gains of the civil rights era, a situation to which we now turn.

Notes

1. This section has benefited greatly from Jason Albright's authoritative master's thesis on the SEIU-University of Miami janitors' campaign (Albright 2010).
2. See "Welcome to YesWeCane.org," http://yeswecane.org (accessed May 5, 2010).
3. Many landmark labor struggles, such as the decertification of the United Steel Workers of America in the Phelps Dodge copper mines of Arizona, involved Mexican union members. Yet that paled in comparison to the

brazen union-busting and legal decertification of the Professional Air Traffic Controllers Organization (PATCO) by President Reagan. Any governmental support for organized labor that was in place during the New Deal or Great Society programs was clearly in retrenchment with the ascendancy of the neoliberal, anti-union Reagan administration. A campaign support letter to PATCO by then presidential candidate Reagan stated that he would be a major supporter of reforming labor relations to ensure better and safer working conditions for the nation's air traffic controllers (see Fantasia and Voss 2004, 67). When it became clear that the Federal Aviation Administration would not concede to PATCO demands, the call to strike was met by a Reagan-sponsored order to hire replacement workers and begin a process that would eventually lead to the decertification of the union.

4. Mexican labor leaders included Reyes Soberanis Moreno, general secretary of the *Sindicato Nacional del Transporte*-COR; Eli Parolari and Rafael Marino of the *Sindicato Industrial Nacional de Trabajadores del Autotransporte*; Alfredo Dominguez of FAT; and the Mexican Action Network on Free Trade.

5. See http://www.ueinternational.org/ v011n05.html.

6. The New York–based worker centers have been the most extensively researched (see Fine 2006; Gordon 2006; Jayaraman and Ness 2005; Ness 2005; Tait 2005), yet we know relatively little about UNITE worker centers in other locales.

7. The National Interfaith Committee on Worker Justice, Korean Immigrant Workers Advocates, Coalition for Humane Immigrant Rights in Los Angeles, *Instituto de Educación Popular del Súr de California*, Casa of Maryland, Virginia's Tenants and Workers United, Denver's *El Centro Humanitario para Los Trabajadores*, and Omaha Together One Community are representative examples of centers devoted to expanding beyond their racial/ethnic base to engage in coalitional politics.

8. See http://www.jerez.com.mx/.

9. A pseudonym.

10. Harold Washington was the first African American mayor of Chicago, serving from 1983 to 1987.

11. Source: http://www.bluelatinos.org/HelpSaul.

12. "The incumbent caucus members whose seats were lost [by] the GOP are Charlie Bass (NH), Bob Beauprez (CO), Jeb Bradley (NH), Gil Gutknecht (MN), J.D. Hayworth (AZ), Joel Hefley (CO), Jim Ryun (KS), John Sweeney (NY), and Charles Taylor (NC)." *People's Weekly World*, January 3, 2009, http://www.pww.org.

Chapter Five

Backlash and Retrenchment (1980s–1990s)

Reactionary politics have been squarely aimed at Mexican immigrant communities. The viciousness of anti-immigrant sentiment is reaching a new level with the largely positive press coverage of the vigilante actions of the Minutemen and American Border Patrol. The 1986 IRCA attempted to deal with the "illegal immigration problem" by giving undocumented immigrants pathways toward legalizing their status and protections against discrimination. For the first time in the history of immigration law, the group most directly responsible for attracting undocumented immigrants — employers — could be held legally culpable for knowingly hiring undocumented laborers and discriminating on the basis of perceived immigration status. However, the H-2 temporary visa program was vastly expanded into the H-2A, H-1B, and H-2B programs to allow a multitude of employers access to temporary immigrant workers. Penalties for employers and immigrants, as well as the increase in funds for border enforcement, set the agenda for immigration legislation from that point forward. The Illegal Immigration Reform and Immigrant Responsibility Act of 1996 (IIRIRA) was particularly punitive in its criminalization and militarization approaches and offered little to no hope for immigrants looking for legal and expedient pathways to naturalization. A backlash against immigrants has been evidenced at the federal level, but reactionary politics are most clearly seen in California where a series of voter propositions have severely limited the rights of Mexican immigrants.

IRCA and the Contradictions of Immigration Policy

The 1980s and 1990s saw a drastic change in public policy and the narrowing of the terms of public debate toward a more unitary focus on nativism, privatization, and neoliberalism. Yet, in spite of the push for free markets

Table 5.1: *Timeline of Backlash and Retrenchment*

1986	Proposition 63, "The California English Language Amendment," passed overwhelmingly by voters (73 to 27 per cent), begins the anti-immigrant proposition movement in California and emboldens the English Only movement nationwide.
November 9, 1994	Proposition 187, the "Save Our State" initiative, is passed by California voters (59 per cent approval rate) to prohibit undocumented immigrants from gaining access to public services in the state. The initiative was struck down as unconstitutional five years later.
1996	The Illegal Immigration Reform and Immigrant Responsibility Act (IIRIRA) is signed by President Bill Clinton. The Act represents a full commitment to the criminalization of immigration and the militarization of immigration enforcement. In addition to increased border controls, Provision 287(g) allows the federal government to deputize local law enforcement as federal immigrant officers.
August 22, 1996	The Personal Responsibility and Work Opportunity Reconciliation Act is signed by President Clinton and "ends welfare as we know it." Specifically, the Act extends the restrictions on immigrant access to public services (originally voiced in California's Proposition 187) to the nation.
November 1996	Proposition 209, the "Civil Rights Initiative," contrary to the name, is designed to end affirmative action in state government of California. It passes 55 to 45 per cent.
November 1998	Proposition 227, "English for the Children," is designed to end bilingual education in California, to be replaced with one-year English immersion programs at the behest of sponsor Ron Unz. It passes 61 to 39 per cent.
December 16, 2005	Sensenbrenner Bill HR 4437 is passed by the US House of Representatives and would make it a felony to reside in the US without legal documentation. The bill does not pass Senate but creates a maelstrom of controversy in immigrant communities.
March 2010	Arizona's racial profiling State Bill 1070 signed into law.

and against governmental controls, restrictionist immigration laws did not fundamentally change. While goods and capital were allowed to flow more easily over borders, the US government sought to further restrict non-citizens' transnational mobility. The irony is that what enabled the legal transnationalization of production and consumption was a continued reliance on the exploitation of immigrant workers, whose presence was increasingly treated as illegal.

During the 1980s, the rhetoric over illegal immigration found appeasement in the alteration of immigration law. A good deal of compromise to deal with the contradiction that immigrant labor was both desired and resented eventually led to the passage of the IRCA in 1986. The law was comprised of five major elements: 1) employer sanctions, 2) amnesty provisions for illegal immigrants who met certain criteria, 3) anti-discrimination measures to appease immigrant rights groups, 4) H-2 temporary visa expansion, and 5) increased fines and punishment for undocumented immigrants and increased funds for the Border Patrol. It sought to provide comprehensive provisions to deal with agricultural labor as well as with undocumented immigration. The employer sanctions provision was designed to close the previous loophole, which absolved employers from responsibility for illegal hiring practices, by holding accountable those who knowingly hired undocumented laborers. Verification of citizenship status became a lasting feature for all new hires. Subsequently, the farm labor contractor became responsible for every facet of meeting the growers' labor needs: hiring and firing, paying wages, certifying legal status, and meeting wage and hour requirements (where they apply). In effect, the contractor assumed responsibility if these state-monitored requirements were not met and took on the role of patsy or fall-guy so that the grower could deny responsibility. The UFW and other farmworker advocacy groups attempted to close this loophole by proposing federal and state legal actions that would hold growers responsible for infractions that occurred in their fields with workers picking their crops.

The legalization provision was designed to grant US citizenship for undocumented immigrants who could prove they had lived in the US continuously for at least the previous ten years. Special rules regarding undocumented migrants and seasonal workers recognized the circular migration trends that predominated. The Seasonal Agricultural Workers program (SAW) and Replenishment Agricultural Worker program (RAW) were designed both to legalize agricultural laborers who could prove 90 days of continuous employment in the previous year and to meet grower concerns that legalized workers would leave agriculture. Sociologist Susan González Baker (1990) notes that the SAW program was expected to net 50,000 applicants, but the number applying was closer to 1.3 million. Growers had lawmakers convinced that once farmworkers were legalized, they would leave agriculture in droves. It was for this reason that IRCA contained a replenishment provision (RAW) to supply temporary workers when the spigot ran dry. In reality, a mass exodus of SAW workers from agriculture never occurred, and the definitive report on post-IRCA farm labor, the 1989–91 National Agricultural Workers Survey, found that legalization did not lead to a departure from agricultural employment. If anything, SAW workers worked more days per year after legalization than before they were documented.

As part of IRCA, a series of antidiscrimination measures were implemented at the behest of immigrant rights and Latino-serving organizations.[1] They feared that the employment verification process would create a situation where prospective employees who "looked foreign" might not be considered for employment. The measures prohibited "employment discrimination based on national origin if the person alleging discrimination is a US citizen or a permanent resident alien, or newly legalized alien who has filed a notice of intent to become a citizen" (Montwieler 1987, 25).

The H-2A Program is in many ways an extension of the Bracero Program. Designed to meet the needs of US growers, it guaranteed the option of employing immigrant workers if citizens were not willing to work in agriculture. When the Bracero Program was terminated in 1964, immigration law was overhauled for the first time since the Quota Acts with the passage of the 1965 INA. Since it removed discriminatory quotas, the act is often hailed as civil rights legislation. But one provision extended the Bracero Program through the development of an H-2 temporary visa program. The H-2 (after 1986, the H-2A) program served largely as the safety valve for large-scale agribusiness and its desire for cheap, pliable, temporary labor. The H-2 program was severely underutilized because the other less bureaucratic option, hiring undocumented immigrants, was never deemed illegal or worthy of sanction until the IRCA was enacted. Its H-2A program expanded to include temporary migrants in two additional categories: H-1B for specialty occupations and H-2B for wage-shortage industries (see below). Employers complained about the requirements they must adhere to when employing H-2A workers.[2] Yet, based on data released by the US Department of Labor in 2003, the H-2A had ballooned to a 45,000-person program utilized by 6,000 US companies in all 50 states (US Department of Labor 2003a).

The vast majority of temporary workers come through the H-1B program, which was capped at 195,000 entries from 2001 to 2003. Social scientist Rafael Alarcón (2003) refers to these specialized workers, primarily computer engineers and scientists, as *cerebreros* since they are recruited for mental labor. A small, but significant, contingent of Mexican citizens has entered the US on H-1B temporary visas, but the majority are from India, China, and Britain. In 2000, approximately 144,000 specialized workers were recruited in the H-1B program. The H-2B program is a left-over category for temporary entry of workers in situations where an employer can demonstrate that no citizen workers are willing to take the jobs at the prevailing wage. Landscaping, hotel cleaning, and other seasonal occupations, which traditionally relied upon undocumented Mexican labor, comprised the majority of the 66,000 eligible visa recipients in the first year of the program. The cap was raised in 2001, and numbers have since exceeded 100,000 visa holders.

Other provisions included state reimbursement for the costs associated with implementation of increased enforcement and service, especially those associated with making sure that state agencies distribute services only to US citizens (the touchstone issue for Proposition 187) and with strengthening the enforcement powers of the INS. Unrecognized at the time, the strengthening of the US Border Patrol, which began with the passage of the IRCA, would shape deterrence policy for the next 20 years.

With the intention of restricting immigration, the IRCA increased enforcement of the US-Mexico border and sanctioned special operations to arrest and deport undocumented immigrants. The border has become a militarized zone, following the LIC approach (Dunn 1996) begun with Operation Wetback, described in Chapter 2. This is evident in the equipment used to patrol the border, the operational tactics and military strategies of border enforcement, and the resultant social control of a targeted civilian population. The most visible physical manifestation of the militarization of the border region has been the construction of walls and fences to separate urban sister cities, first suggested by Lieutenant General Joseph Swing at the time of Operation Wetback. A series of INS border campaigns from 1993 to the present (to be discussed in Chapter 9) have all physically defined the lines in the sand or the rivers that symbolically mark the divisions between Mexico and the US.

Subsequent immigration legislation has taken a markedly restrictionist cast. The 1996 IIRIRA placed blame and "responsibility" for the flawed immigration system on immigrants themselves so as to appease nativists' ire. The act provides substantial allocations to increase border enforcement, further restricts apprehended undocumented immigrants by creating life-long bars for entering the US via legal means, and creates a pilot program to verify the citizenship status of job applicants. Section 287(g) allows the federal government to deputize state and local law enforcement to administer deportations and conduct workplace raids, immigration verification checkpoints or roundups, and deal with other immigration matters. The result is the social construction of illegality, in which immigrants are blamed and punished for all the complex relations of illegal immigration.

The overall effect of criminalization of the undocumented is that entry into the US has become much more dangerous. With increased enforcement, immigrants have been forced to cross in the least defended stretches of the 2,000-mile border, which are the most treacherous and dangerous crossing points. Researchers at the University of Houston estimate that nearly 5,000 immigrants have died on the US side of the border from 1985 to 2002. The deadly consequences of border enforcement are reinforced in states like California where anti-immigrant sentiments have boiled over into politics and vigilantism.

California Propositions and Immigrant Bashing

In California, a series of voter-approved propositions have created an environment of racialization and immigrant bashing, fostering a fear of Latinos and other minorities and immigrants, and suggesting that their presence is the cause of the state's economic woes. Political elites overseeing one of California's worst recessions in 1994 found an easy scapegoat in the form of the "illegal alien." Proposition 187, the so-called Save Our State initiative, was designed to deny public services to undocumented immigrants. Then-governor Pete Wilson was a staunch supporter; during the campaign, news surfaced that his family employed undocumented laborers as maids and household workers. This hypocrisy was lost on the voters who overwhelmingly passed the proposition mandating state employees to turn in suspected undocumented immigrants and refuse education, medical, and social services to those who could not provide sufficient documentation. Proposition 187 was preceded in 1986 by California Proposition 63, which was designed to make English the "official language of the state," and was followed by Proposition 227 in 1998, the so-called Save Our Children initiative, which required the placement of Limited English Proficiency students into English-only classrooms (so-called immersion programs) after one year of English as a Second Language instruction. In 1996, voters passed Proposition 209, effectively ending affirmative action in state hiring and school admittance decisions. The hostile climate in California has prompted cultural critic George Lipsitz (1998, xviii) to view "California in the 1990s as the human rights equivalent of Mississippi in the 1960s."

In the 1970s and 1980s, the dominant public discourse on immigration was one of mounting hysteria over undocumented immigrants, who were framed not only as a drain on the US economy, social services, health care system, and criminal justice system, but also as drug smugglers (Chavez 2001; Mize and Leedham 2000). Chavez surveyed 76 popular magazine covers from 1965 to 1999 and found that the vast majority, 66 per cent, used alarmist imagery and words to convey a sense of immigration as a problem (Chavez 2001, 23). Mize and Leedham found that of the 146 articles surveyed from 1992 to 1993 in four daily Colorado newspapers, 62 per cent framed Latino immigrants in negative terms as users of social services, drains on the economy, destroying US culture, more prone to commit criminal acts, and requiring stricter legislation to deter their entry. Even though their sample was limited to Colorado, 80 per cent of all the stories were pulled off the Associated Press Wire, indicating what average newspaper readers were exposed to across the nation. Both analyses find that levels of immigration do not determine the amount or tone of media coverage. The larger political debate and calls for immigration reform seem to stoke the fires of alarmist and negative media portrayals.

One example of the illegal drug–immigrant link is the story of a tunnel that drug smugglers built to transport narcotics under the border. Because of the hysteria over border crossers, the story was reported in Colorado newspaper editorials as the tunnel that brought "illegal aliens and drugs into our homeland." It is important to note that federal agents never reported that people were transported through this tunnel, but the link was made nevertheless. The War on Drugs became the war on Mexican immigrants along the border, and the two became synonymous in the popular imagination as well as in INS strategies to stop both perceived threats. In Lamm and Imhoff's *The Immigration Time Bomb* (1986), the authors declare, without evidence, that illegal aliens are used as "pack mules" for drug smugglers and carry drugs on and in their bodies. In many ways, the INS and Border Patrol benefited greatly from the War on Drugs, given the vast increase in funding for border enforcement.

Similarly, drug discourse prompted the US House of Representatives to essentially redefine borders when it passed an amendment mandating that US military forces "seal land, air, and sea borders" within 45 days. Surveillance blimps suspended 1,000 feet above ground and stationed every few hundred miles along the US-Mexico border epitomize this militarization. These blimps ostensibly scour the terrain for low-flying airplanes. More frequently, however, they appear as both expensive tools to spot straggling migrant workers and as yet another military experiment. (Brady 1998, 118)

As alarmist accusations heighten the spurious drug–immigrant link in these early years of the twenty-first century, terrorism has been wantonly connected to the calls for increased border militarization. As part of the Homeland Security Act of 2002 that followed the USA Patriot Act, the reorganization and renaming of INS as Immigration and Customs Enforcement (ICE) under the auspices of the DHS has meant a change in name but not its mission to enforce immigration law. Yet, according to its website, the rationale for both the DHS and ICE is to thwart terrorism and crime even though the unit focuses on immigration:

> By bringing together customs and immigration enforcement authorities under one roof, ICE can fight crime and terrorist activity in ways not possible prior to the founding of DHS. Investigators on immigration cases can track the money trails that support smuggling and document fraud operations; financial investigators have additional tools in using immigration violations to build cases against criminals; sexual predators that prey on the innocent are more readily targeted than ever before.[3]

A terrorist has never entered the US via the US-Mexico border; the group responsible for 9/11 all entered legally on visas via air travel. Yet the justification for increased border enforcement and criminalization of immigrants is the larger effort to fight crime and terrorism. The DHS website even links sexual predators to immigration. In framing immigrants as social problems, there seem to be an endless number of possible false associations.

"Save our State" and "Save Our Children": Propositions 187 and 227
In 1994, California voters overwhelmingly passed Proposition 187 in order to deny public services to undocumented immigrants. Not recognizing the

social costs of reproduction paid in Mexico, the mass media clamored about how undocumented immigrants were draining the social services of the US. The sales-tax dollars that Mexican immigrants contributed to the economy were ignored in favor of focusing on highly publicized welfare fraud campaigns or on Mexican women who bore children in US hospitals. In many ways, the economic recession, which California endured as a result of deindustrialization and the state's reliance on shrinking military contracts, was easier to blame on undocumented immigrants. Scapegoating Mexican immigrants represented a return to a nativism that has spelled disaster for present and earlier generations of immigrants.

With the overall climate of nativist sentiment and immigrant bashing, the demographic shifts in California quickly became the popular scapegoat for the state's economic woes. The authors of Proposition 187 worded the required background section on the ballot in the following manner: "According to the 1990 census, more than one in five Californians were born in another country. The number of California residents who are foreign-born now totals about 7 million. Currently, about 300,000 new residents enter the state each year from foreign countries" (cited in Ono and Sloop 2002, 170). The stated goal of the proposition was to bar undocumented immigrants from receiving public services and to require state officials to report them. Its authors skillfully constructed and played off popular fears to craft a ballot measure that would supposedly end this enemy threat. Anti-immigrant leaders Ron Prince and Barbara Coe, state representative Richard Mountjoy, former INS commissioners Harold Ezell and Alan Nelson, and Orange County mayor Barbara Kiley were key figures in drafting and promoting the 187 campaign. All registered particularly disparaging remarks against "illegal aliens" and most often equated them with Mexicans. "You get illegal alien children, Third World children, out of our schools, and you will reduce the violence.... You're dealing with Third World cultures who come in, they shoot, they beat, they stab, and they spread their drugs around in our school system. And we're paying for them to do it" (Coe, cited in Johnson 1998, 114). Coe often invoked "our laws, our language, our culture, and our history" in her rhetoric. Apparently, her history is not the history of the California that was once part of Mexico; that required until Proposition 63 that all government documents be published in English and Spanish; and that credits its economy, much of its architectural history, public names, and culture to Mexican contributions. The 187 proponents claimed that their political positions had nothing to do with race. This could not have been more elo-quently and accurately reflected than Don Barrington's statement while he defended his promotion of an Arizona proposition similar to 187. "My friends have never heard a racist word out of me. *I just don't like wetbacks*" (cited in Johnson 2004, 45; emphasis in original).

The push to spread 187 legislation across the nation at the state level, however, was pre-empted by the welfare reform legislation passed at the federal level. "[P]assage of the federal Personal Responsibility and Work Opportunity Reconciliation Act of 1996 in many ways ended the need for states to establish individual policies. President Bill Clinton signed the bipartisan welfare reform legislation into law 22 August 1996. The federal restrictions on immigration benefits in the bill duplicated many of the provisions of Proposition 187" (Ono and Sloop 2002, 5). In IIRIRA, the explicit bars on undocumented immigrant access to public services fin-ished what welfare reform started. By retroactively applying the law to any immigrant who had committed a crime (even minor legal infractions), the intent was both to further reduce those immigrants eligible for bene-fits and services by means of deportation and to provide the mechanisms and rationales for mass deportations, harkening back to the eras of the Great Depression repatriation campaigns and Operation Wetback. Today, California's Proposition 187 is, for all intents and purposes, federal law.

The spurious claims of the proponents of Proposition 227, the Prop-osition 187-inspired "Save Our Children" initiative, could not be farther from what scholars of language and learning recommend as best practices. The proposition's main advocate, a self-described humble immigrant turned millionaire, was Ron Unz, and his support of English immersion had no basis in scholarship. Instead, his was an ideological drive to ensure that immigrants properly assimilated to the US so that they could follow his "pull yourself up by your bootstraps" example. Recent research on bilin-gual education can be viewed as an attempt to transcend a political debate that is mired in an ideological debate on assimilation vs. cultural pluralism by attempting to understand how language acquisition impacts learning.

The ideologues that oppose bilingual education believe English is under attack because of recent immigration flows from Latin America and Asia. Yet, according to Census data, in 1990 only 13.8 per cent of the pop-ulation spoke a language other than English (US Census 1990). In 1910, 23 per cent of the US population age 10 and over did not speak English. Those who fear the loss of English predominance rarely recognize that the

---

Politics of English Only

The agenda of the English Only movement was made public when John Tanton, the founder of both US English and the Federation for American Immigration Reform, and former president of Zero Population Growth, authored a memo that decried the presence of too many Hispanics and Asians by concluding: "Perhaps this is the first instance in which those with their pants up are going to get caught by those with their pants down!" (Tatalovich 1997, 87). At the time, Linda Chavez was the president of US English and resigned her position over Tanton's overtly racist statements. US English claims that 30 states have adopted "official English" laws. The organization is also lobbying for federal legislation that would create English as the official language of the US. In 2006, the US House of Representatives inserted official English wording into their anti-immigrant bill to ensure that the link between anti-immigrant border enforcement and preservation of the English language were inextricably linked. (See US English 2006.)

US has been a multilingual nation from its inception; consider, for instance, the early role of the German language in many Midwestern states. Furthermore, the original California State Constitution was in English *and* Spanish, and it ensured that the state's official documents would be available in both languages.

In a bilingual context, many educators believe that the optimal way to learn English requires first-language retention (see Feliciano 2001). Research conducted on cohorts of students in San Diego Unified School District found that among Latino and Asian students, those most likely to score highly on predictors of high-school success were those with bilingual abilities (Portes and Rumbaut 1996). As expected, Limited English Proficiency students were likely to drop out and have lower grade point averages, but the same was true for students with English-only proficiency. All too often, literacy is assumed to be the same as English literacy and illiteracy a sign of low intelligence. Yet, in the current global labor market, bilingual and multilingual abilities have become highly marketable job skills.

Many English Only proponents assume that English illiteracy is high because language minorities are not eager to learn the language. On the day that California Proposition 63 passed, making English the official language of the state, more than 40,000 adults were on waiting lists for ESL classes in Los Angeles alone. The scholarly literature does not support the claim that the best way to promote English literacy is through English

Only or immersion programs. Yet this research is rarely aired in the highly charged realm of California politics. In his failed bid for the presidency, Governor Pete Wilson touted his role in securing the passage of Propositions 187 and 227 until the national newspaper ads and coverage of his hiring of undocumented Latino help was too much for the Republican National Committee to tolerate.

Conclusion

In an era of backlash and retrenchment, the assumed wisdom of the 1990s was that minorities were unfairly benefiting from government programs like affirmative action and that somehow, after 25 years of legislation, all legacies of racial discrimination had been miraculously wiped away. The decade's buzzwords were "reverse discrimination" and "color-blindness," but a look at Equal Employment Opportunity Commission complaints suggests that claims that affirmative action led to discrimination against whites are more conservative rhetoric than reality: "White men averaged only 1.7% of discrimination charges filed at the Equal Employment Opportunity Commission in the fiscal years between 1987 and 1994. This is certainly not because of a reluctance to file; white men file the lion's share of age discrimination complaints... (6,541 of 8,026 in 1994)" (Holmes Norton 1996, 45).

Migrant farmworkers in the US are consistently the most economically disadvantaged of any employed class because of the seasonal and migrant nature of their work. They are overwhelmingly Mexican and earn an average annual income of $7,500. Research on this population, arguably the most marginal workers in the nation, provides important insight into a nearly invisible workforce. The National Agricultural Workers Survey was the first systematic attempt by US government data collection agencies to survey migrant workers. Based on interviews with over 7,200 workers from 1989–92, the survey notes that the farm labor force is increasingly reliant upon Latino immigrants. Seventy per cent of those surveyed are Latino; of the immigrant population, 96 per cent of the foreign-born are Latino. The situation in California portrays the increasing reliance on Mexican immigrant workers in agriculture: in 1965, 46 per cent of farmworkers were Latino; in 1988 they accounted for 88 per cent; and from 1989–91, 92 per cent were Latino (US Department of Labor 1993, 14).

The National Agricultural Workers Survey found that the migrant labor force is overwhelmingly male (73 per cent) and relatively young (median age 31). As a result of these two factors combined, costs associated with labor reproduction and family survival (health care, education services, food, shelter, clothing) are separated from the costs of production for profit. In effect, sending communities in Mexico bear the costs of maintaining the family while receiving communities in the US reap the benefits of cheap labor of those who come to make enough money to send back to Mexico for their families' subsistence.

One would think, given the current rhetoric of backlash against educational access programs for the historically excluded, that early desegregation cases such as *Brown v. Board of Education* (1954) and lesser known precedents involving Mexicans such as *Alvarez v. Lemon Grove (CA) School District* (1929), *Del Rio (TX) ISD vs. Salvatierra* (1930), *Mendez v. Westminster (CA) School District* (1946), and *Delgado v. Bastrop (TX) ISD* (1948) were successful in ensuring equal educational outcomes. However, the continued lack of educational opportunities contributes to the marginal status of many Mexicans in the US economy, regardless of citizenship status. According to the 1990 Census, Latinos over 25 had a high-school graduation rate of 49.8 per cent as compared to Whites, who completed high school at a rate of 79.1 per cent. Similarly, 9.2 per cent of Latinos hold bachelor's degrees, compared to 22 per cent of Whites. These national disparities are symptomatic of the larger endemic crises in public education, affecting all low-income students. Latinos are left behind on every measure. The high-school completion rate looked to be improving during the 1990s but has sunk back to the 50 per cent range, according to the 2000 Census. There was a 50 per cent attrition rate of Latinos at college level that year, and even though one-quarter of the non-Latino population held a college degree in 2000, only 10 per cent of the Latino population could make the same claim.

The rates should be startling to those who profess that the US is a nation of equal opportunity through education; all they need do is look at the learning conditions of all-Latino schools. Latinos face systematic barriers to their educational success, including public school funding inequities, grade retention and suspensions, tracking, segregation, lack of college preparatory courses, lowered expectations, outdated and culturally and linguistically inappropriate curricula, lack of computer technology, and uncertified teachers. If Latinos do make it to college, they often face major financial constraints. They may be socially isolated and face discrimination and lowered expectations from some teachers (Nora 2003,

55). Schools predominately attended by Mexicans in California and Texas are chronically overcrowded and underfunded. As Kozol notes: "Now Hispanic students also, mostly female, are encouraged or required to take classes such as [hair-dressing and sewing], as we have seen at [Los Angeles] Freemont High, while children of the white and middle class are likely to be learning algebra and chemistry and government and history and all those other subjects that enable them to set their sights on universities and colleges" (2005, 186).

One of the few legal cases ruled in favor of undocumented Mexican immigrants offers some alternatives to the segregated, unequal education afforded to the majority of Latinos. In *Plyler v. Doe* (1982), the US Supreme Court ruled that undocumented children have the same right to basic education as citizens, due to their relative innocence in the making of their citizenship status. Even though IIRIRA sought to restrict benefits and services to undocumented children seeking higher education, the precedent of *Plyler* has stood up to its challengers. In this book's Conclusion, we will discuss the proposed DREAM Act that would provide a pathway to legalization for undocumented children who seek higher education or military options and that thwarts the intent of IIRIRA's restrictionist thrust.

Anti-immigrant rhetoric and actions, anti-affirmative action rulings and propositions, English-only initiatives, and separate and unequal schools together make for an inhospitable climate for Mexicans residing in the US. Anti-immigrant rhetoric has become increasingly vitriolic with the rise of vigilantism and right-wing spin machines that have created the twenty-first-century witch-hunts that scapegoat "illegal aliens." In the following chapters, the climate of nativism is the backdrop for each geographical region as we consider how Mexican immigrants fare where they are so coveted as laborers.

Notes

1. The organizations that lobbied for the antidiscrimination measures included the League of United Latin American Citizens, National Council of La Raza, Mexican American Legal Defense Fund, Commission on Migrants and Refugees of the Church World Service, Immigration and Refugee Organization of Chinese Americans, Task Force on United States-Asia Institute, Caribbean Action Lobby and Haiti, and the American Civil Liberties Union. At the time,

the NAACP and AFL-CIO aligned with anti-immigration groups because of their fear that immigrants might take jobs from union and African American workers. Both organizations have come a long way in the last few years to deal with the nativist currents within their ranks.

2. These requirements are: 1) recruitment efforts in local labor market must first be exhausted; 2) wages must match the state's adverse effect wage rate (from $6.60 in Kentucky, Tennessee, and West Virginia to $8.17 in the New England states to $9.05 in Hawaii); 3) free housing; 4) free transportation; 5) meals provided at a pre-established state rate; 6) free and reimbursed transportation; 7) workers' compensation insurance; 8) free tools and supplies; 9) three-fourths of the workdays contracted guaranteed; 10) workers cannot be used to replace striking or locked out domestic workers; 11) pay records and work contracts must be provided; and 12) an employer certification fee must be paid (maximum $1,000).

3. "Homepage—Immigration and Customs Enforcement," 2008, http://www. dhs.gov/index.shtm.

part III
Regions

Introduction

Although Mexicans are found in every income bracket and in every industry and occupation in North America, they tend to be concentrated in service, construction, non-union manufacturing, transportation, and agricultural industries for reasons that we will discuss in the chapters in Part III.

Chapter 6: Mexican Labor in *Aztlán* discusses the contemporary labor trends for Mexicanos living in the US Southwest. *Aztlán* is the name of the original homeland of the *Mexicas* whose origins story has them ascending from caves in the North. Chicano activists seized upon this imagery to rename the Southwest for its indigenous origins. Our analysis explores the demographic reclamation and the marginalization, deprivation, and systematic violent treatment of migrants that has occurred with de-industrialization and the expanding service economy in the Southwest. Increasingly, service-based jobs are heavily segregated as low-wage, Mexican immigrant workers toil for long hours in unreliable jobs, such as in restaurants and hotels, for poverty wages. We examine the formal sweatshop jobs that maintain labor relations that most of us imagine have been

Table III.1: *Timeline of Regions*

1966	The Canadian government initiates the Seasonal Agricultural Worker Program (SAWP) to allow for the employment of migrant farm workers from the British Caribbean. An explicitly temporary worker program, SAWP continues the long-standing policy of restricting Canadian naturalization to Europeans.
1974	The Canadian government initiates the Mexican Seasonal Agricultural Worker Program (SAWP) to allow for temporary labor migration from Mexico.
January 1, 1994	NAFTA is ratified.
January 1, 1994	In the southern state of Chiapas, the EZLN rises up to condemn NAFTA.
2001	The Plan Puebla-Panamá (PPP) is a public investment plan introduced by president Vicente Fox. It includes large-scale infrastructure and industrial development programs to alleviate poverty, protect ecological zones, and promote tourism projects from central Mexico to Panamá.
December 12, 2006	ICE raids of Swift and Company meat-packing plants in Greeley, CO, Grand Island, NE, Cactus, TX, Hyrum, UT, Marshalltown, IA, and Worthington, MN, commence in spite of Swift's participation in a pilot employee verification program. Deportations include 2,282 arrested, yet no charges are filed against the company. The raids are dubbed "Operation Wagon Train."
January–August 2007	Smithfield pork processors in Tar Heel, North Carolina, are raided by ICE because of social security no-match lists. Workers hold a wildcat strike in solidarity with fired co-workers.
May 12, 2008	ICE raids of Agriprocessors kosher facility in Postville, IA, yield hundreds of arrests and deportations.
September 2009	American Apparel is subjected to the "no-match" ICE program that results in firings (*de facto* raids) of 1,800 employees. By targeting a "sweat-free" clothes producer, the Obama administration's crackdowns are in line with the Bush-era meat-packing raids.

relegated to history, the semi-formal temporary employment sector, and the informal sector that employs day laborers and domestic workers.

In Chapter 7: Mexican Labor in the Heartland, we examine the central role that labor contractors are playing in this new era when not only agriculture but the meat-packing industry are increasingly relying on an undocumented workforce. We discuss how the Bracero Programs and the

H-2A temporary visa program have facilitated the flow of Mexican immigrants to the Midwest and why employers shifted to illegal means in their hiring practices. Finally, we analyze how Mexican social networks are mapped onto these recruitment processes and how a seemingly self-sustaining social network system of labor recruitment is still facilitated by the use of employer monetary incentives. As discussed in Chapter 3, the Midwest hosts long-standing, innovative organizations that fought for the rights of migrant workers and undocumented immigrants. The Toledo-based FLOC has been a crucial source for unionizing farmworkers and organizing large-scale boycotts of Campbell Soup, Dean Foods, Libby, and Heinz. As a result, FLOC has successfully entered into third-party contracts with food processors, the growers that supply them, and the workers that tend to the crops. Chicago-based activist Emma Lozano and the organizations she has created in defense of immigrants (*Pueblos Sin Fronteras, El Centro Sin Fronteras*, and *Sin Fronteras*) have been at the forefront of the recent mass mobilizations for immigrant rights.

In Chapter 8, Mexican Labor in the Hinterlands, we discuss the historical conditions that gave rise to the recent Mexican influx into the nation's hinterlands — those regions that have not had the long-standing historical concentrations of Mexican residents as have the lands formerly under Mexican domain (the current Southwestern US) and the Midwest. We consider the formation of agricultural migrant streams and the shift toward large-scale agribusiness that are changing land and labor relations in the South and to a lesser degree in the Northeast. The days of the Black or White sharecropper or Caribbean sojourner are seemingly over, as these workers are being replaced predominately by Mexicans who are now picking North Carolina's tobacco, Florida's oranges and tomatoes, Georgia's peaches, and New York's apples. The little-known H-2A temporary visa program is responsible for a portion of the laborers, but undocumented Mexicans are doing much of this work. Illustrative case studies of particular communities reveal working conditions, exploitation and prejudice, and the hope that labor relations can be ameliorated through the efforts of organizations like FLOC.

Chapter 9: Mexican Labor *en la Frontera* focuses on the role of labor along the US-Mexico border. We discuss NAFTA's role in developing the *maquiladora* system in an age of globalization. An oft-neglected aspect of the production system are *las maquilas del norte,* the sister distribution plants located on the US side of the border. The border is a unique social, political, geographic, and economic entity that reshapes relationships and definitions in a way distinct from any other part of the nation-state configuration. As the largest land border between an underdeveloped and overdeveloped nation, the nearly 2,000-mile US-Mexico border serves as the vantage point from which one can best see and feel how globalization is impacting the life chances of all global citizens. The experience of consuming Mexican labor cannot be underestimated along this border.

Chapter 10: Mexican Labor in Mexico: The Impact of NAFTA from *Chiapas* to *Turismo* considers the relationship between North American consumption and Mexican labor practices in Mexico. In particular, we address the impact of NAFTA in Southern Mexico and on Mexican workers who migrate to the US. NAFTA was designed to end collective subsistence farming and replace it with heavy pesticide-based agricultural export crops. The impacts of trade liberalization reach all the way from Mexico's industrial triangle to the tourist industry and the indigenous farmworker uprisings in Chiapas. We will discuss land and agricultural policies and examine the reforms that prepared the country for NAFTA, detailing its impact on structural adjustment policies in rural and urban areas in Mexico. What becomes clear is that "immigration," perceived as a social problem by many, is a logical result of the destabilization of Mexico's economy that began with Spanish colonialism, continued with export-oriented development policies, and most recently has been exacerbated by neoliberal policies. Immigration by Mexicans to the US cannot be understood only by studying social problems in Mexico, but rather requires a hemispheric and historical perspective. We recognize the Mexican government's labor-exporting penchant, but that fact alone does not explain the vastly distinct migration flows to the US and Canada. The US has created its own "illegal" immigrant problem by allowing employers to heavily recruit low-wage workers with relative impunity. Canada has traditionally protected its working class by both a strong welfare state and an immigration policy, albeit racist, that favors highly educated, skilled immigrants. As all three nations converge in the neoliberal NAFTA era, there is an increasingly hemispheric reliance upon low-wage Mexican laborers to provide the basic services that the privileged consume.

In Chapter 11: Mexican Labor in Canada: From Temporary Workers to Precarious Labor, we discuss the recent migration of Mexicans to Canada and distinguish this flow from patterns defining Mexican migration to the US. We find important points of convergence when exploring the

Canadian consumption and exploitation of Mexican labor. Particularly in agriculture, but increasingly in urban locales and industries such as meat-packing, the growing Mexican presence is directly related to the pressures of Canadian consumers and the interconnected political economies of all three NAFTA nations. Because Canada has experienced Mexican labor migration much differently than the US, we begin with the recent history of Mexican migration to Canada. We draw on Citizenship and Immigration Canada government statistics to differentiate earlier eras from the current NAFTA era of a more sizeable Mexican influx. NAFTA's relationship to migration is manifest in the macrostructures that facilitate the flow of capital and integrated firms but also, more and more, the flow of labor. Canadian and US immigration laws differ markedly, so we examine what factors define Mexicans in Canada as seasonal laborers, family class, economic immigrants, and humanitarian cases or refugees. The safeguards and worker guarantees in the Mexican Seasonal Agricultural Worker Program (SAWP) represent an exceptional approach to utilizing temporary laborers that contrasts sharply with US state-sanctioned programs. However, we do not wish to take the Canadian exceptionalism argument too far, so we connect the agricultural program to the "precarious status" of Mexican immigrants as defined by Canadian immigration law. Finally, we present regional analyses of the Mexican presence in Canadian labor markets to demonstrate how patterns of Canadian consumption and labor exploitation are defining Mexican labor migration in this post-NAFTA era.

Chapter Six

Mexican Labor in *Aztlán*

"As California goes, so goes the rest of the nation."[1] The popular saying is often spouted by pundits referring to the latest fashion trends or citing the influence of popular entertainment. But in matters that are much more germane to the rest of nation, the saying is apropos to fundamental changes. The suburbanization of major metropolitan areas may have begun in Levittown, New York, but it has sprawled from the San Fernando Valley to San Juan Capistrano. The malling of America may have begun in the Midwest but was taken to its extreme in the Mission Valley of San Diego where two mega-malls (Fashion Valley and Mission Valley) are built right next door to each other on the I-8 corridor with two additional malls located five miles to the east in La Mesa and El Cajon. What sociologist George Ritzer refers to as the "McDonaldization of America" is on display prominently in San Bernardino where the first McDonald's opened in 1948. Today, one can find a McDonald's every two to four major blocks in most cities; from one restaurant, McDonald's has spread worldwide to over 30,000 franchises (Ritzer 2004). "In 1970, Americans spent about $6 billion on fast food; in 2001, they spent more than $110 billion" (Schlosser 2002, 3, 19). The consumer tastes of the nation are defined in California, and the demographic shifts that mark the state are inextricably linked to its political economy. Demographers, in the early 1990s, began talking about the majority minority possibility for California by 2010. The surprise was the rapidity of the Latino and Asian immigrant boom; by 2000, the state's population had more minorities than majority residents. The nativist backlash against this current demographic reality reached fevered pitches in Hazelton, Pennsylvania, and Farmers Branch, Texas, but originated in the California state propositions that ended affirmative action and bilingual education and barred undocumented immigrants from receiving services.

With the settlement of the US-Mexico War of 1846–48, nearly one-half of Mexico's northern territories was ceded to the US and became the states of California, Texas, New Mexico, Arizona, Colorado, Nevada, and Utah. According to the 2000 Census, three-quarters of the Mexican population resided in these seven states as of 2000: 15.8 million Mexicans out of a nationwide total of 20.6 million.[2] In 2004, 76 per cent of all Latinos resided in the Southwest. The first Bracero era, the mass repatriation program of the Great Depression, the second Bracero Program, and the illegality associated with border militarization and immigrant criminalization heavily impacted the Mexican population of the Southwest. Thus, the Southwest— dubbed *Aztlán* by Chicano activists—has defined the history of Mexican immigration.

Demographic Reclamation of *Aztlán*

Xenophobes, such as media fear-mongers Glenn Beck, Lou Dobbs, and Bill O'Reilly, fret about the Mexican immigration issue in the Southwest in terms of the "*reconquista*." The term, deployed during the Chicano Movement, describes local community control and a sense that Chicanos' shared fates should be in their hands, not in those of the Anglo power structure.

We discuss Mexican immigration to *Aztlán* in terms of a demographic reclamation, which captures the population shifts but rejects a pejorative assessment of those shifts. Dramatic Latino population increases are occurring in Nevada and Utah, but the states with the largest Mexican populations are not seeing the population explosions that are so often attributed to them (see Table 6.1). California and Texas have seen population increases of 65 and 68 per cent, well below the growth rates witnessed in the South and Midwest regions. The absolute numerical increase is quite large (California's Mexican population increased by nearly 4 million and Texas's by almost 2 million), but because Mexican populations were already present with a combined 1 million residents in 1990, their presence was already well established. Arizona now has more than 1 million Mexicans, and 1 million more live in New Mexico and Colorado combined. Due to their numbers, the range in socio-economic status is broad, although they tend to congregate at the bottom end of the spectrum.

The North County of San Diego illustrates the range of socio-economic positions among Mexicans. A small handful of upper-class Mexicans reside in gated communities and million-dollar homes in Rancho Santa Fe, Cardiff-by-the-Sea, Encinitas, Leucadia, Poway,

Table 6.1: *Demographic Distribution of Mexicans in Southwest US*

	2004	2000	1990	Per cent Increase 1990–2004
US	25,894,763	20,320,095	13,495,938	92
Arizona	1,433,823	1,041,777	616,195	133
California	10,069,145	8,367,070	6,118,996	65
Colorado	643,235	442,659	282,478	128
Nevada	410,010	280,308	85,287	381
New Mexico	439,746	322,003	328,836	34
Texas	6,546,502	4,977,163	3,890,820	68
Utah	188,430	134,888	56,842	231

Source: US Census 1990; US Census 2000, Summary File 3; US Census 2005.

Carlsbad, and Del Mar. In close proximity in the hills below is the migrant population, who scratch out a temporary existence with no access to housing, water, sewage, electricity, or the other modern conveniences taken for granted by those with ocean views and perfectly manicured lawns.

Many undocumented migrants are drawn to northern San Diego County by the demand for labor and the strawberry, tomato, and avocado fields, as well as in large nurseries and flower farms.... [W]orkers set up makeshift sleeping shelters of plastic, cardboard tar paper, discarded wood, and anything else that is handy. These encampments can be found on hillsides covered by dense brush, and in canyons with pleasant sounding names like McGonigle Canyon and Deer Canyon. Even though they are just moments away from middle- and upper-middle-class neighborhoods and communities, they stand in stark contrast to the growing affluence of North San Diego County. (Chavez 1992, 67)

McGonigle Canyon, at the base of mid- to upper-income Rancho Penasquitos, has turned into a battleground for anti-immigrant forces and registered national attention in 2000 when migrants living in cardboard colonies were beaten by a group of young people. "On July 7, 2000, eight teenagers from Mount Carmel High School in Rancho Penasquitos dragged five elderly migrants from their camp huts, beat them with pipes and stakes, and shot them each with pellet guns. One of the teens pitch-forked each of his victims.... The attack occurred in McGonigle Canyon, site of the original Rancho de los Diablos camp. The camp's celebrated abatement and relocation five years earlier had been widely reported as evidence that the camps were now 'history'" (Caldwell 2003, 222). Seven were privileged Anglo teens; the eighth was Latino. The land is owned by wealthy developers and sits fallow until the housing market warrants the building of even more sprawling suburban "McMansions." In the mean-time, growers lease the land for tomato and avocado crops. Everyone seems to be making a hefty profit from the arrangement, except the Mexican migrant workers who toil for under-the-table wages and have no access to housing. In late 2006, tensions escalated when anti-immigrant groups used the site of the earlier beating to make their pitch that immi-grants are a menace and should not be in the US. A local news article cap-tured the tone of the situation:

> They tend lawns, build homes and harvest produce, but the workers that lived in shanties at McGonigle Canyon near Rancho Penasquitos are now homeless and scattered. Again. Police and landowners blocked the entrance to their canyon homes a week ago, citing concerns over a highly publicized protest by anti-illegal immigrant activists. Most of the workers left last week before the protest on Saturday, police said.... An estimated 300 to 500 workers lived in the canyon camps near Torrey Santa Fe Road and State Route 56. Most toiled in nearby fields, nurseries and construction sites. Many of the products they help harvest are sold in prominent grocery stores throughout southern California. (Sifuentes 2006)

Proposition 21 and Migrant Beating

Most of the media attention on the migrant beatings focused on the youth, who were tried under California Proposition 21, which required children to be tried as adults if they were accused of felonies. The never-subtle assertion was that the proposition was not intended for "these" types of kids. Proposition 21 received much initial support in affluent communities like Rancho Penasquitos because their residents believed the law allowed "gangbangers" (read: poor Brown and Black kids) to be tried as adults. The reason for the brutal attack on the elderly men was rarely questioned, although it did elicit mandatory hand-wringing. Rarely identified as a surprising event, it was almost expected, given the consistent and pervasive dehumanization of illegal immigrants in San Diego. Border militarization, immigrant criminalization, the rhetoric of immigrant scapegoating, and the callous view of labor as disposable all came together when the kids picked up baseball bats and a pitchfork to senselessly attack the most vulnerable.

Very rarely does the US consumption of Mexican labor find such prominent expression in media coverage, which is why *North County Times* reporter Edward Sifuentes is on the list of most hated "raza" members by anti-immigrant xenophobes. The San Diego Minutemen, with support from area Republican congressmen Brian Bilbray, Bill Morrow, and Mark Wyland, organized several protests to intimidate day laborers. Lately, their main targets of ire have become the homeless migrants living in the hills. They use coded racialized language to both dehumanize immigrant workers and debase their detractors. They identify any person opposing their views as "la raza," another Chicano Movement term used to connote "the people" or "the community" but colloquially translated as "the race." The anti-immigrant movement is quite adept at code-switching. They use the self-expressed justification that they are not a hate group engaging in intimidation, hate-mongering, and fostering an anti-Mexican climate by questioning Mexicans' basic rights to claim "American" citizenship.

In South Texas and the Imperial Valley of California, as well as in border communities in Arizona and New Mexico, Mexicans' marginality is visible in areas known as *las colonias*. In these remote areas, the lack of infrastructure, basic services, and formal property titles approach Third World conditions. "*Colonias* are rural communities and neighborhoods within 150 miles of the US-Mexico border that lack adequate infrastructure and frequently also lack other basic services.... These single or double room dwellings were placed on land that was never registered with any city or county. As a result these communities exist without fundamental services such as water and electricity" (Galan Productions 2000). Unpaved roads, no electricity, no running water or sewers, and frequent exposure to the natural elements reflect the displacement and dispossession of the most marginalized of the marginalized (Davis 2007; Harvey 2003). The most economically disadvantaged group in the US, *colonia* dwellers earn $1,636 dollars per year and live in counties where unemployment rates are as high as 25 to 40 per cent (Coronado 2003, 195). The Rio Grande Valley of South Texas and California's Imperial Valley are the two areas of the US that still, to this day, send Mexican Americans along the migrant trail to toil for long hours and low pay in agriculture. The seasonality of employment is exacerbated by the dwindling availability of employment opportunities.

Part of this trend can be attributed to the massive transformation of the rural US economy and the resultant dwindling of agricultural employment options. Nationwide, Census data confirm the strong relationship between concentration, mechanization, and worker displacement in agriculture. In 1947, 7.9 million people were listed by profession as farmworkers. In 1994, there was less than one-half of that number (3.4 million) (Briggs 1996, 192). The proportion of the labor force involved in agriculture has shrunk to less than 2 per cent as of 1988. In that same year, those designated as "farmworkers" comprised 0.8 per cent of the total employed labor force (US Census 1990). The Census no longer reports on farmworkers, but every year the rate of those employed in agriculture has slowly but steadily decreased to the 2004 rate of 1.6 per cent (US Census 2006, 407).

In California, most job opportunities are in the counties of the Central Valley where farmworkers can still find employment (56 per cent of farmworkers work in the valley). Estimates by the California Institute for Rural Studies (see Table 6.2) identify a farmworker population of about 744,000 in the late 1990s, with the heaviest concentration employed in the San Joaquin Valley. In the Central Valley, Fresno County, where every conceivable fruit and vegetable is grown, is the largest and most profitable agricultural producing county in the world. The Central Coast, where nearly 20 per cent of the state's farmworkers are employed, is host to specialty labor-intensive crops such as roses and strawberries.

Table 6.2 shows that the Mexican sending states of California's farmworker population are quite varied, with Guanajuato, Michoacán, and Jalisco together constituting over 60 per cent of California's farm labor force. The large Oaxacan population, most often indigenous, is a direct result of NAFTA displacement from *ejido* farming practices, which we will examine further in Chapter 10.

Farm work is one of the most dangerous occupations in the US. In 1988, agriculture had the highest rate of work-related deaths (48 per 100,000 workers) of any sector of the economy (US Census 1990). The second highest death rate was construction (34 per 100,000), and the rate among all industries was nine per 100,000 workers. The death rate in manufactur-

Table 6.2: *Place of Origin of California Farmworkers*

Michoacán	28.7%
Guanajuato	20.3%
Jalisco	12.9%
Baja California	4.9%
Guerrero	4.6%
Sinaloa	4.1%
Oaxaca	3.9%
Zacatecas	3.8%
Nayarit	2.6%
Other	14.2%

Source: California NAWS data 1995–99, http://www.cirsinc.org/CPAC.pdf, 13.

ing was six per 100,000 workers. In 2003, work-related deaths occurred most frequently in the following three industries: mining and quarrying (22.3 per 100,000), agriculture (20.9), and construction (11.4) (US Census 2006, 433).

Economic restructuring—referred to as "deindustrialization"—has also had a major impact on Southwestern metropolitan areas. Unlike the Northeast and Midwest Rust Belts that are still surviving though reeling, the Southwest's base was quickly subsumed by an ascendant low-wage service sector, which represents the vast majority of today's employment opportunities for immigrants. The restructuring of the Los Angeles economy includes, on the one hand, the decline of traditional, highly unionized, high-wage manufacturing employment and, on the other, the growth of employment in high-technology manufacturing, craft specialties, and advanced services sectors. South Central Los Angeles—the traditional industrial core of the city—bore the brunt of the decline in heavy manufacturing employment, losing 70,000 high-wage stable jobs between 1978 and 1982 and another 200,000 between 1982 and 1989 (Johnson, Ferrell, and Guinn 1997, 1073).

As the gateway to middle-class living closed, the loss of steady manufacturing employment has contributed to a widening gap between rich and poor. In the wake of deindustrialization, minimum-wage, no-benefits jobs are created in the top three industries—restaurants, garment producers, and private households—that employ immigrants in Los Angeles (Waldinger 1996, 1081). According to Saskia Sassen (2005), these economic niches constitute the new "serving classes" in global cities. To serve the needs of the wealthy or those aspiring to the elitist standards of conspicuous consumption, the serving-class jobs of gardeners, general laborers, garment workers, domestics, restaurant workers, farmworkers, hotel maids, janitors, and day laborers are increasingly filled by Mexican immigrants. The restructuring of the economy means that it should be no surprise that Mexican workers in the Southwest frequently face underemployment and are pushed to the margins or to *colonias* where living conditions are precarious.

The Serving Classes in the Service Economy

In the new economy of the post-industrial Southwest, US consumption patterns rely, at least in terms of maintaining elite consumer demand, on labor-intensive services steeped in neo-bourgeois tastes and sensibilities. "This has reintroduced—to an extent not seen in a very long time—the whole notion of the 'serving classes' in contemporary high-income households. The immigrant woman has replaced the traditional image of the African-American female servant serving the white master" (Sassen 2005, 205). Both Saskia Sassen and Mike Davis, prior to the 2006 immigrant marches, warned of the increasing social polarization and civil unrest that were a response to the crass US consumption of Mexican labor. "In Los Angeles's new ethnic division of labor, Anglos tend to be concentrated in private-sector and management and entertainment production, Asians in professions and light industry, African-Americans in civil service occupations, and Latinos in labor-intensive services and manufacture" (Davis 2001, 56).

Mexican immigrants increasingly find themselves locked out of the best that the "new" economy has to offer. Well-paying jobs in research and development, biotechnology, and computer information systems are unavailable to immigrants with little formal education. Even with requisite education, Mexicans are finding it difficult to crack the barriers that reproduce racial and class cleavages. "Indeed, some of the worst offenders are cyber-capital icons like Apple, Sun, Adobe, Netscape and Oracle, all of whom have been fined or sued for racial discrimination or failure to meet federal diversity deadlines. Three of the largest firms lacked even a single

Latino official or manager. 'It is pretty clear,' says UC Santa Cruz's Manuel Pastor, 'that there's ethnic and occupation segregation going on in Silicon Valley'" (Davis 2001, 121).

At the bottom end of the new economy, a plethora of jobs are available for Mexicans seeking janitorial, domestic, receptionist, mail room, restaurant and hotel service, and truck driver positions, but occupational mobility is elusive to non-existent. The US government filled these low-wage jobs through the creation of the H-2B program, the majority of whose workers are employed in seasonal (non-agricultural) jobs in nurseries, landscaping, hospitality, and cleaning. Rural counties experiencing high-growth Latino residential settlement are predominately associated with the meat, poultry, and pork processing industries, but in the Southwest the mountain resorts are the main draw for Mexicans and other Latinos. When the rich play, they expect the same degree of pampering and consumption that they enjoy at home. Mountain resort communities have seen a rise in Mexican immigrants as the serving classes are transplanted to fulfill the needs of bourgeois second-home owners and vacationers. The H-2B program supplies a ready supply of cheap labor to be exploited when the social networks that bring in undocumented workers do not suffice. Kandel and Cromartie (2004, 14–15) identify as "high-amenity resort areas that attract low-wage service workers" the 10 counties of Jackson, Wyoming, Park City, Utah, Lake Tahoe-Reno, Nevada, and the I-70 Aspen-Vail-Breckenridge ski corridor. Most often, it is not the counties with resorts that deal with the Mexican serving classes. Because of their low wages, they find it impossible to pay the exorbitant costs of living in the communities where they work. Resorts such as Vail and Beaver Creek are in Summit County, but housing, health care, and education costs for the Mexican service workers are displaced onto more affordable neighboring counties such as Lake and Eagle.

In Lake County, the mountain town of Leadville was founded in 1878 by prospectors who located silver deposits. The city quickly boomed when mining companies staked out claims, and Leadville became the second largest city in Colorado, behind Denver, by the turn of the century. Miners were recruited from European and Mexican immigrant communities, as well as from Mexican American communities in Northern New Mexico. The mine was in operation until 1982 and was the main employer in the community. After it closed, the city's population dwindled to 3,822; even

Table 6.3: *Leadville/Lake County Census Data, 1930–2000, on Mexican Re-Emergence*

Year	Total Population		Total Mexican Population		Per cent Mexican Population	
	Leadville	Lake	Leadville	Lake	Leadville	Lake
2000	4,763	7,812	1,381	2,823	29.00	36.1
1990	4,386	6,007	677	1,434	15.44	23.9
1980	3,879	8,830	6	6	0.15	0.07
1930	3,722	4,899	74	282	1.99	5.8

by 1980, most residents had left. In the mid-1990s, when large hotel chain employers in the nearby ski resort towns of Vail and Beaver Creek began recruiting undocumented and H-2B temporary visa workers in the hospitality industry, Leadville was one of the closest communities where they were able to find affordable housing. In 2000, Latinos constituted 36.1 per cent of Lake County's population and 29 per cent of Leadville's population. Leadville constitutes a re-emerging Latino destination due to boom-bust cycles of the rural community and the shift in the economy from extractive industry to resort bedroom community (see Table 6.3). These shifts have major impacts on the health care, education, and social service systems, and resentment arises toward the newcomers from established residents even though corporations and consumer demand are the major motors of change.

Nevada's urban locales in the postwar era dramatically illustrate the Southwest's urbanization and suburbanization trends and resulting need for service workers in a post-industrial economy. Las Vegas is perhaps the crassest example of a consumerist society that caters to hedonistic consumers. "What happens in Vegas stays in Vegas" is how the travel industry touts the excesses. Casino development, urbanization, and suburban sprawl bring Mexicans to work in Vegas's construction industry, but the state of Nevada in many ways represents a destination for Mexicans from the miners in yesterday's boomtowns to today's residential construction workers, janitors, and hotel cleaners employed in the thriving hospitality industry.

Sweating It Out: Sweatshops and the Garment Industry

Although many think that sweatshops are things of the past, they have become prevalent again in the US garment industry over the past 30 years. In Chapter 4, we detailed the unsuccessful attempts by UNITE to secure a contract with Guess jeans after a public and well-coordinated campaign. The larger context of de-unionization and the offshoring of the apparel industry made the race to the bottom even more virulent. Workers, both domestic and international, paid the price. A sweatshop is "a factory or a homework operation that engages in multiple violations of the law, typically the non-payment of minimum or overtime wages and various violations of health and safety regulations" (Bonacich and Applebaum 2000, 3). This definition qualifies many garment factories in Los Angeles as sweatshops.

In a sample survey conducted by the US Department of Labor in January 1998, 61 per cent of the garment firms in Los Angeles were found to be violating wage and hour regulations. Workers were underpaid by an estimated $73 million per year. Health and safety violations were not examined in that study, but in a survey completed in 1997, 96 per cent of the firms were found to be in violation, 54 per cent with deficiencies that could lead to serious injuries or death (Bonacich and Applebaum 2000, 3). These sweatshop conditions were occurring in an industry that was ascendant at the time in Los Angeles. De-unionization was certainly impacting the workforce, but offshoring was less relevant. "Between 1971 and 1992, the number of garment workers [in LA] nearly doubled, in sharp contrast to New York City, where it fell by over one-third during those years" (Milkman 2006, 88).

Los Angeles was becoming the garment capital of the US largely due to the city's comparatively low wages and high supply of exploitable workers— undocumented immigrants. Asian, Central American, and Mexican women toiled in conditions not experienced since the early 1900s, when sweatshops operated by exploiting Southern and Eastern European women and children. The sweatshops of that period are engraved in popular memory by the 1911 Triangle Shirtwaist Fire in Greenwich Village. Because of a lack of workplace safety measures such as emergency exits, 123 women and 23 men were burned or jumped to death when the exits were blocked and firefighters could not reach the high-rise's windows. The plight of today's immigrant sweatshop workers was brought into sharp relief by the discovery of a slavery ring in El Monte, California, where 72

Thai garment workers were locked in their apartment complex and forced to work 18-hour days. The ring operated undetected for 17 years even though the apartment had armed guards at its exits and barbed wire lining its windows and balconies. Though this incident was universally condemned, the reality of slave wages paid to garment workers seems to be less important to the public than the latest fashion trends.

The wholesale cost of a $100 dress made in the US is about $50; half of the $100 sales price goes to the retailer. Of the $50 wholesale cost, 45 per cent, or $22.50, is spent by the manufacturer on the fabric, while 25 per cent, or $12.50, is profit and overhead. The remaining 30 per cent, or $15, goes to the contractor and covers the cost of direct labor and other expenses and profit. Only 6 per cent — $6.00 — goes to the person who actually sewed the garment. Furthermore, this individual is more than likely to have been paid by the number of sewing operations performed than by the hour and to have received no benefits of any kind (Bonacich and Applebaum 2000, 1–2).

Piece rates, or pay per garment produced, are one strategy contractors use to maximize the goods produced per hour. Workers are compelled to sew and assemble at the fastest speed possible in order to maximize their earnings. Only agriculture and sales allow piece rates in lieu of hourly wages. Often, piece rates in the garment industry do not allow workers to earn even the federally mandated minimum wage. Bonacich and Applebaum (2000) note that the Department of Labor found that standard businesses are operating in violation of applicable labor laws, and garment suppliers would rather take their chances with fines rather than provide a minimum, let alone a living, wage. Even those companies that do try to treat their laborers, whether legal or undocumented, in a fair manner are subject to penalty. In September 2009, the largest employer of sweat-free labor, Los Angeles-based American Apparel, was targeted by the DHS for hiring workers whose names did not match their documents. The DHS required the company, one of the most outspoken proponents of legalizing undocumented workers, to fire 1,800 employees. Immigrant advocates have universally condemned the Obama administration for this action.

Just Tempin' It: (Not) Getting By in the Flexible Economy
Southwestern Mexican communities are at a disadvantage in this era of flexible specialization that forces workers to put together employment options like a patchwork quilt, as steady work at a living wage is increas-

ingly difficult to secure. Unfortunately, the US government does not systematically collect data on the number of temporary workers in casual employment contracts. With a lack of full-time, gainful employment options, the type of work available on a temporary basis includes industrial, light industrial, clerical, customer service, and administrative work. Estimates by the American Staffing Association (2009), which represents the temporary employment services industry, are that 35 per cent of employment options are in the industrial sector and one-fifth each are in office-clerical and professional-managerial contingent employment. The temporary industry tends to be highly gendered in offering low-wage, "unskilled" work,[3] but even high-income industries, such as software development, health care, programming, engineering, applied sciences, sales, marketing, financial services, and management are pursuing contingent labor routes.

A flexible workforce is designed for optimality and efficiency by cutting labor costs to a minimum and expanding only when consumer demand requires it. In the words of the world's largest employer, Manpower, "The use of lower-skilled temporary employees in administrative and industrial roles has continued to be a reliable means of finding quality supplemental staff either on short notice during absences of permanent employees, or when workloads increase periodically due to customer demand" (Manpower 2006, 2). Manpower equates contingent workers with temporary workers, contractors, consultants, and outsourcing. Those who do the work that is outsourced by the post-Fordist global economy have counterparts in the US, as industries increasingly rely upon temporary workers. Outsourcing and temporary employment are two approaches to the same end — casualizing employment contracts to maximize labor savings.

In the Southwest, temporary employment agencies such as Manpower, Express Personnel, Volt, Kelly Services, Helpmates, Rush, Westaff, TLC, and AtWork supply contingent workers to companies of all sizes. They recruit temporary workers for once-per-year replacement as well as for companies that maintain a permanent temporary workforce. Manpower (2006, 4) estimates that it represents approximately 20 per cent of the average company's total workforce. The American Management Association (2000) estimates that 93 per cent of US firms employ some type of contingent workers. In San Diego and Denver, Mize made a research virtue out of economic necessity and worked as a temporary employee from 1986 to 2000. He had approximately 50 different employers over an intermittent period of 14 years. He worked for a multinational battery corporation that kept its employment commitments as flexible as possible to respond to consumer demand — the US equivalent of Japan's "just-in-time" production model. An educational supply company supplemented its warehouse division of approximately five shippers with anywhere from two to ten temporary workers who pulled products off the shelves and filled orders. Mize also worked as an administrative assistant for two water companies in South San Diego. He never knew beyond a week if he would have work the next week. The constant treadmill of new companies, new bosses, and minimum wage pay without benefits was a difficult way to live as a student but was even more precarious as an adult providing for a family. Occupational segregation was racialized as well as gendered, as Mize noticed when he was working at "Mexican shops" and "Anglo workplaces." The public water companies were the most diverse in terms of employees, but in general non-Whites were hired for less skilled and entry level positions while Whites were concentrated in highly skilled and managerial positions. Warehouse work was the exclusive domain of Mexican American males in all of the San Diego companies in which he worked.

For Mexican immigrants unable to secure work documents, possibilities for secure employment are even more limited:

> On the supply side of urban labor markets, workers are increasingly turning to day labor hiring sites, and other sources of contingent work like temp agencies and labor brokers, following the deterioration of job opportunities in the local economy. Plant closings and mass layoffs continue to plague many cities, particularly old industrial centers, which have seen the widespread loss of manufacturing jobs and employment in ancillary industries. (Valenzuela *et al.* 2006, 1)

Informalizing Immigrant Work: Attempts at Formalization by Day Laborers and Worker Centers

The work conducted by day laborers can be characterized by its temporary nature, but that does not capture the precariousness of their existence. The 2004 Day Labor National Survey provides a shocking glimpse into the working lives of the men congregating on street corners or outside Home Depot stores who hustle work on a daily basis in unregulated, informal, and dangerous environments. "The inescapable conclusions are that day laborers are hired to undertake some of the most dangerous jobs at a worksite and there is little, if any, meaningful enforcement of health and safety laws. Day laborers continue to endure unsafe working conditions, mainly because they fear that if they speak up, complain, or otherwise challenge these conditions, they will either be fired or not paid for their work" (Valenzuela *et al.* 2006, 12). When examining the distribution of day laborers, the Survey found that 42 per cent, or nearly 50,000 *jornaleros*, seek employment in the Western US.

One begins to see the casualization of the Southwest construction industry by the high rate of day laborers in this sector. Construction contractors or private individuals hire 92 per cent of workers by the day. Most have engaged in a plethora of job tasks but are generally characterized as unskilled labor. Most work is designed to be short term, but since 44 per cent of the work is secured by companies or contractors, day laborers' marginalization is clearly the source of profit for middlemen contractors.

High rates of abuse make day laborers' situations extremely precarious. As can be seen in Table 6.4, abuse by employers, merchants, police, and security guards is not overwhelming but is sizeable enough to be considered problematic. Non-payment or underpayment of wages is by far the most widespread and serious repercussion of securing work through informal means. Since 70 per cent of day laborers do not know where they should report such abuses, most of these crimes go unpunished and unreported and will continue to do so without substantial intervention and worker education.

Following the national trend we outlined in Chapter 4, worker centers have developed across the Southwest to fill this void. Both union-sponsored and independent worker centers are designed to provide legal assistance, education, and worker solidarity to defend the day laborers' basic rights. Worker centers in California, Colorado, Texas, Arizona, and Nevada contribute to formalizing the day labor industry. They collectively provide venues for securing work contracts, establish baseline wage rates, and provide enforceable contracts to guard against abusing workers' rights. *Macehualli* Worker Center in Phoenix, *El Centro Humanitario para los Trabajadores* in Denver, the Workers Defense Project/*Proyecto Defensa Laboral* (PDL) in Austin, the Alliance for Workers' Rights in Reno, Oscar Romero Day Labor Center in Houston, and about 30 worker centers in California support day laborers' struggles for respect and dignity. Fair wages and human rights can become important components in a larger campaign against those who vilify and criminalize day laborers.

Table 6.4: *Day Labor Abuses, Two-Month Period Incidence Rate, 2004*

	Total (%)	West (%)	Midwest (%)	Southwest (%)	South (%)	East %)
Experienced at least one instance of employer abuse						
Non-payment of wages	49	44	66	52	50	54
Underpayment of wages	48	46	53	49	37	54
Worked extra hours	32	32	31	26	26	39
Abandoned	27	28	23	20	30	31
No food and/or breaks	44	46	41	37	41	46
Violence	18	17	27	15	9	25
Insulted	28	24	36	24	33	35
Experienced at least one instance of merchant abuse						
Insulted	19	19	21	23	19	16
Threats	9	10	10	9	10	6
Violence	4	4	4	4	4	4
Refused services	14	17	34	8	11	13
Called police	24	25	27	29	20	19
Experienced at least one instance of police abuse						
Insulted	16	15	11	19	25	11
Arrested	9	9	16	5	16	6
Cited	11	15	25	5	13	7
Confiscated papers	3	3	9	2	3	3
Forced to leave site	37	39	34	42	38	28
Immigration status check	15	17	27	14	12	12
Photographed and/ or videotaped	13	17	24	11	8	10

	Total (%)	West (%)	Midwest (%)	Southwest (%)	South (%)	East %)
Experienced at least one instance of security guard abuse						
Insulted, harassed, or threatened	9	12	12	8	6	7
Violence	4	4	7	2	4	4
Robbery	2	2	7	0.5	2	3
Called police or immigration authorities	12	15	6	9	7	8
Do not know where to report workplace abuses	70	70	56	75	67	69

Source: Valenzuela *et al.* 2006.

Maid in Aztlán: *Domestics on the Fringes of the Formal Economy*

The resurgence in the number of maids, housecleaners, nannies, and childcare providers is related to both economic restructuring and the new gender division of labor. The new economy has placed incredible strains on working families, and those with requisite disposable incomes out-source their domestic and childcare needs to a paid labor force most often supplied by immigrant women. "In Los Angeles, for example, the percentage of African American women working as domestics in private households fell from 35 per cent to 4 per cent from 1970 to 1990, while foreign-born Latinas increased their representation from 9 per cent to 68 per cent" (Hondagneu-Sotelo 2007, 16–17). Hondagneu-Sotelo (2007, 29) notes three types of domestic arrangements: live-in nanny/housekeeper, live-out nanny/housekeeper, and housecleaner. The informality of work arrangements is often detrimental to domestics since wages are not clearly determined, hours go beyond agreed-upon start and/or end times, and the intensity of work varies based on the employing family's needs, not the worker's.

Household workers in El Paso's suburbs include both commuter maids with green cards and undocumented Mexicanas who dodge *la Migra* (the Border Patrol and INS agents) as they cross the border. The extent of economic interdependency was demonstrated in March 1979 when Mexican nationals blockaded the bridge between Mexico and the US to protest *la Migra*'s deportation of some 140 maids: "Some of the Mexican border towns seem to have only one reason for being where they are: to supply the US with cheap temporary workers. They supply the maids for Juarez, who earn enough money in El Paso to support their families" (Romero 1992, 91).

As the employment of domestics becomes a major status distinction for the US wealthy and wealthy-aspirant, the poorly remunerated labor performed by Mexican immigrant women is taken for granted. "Like the privilege of whiteness in US society, the privilege of employing a domestic worker is barely noticed by those who have it. While they obviously do not deny that they pay someone to clean their home and care for their children, they tend to approach these arrangements not as employers, with a particular set of obligations and responsibilities, but as consumers" (Hondagneu-Sotelo 2007, 12).

Building on the Backs of Mexicans: Construction Trades and Regional Development

By comparison, work in the construction industry is well remunerated, and for regions of the Southwest where weather does not preclude seasonal layoffs, the good pay is very enticing to those with few options because of their limited education. Yet good wages cannot compensate for the long-term impacts of construction work. Construction is one of the most dangerous — in 2003 *the* most dangerous — occupations. The most visible sign of this danger is the high rate of occupational deaths. Long-term health impacts of construction work are rarely studied but nonetheless a serious problem. In the Southwest, the housing boom was built on the backs of Mexican construction workers. The growth of new firms in the post-industrial economy did not result in Mexican upward mobility but did secure steady work in first the construction industry and later in janitorial and landscaping industries. The building trades tend to be much more diverse but still overwhelmingly dependent upon Mexican labor.

In the booming Las Vegas construction industry, an interesting dichotomy has arisen that stratifies construction work along citizenship lines. Morales (2009) notes that the casino and hotel boom provides employment opportunities for union-affiliated construction workers, often though not exclusively of Mexican American descent, whereas the residential construction boom is characterized by non-union, subcontracted, and flexible work that is mostly dominated by undocumented Mexican immigrants. As a result, the opportunities for stable employment with high wages are simply missing in the residential home construction industry.

Mexican immigrant workers tend to be relegated to the low-end, worst-paying, and least-desirable job tasks in the construction industry. As reported by the Giannini Foundation of Agricultural Economics (1982, 36), "certain microsectors become dominated entirely by illegal, temporary workers—for example, [in] the construction cleanup in Southern California...the low wages and poor working conditions have eliminated domestic workers for many years." Mexicans found gainful employment in the building trades precisely when the industry was in the throes of de-unionization and deindustrialization. Milkman (2006, 94) notes, "deunionization led to rapid deterioration in wages, conditions, and benefits, especially in the residential sector. Pay rates were cut by as much as half over the course of the 1980s, overtime work remained common but was rarely properly compensated, and fringe benefits became a distant memory."

When the Los Angeles construction corporations sought to end contracts with labor unions, the industry looked to contractors. Milkman (2006, 195) found that informal recruitment of Mexican immigrants by Latino contractors filled the void created by the open shop movement when unions were blocked out of competition. It was within this context that the successful drywallers' strike occurred, which undercut the Anglo union line that Mexican construction workers could not be organized and that Mexican workers would passively accept inferior work conditions at low wages. In the following chapters, we discuss the deleterious working conditions Mexican immigrant workers experience as well as their organized responses for equal treatment, respect, and dignity in other regions of North America.

Notes

1. Most recently, California Republican governor Arnold Schwarzenegger used the saying in his 2007 State of the State address.
2. Texas is considered a Southern state by the US Census, which does not recognize a Southwest region category; therefore, our calculations differ from official Census reports.

3. Having worked as a temp for 14 years, Mize disputes the characterization of poorly paid temp jobs as low skill. Standing on concrete all day sorting aluminum supports to make sure they are free from defects or scratches may not require a great deal of physical or mental ability; however, it often requires great mental restraint to avoid smashing the beams over the head of managers breathing down one's neck or to keep one's mind intact while doing drone work.

Chapter Seven

Mexican Labor in the Heartland

When "Roberto Salinas" was born in Mexicali, Baja California, in 1950, he planned to farm on the family plot from a very early age.[1] His mother's death in 1963 pre-empted these plans, so to help care for his extended family of 30 cousins and brothers, Roberto traveled with his father and one brother to the US to find employment as a migrant farmworker. Looking for better employment options, the men moved to Los Angeles but were convinced to relocate by advertisements in an LA Spanish newspaper by the Iowa Beef Processors (IBP), who were soliciting meat-packing workers willing to relocate to Perry, Iowa. The company hired on the spot, provided free bus tickets to nearby Des Moines, and offered two weeks of free lodging at a local motel. Since Roberto was older, had earned his high-school equivalency diploma, and spoke English, he became the company-appointed leader and translator of this recruited community. Always the creative entrepreneur, Roberto frequently traveled to Los Angeles to secure goods to resell or trade in Perry. He also maximized his earnings by taking full advantage of IBP's subsequent recruiting policy of paying workers $150 for every referred applicant they hired. Roberto's life in Iowa is becoming a much more common story for Mexican immigrants who are willing to move where the jobs are.

The draw of Mexican labor to the agricultural, meat-packing, and increasingly rural factory production industries is the main economic motivation for the most recent Mexican immigrant influx to the Midwest. One would think that Mexicans were unwanted newcomers to the Midwestern US if one relied solely on local newspaper accounts by the White community. As a Latina focus group respondent stated in Millard and Chapa (2004, 114–15):

> In this area [Falls County, Michigan], there is still prejudice against Mexicans. It's probably the hardest prejudice to change. It's a kind of subtle racism. I work

with a [White] American woman. One day she said, "Julia, you and your family are different compared to the other Mexicans. You, you're not poor; you don't take advantage of public assistance. You're not draining society of resources."

In addition to this stereotypical image, Julia notes the commonsense understandings of who are deemed the rightful residents of the heartland: "Americans" and "foreigners," productive citizens and those draining resources, wanted and not wanted. In the Midwest, too often White is synonymous with American and a *de facto* "alien-ization" of non-Whites becomes rooted in the vernacular of both Whites and non-Whites, regardless of citizenship status. The reality is that most of these migrant streams began in either the early part of the 1900s or during the second Bracero Program.

In fact, Mexican laborers have been doing the bulk of the arduous, low-paying, and dangerous work in the fields and factories of the Midwest for over 100 years. The major rural draw was the sugar-beet industry that came to rely on Mexican labor for the bulk of crop cultivation. In metropolitan areas such as Gary, Chicago, and Detroit, the major recruitment of Mexicans for work in the steel mills, meat-packing houses, and automobile industry can be traced back to the World War I era. As the processes of deindustrialization and economic restructuring impact the Midwest portion of the Rust Belt, demographic patterns have similarly changed. After the 1970s, the majority of new job creation has been concentrated in the service economy.

The rural Midwest has been impacted particularly harshly, given the limited economic opportunities available before deindustrialization. Rural communities throughout the heartland have witnessed their resident White population decline and at the same time have seen a rise in the number of Latino in-migrants who are, like Roberto, recruited to work in the reconstituted meat-packing industry. A small-scale proliferation of rural factories has also heavily recruited Mexican immigrant workers. Once exclusively restricted to Mexican migrant farmworkers, the rural heartland has become the new destination for Mexican workers seeking factory jobs as well as jobs in agriculture. These economic shifts are occurring in an environment of heightened fears of White citizens and of racialization and marginalization of Mexican immigrant workers.

The forces of economic restructuring are shifting meat-packing centers away from Chicago and Kansas City and relocating them in the feedlots of the rural Midwest. What is left in the urban Midwest is a rise in service sector employment that also finds Mexicans overrepresented in low-wage, flexible-hour, blue-collar work. Yet Mexican immigrant laborers are continuing their long-standing connections to the industry, and as a result, the growth of the Latino population in the rural Midwest has risen as the meat-packing industry shifts its slaughter and processing facilities closer to pastures. The direct employer recruitment strategies that brought Mexican immigrant laborers have profoundly shaped the migrant streams into the Midwest. Many of these were codified during the first and second Bracero Programs. Most academic discourse on migration talks about social networks or self-generating conduits of immigrants into new receiving areas, but when considering the Midwest, the long-standing presence of Mexican immigrants attests to the primary role that labor recruiters and state-sponsored temporary worker programs have played in developing the initial connections and conditions upon which social networks are operating.

Socio-Economic Restructuring and Factories in the Feedlots

Meat-packing has a long and storied history in the US Midwest. From the first whole-scale indictment of the cruel and unusual punishment of animals and workers in Upton Sinclair's *The Jungle* (1985 [1906]) to the recent indictment of the industry's dangerous workplace conditions and the new construction of factories in feedlots as documented in Eric Schlosser's *Fast Food Nation* (2002), the US public has been frequently exposed to the meat-packing industry's most despicable characteristics. The industry is tied inextricably to the development of the Midwestern economy through the region's devotion to growing corn (primarily for livestock consumption); the factory farms in rural areas that feed corn to pigs and cows; and the large meat-packing districts in Chicago, Kansas City, Saint Louis, Omaha, and Des Moines where the nation's beef and pork industries originated. Meat-packing is necessarily bloody and messy, but today's dangerous working conditions are more directly related to the ever-increasing pace of production and the difficulties of working on a disassembly line that sets the pace of work. As a hog butcher notes, "The line is so fast there is no time to sharpen the knife. The knife gets dull and you have to cut harder. That's when you cut yourself" (Compa 2005, 35). The conditions make meat-packing the most dangerous factory job in the US. The dangers have been fairly consistent over the past century, but novel developments are the new locations of meat-packing factories and the overwhelming reliance on undocumented labor by Mexicans and, to a lesser extent, Central American and Southeast Asian immigrants whose irregular status makes them vulnerable.

In the Great Plains states, the major non-metropolitan shifts have been the location of meat-packing plants closer to feedlots and farms and a monopolistic industry that has relied almost exclusively on Mexican labor. Research on Greeley, Colorado (Andreas 1994), Lexington, Nebraska (Gouveia and Stull 1995), Garden City, Kansas (Gouveia and Stull 1995; Stull, Broadway, and Erickson 1992; Stull and Broadway 2004), and various other Midwestern locales in Iowa, Minnesota, Kansas, Oklahoma, and Nebraska where meat and poultry are slaughtered (Fink 1998; Stull, Broadway, and Griffith 1995; Stull and Broadway 2004) have documented the major transformations local communities are undergoing. As Gouveia and Saenz (2000, 306) note: "While the growth of the Latino population is widespread, perhaps no other region of the nation better epitomizes the tremendous growth of the Latino population than the Midwest, especially because it is in this region that growth has taken place alongside slow growth in the general population." In some meat-packing communities such as Gering, Nebraska, the overall population actually declined by 2.5 per cent from 1990 to 2000, yet the Latino population increased by 10.1 per cent (see Carranza 2004, 144). Other meat-packing communities in Nebraska, such as Lexington and Schuyler, have ten-year Latino growth rates of 1,456.5 and 1,377.4 per cent respectively (see Table 7.1). Including the meat-packing towns of Grand Island and Gering, the four Nebraska small towns are experiencing growth due exclusively to their Latino in-migrant population, while the non-Latino, primarily White population is in a state of decline. Nebraska has approximately 165 meat-packing plants, mostly located in rural areas, and the majority of the state's Latino in-migrants are filling the jobs created by the economic restructuring of the industry. Grand Island, Nebraska, is currently 16 per cent Latino and home to a Swift and Company meat-packing plant. There has been a significant backlash against the Mexican influx, and public pressure has led to a permanent INS-ICE office and a jail expansion project to hold undocumented workers.

One can glean a great deal about what life is like in these small towns by examining the demographic data of the local and surrounding area. Though Grand Island is approximately 16 per cent Latino, the Census 2000 tracts (designed to approximate neighborhoods by using major dividing lines such as main streets and railroad tracks as their lines of demarcation) demonstrate that the Latino population is clustered in the

Table 7.1: *Latino Population Growth Rates in Select Nebraska Cities, 1990–2000*

Cities	1990 Total	1990 Latino	2000 Total	2000 Latino	% Change 1990–2000 Total	% Change 1990–2000 Latino	% of Total Change Explained by Latino Growth*
Bellevue	30,928	1,213	44,382	2,609	43.5	115.1	12.6
Columbus	19,480	167	20,971	1,395	7.7	735.3	82.4
Fremont	23,680	165	25,174	1,085	6.3	557.6	61.6
Gering	7,946	944	7,751	1,039	-2.5	10.1	102.5
Grand Island	39,386	1,887	429,70	6,845	9	262.7	138.3
Hastings	22,837	268	24,064	1,343	5.4	401.1	87.6
Kearney	24,396	667	27,431	1,118	12.4	67.6	14.9
Lexington	6,601	329	10,011	5,121	51.6	1,456.5	140.5
Lincoln	191,972	3,764	225,581	8,154	17.5	116.6	13.1
Norfolk	21,476	299	23,516	1,790	9.5	498.7	73.1
North Platte	22,605	1,355	23,878	1,596	5.6	17.8	18.9
Omaha	335,719	10,288	390,007	29,397	16.2	185.7	35.2
Schuyler	4,052	164	5,371	2,423	32.6	1,377.4	171.3
Scottsbluff	13,711	2,720	14,732	3,476	7.4	27.8	74.0
S. Sioux City	9,677	545	11,925	2,958	23.2	442.8	107.3

* Figures over 100 per cent signify that non-Latinos are dying or moving away while Latinos are moving in at rates exceeding the total population growth rate.
Source: Adapted from Carranza 2004, 144.

northeast quadrant; one tract is a neighborhood where 38.7 per cent of the population is Latino.

In Lexington, the Latino population is similarly segregated, though because the overall population of the town is majority Latino, the comparison between the city and county is particularly illustrative. Lexington is separated into two tracts with 46 and 55 per cent Latino concentrations. The community is 51.2 per cent Latino, so the tract differences are not particularly significant. But Dawson County is only 25.4 per cent Latino. Thus, the majority Latino city of Lexington is surrounded by a White county, and the segregation of Latinos to the city limits becomes apparent.

These demographic trends have been partially disturbed by a recent DHS-ICE decision to conduct mass roundups of suspected undocumented workers and deport them to their country of origin. The raids beginning in late 2006 have continued in spite of legal challenges to the deportation charges and detainment tactics deployed by ICE officers. The first mass deportation targeted the Swift Corporation, which at the time was cooperating with ICE by piloting an automated social security registry designed to detect fraudulent documents. Brief national news items on December 12, 2006, on channels such as MSNBC reported that raids took place on six Swift facilities in Colorado, Nebraska, Texas, Utah, Iowa, and Minnesota, representing all of Swift's domestic beef-processing capacity and 77 per cent of its pork-processing capacity, although no charges were filed against the company. Dubbed "Operation Wagon Train," 1,282 arrests were made on one single day, and subsequent raids on Smithfield pork processors in Tar Heel, North Carolina (on January 24 and August 23, 2007), and Agriprocessors kosher facility in Postville, Iowa (May 12, 2008), yielded hundreds of arrests and deportations.

In each case, no charges were laid for breaking the 1986 IRCA provision that made it illegal for employers to knowingly hire undocumented workers. ICE shifted the burden of blame by claiming, in a stretch of the law, that those with fraudulent documents were committing identity theft. In Postville, the company was found to not *knowingly* hire undocumented workers but was charged for workplace safety and child labor violations. The workers who were detained were charged with aggravated identity theft, which would result in a jail sentence and felony conviction that would bar any future opportunity to enter the US, but were also offered a plea bargain of swift and immediate deportation. The nation's largest kosher plant had 390 of its 938 employees arrested in a town of 2,273 residents.[2] Every major meat-packing town is now in danger of being affected by this kangaroo court model of justice that ignores the fact that employers are fully aware of the legal status of those they employ and that Mexican immigrants would not be moving there if not for the guarantee of employment. Ironically, the ICE ideology of national security and increasing enforcement to deter terrorists means that it is now detaining and deporting those who come to the US at the behest of corporations that are responding to and constructing US consumer tastes. It is only the immigrants who are paying the social costs of this arrangement.

Southwest Kansas is increasingly becoming the new face of meat-packing in terms of both corporate conglomerations and their employment of Mexican immigrant labor. In addition to the multiple slaughterhouses owned by Swift and Company, Tyson, and Cargill in Dodge City, Liberal, and Garden City (and just over the state border in Guymon, Oklahoma), the nearby IBP-Holcomb plant is the largest meat-packing plant in the world. In the 1990s, the area had the "largest concentration of beefpacking plants in North America. The five plants in the Golden Triangle had a combined slaughter capacity of 23,500 head a day and employed more than 10,000 workers" (Stull and Broadway 2004, 99). The standard measure of monopoly control, according to the Sherman Anti Trust Act of 1890, was the Big Four (Swift, Hammond, Armour, and Morris) market share that controlled 30 per cent of the market at that time but wielded tremendous control over it. With recent mergers and acquisitions, it is more appropriate to think of meat-packing in terms of the big three monopolies. ConAgra (now owned by Swift and Company), Cargill (recent purchasers of Excel), and IBP (now owned by Tyson), together control more than 85 per cent of the beef market. Swift and Company (purchasers of ConAgra in 2002, which in turn had bought Monfort a few years earlier) was nineteenth on the 2007 Forbes Fortune 500 List of companies but has since slipped to 188th. Cargill is the second-largest private corporation in the world with 2005 revenues of $69.9 billion dollars. Tyson represents the precariousness of these horizontally integrated companies as it has consistently fallen off the Fortune 500 (from 578th in 2005 to 755th in 2006 to 89th in 2009) as it moves simultaneously to corner the poultry and beef markets.[3]

The corporations share a similar strategy of establishing meat-packing plants next to feedlots, so both the employment base and demographic composition of Southwestern Kansas have dramatically shifted. The meat-packing towns of Liberal, Garden City, Dodge City, and Guymon are all quickly approaching populations that will be majority Latino by the end of the decade if current White out-migration and Latino in-migration trends continue. The 2000 Census reports that the Latino influx is quite pronounced in Garden City at 43.9 per cent Latino (12,492 Latinos out of a total population of 28,451), Dodge City at 42.9 per cent (10,793 of 25,176), Liberal at 43.3 per cent (8,513 of 19,666), and Guymon, Oklahoma, at 38.4

per cent (4,018 of 10,472) (US Census 2000). It is possible that some of these communities are already majority Latino since the Census does not report its most recently collected data for non-metropolitan areas; however, persistent immigration raids result in the fluctuation of the number of Latino residents often from month to month. Meat-packing towns in both Nebraska and Kansas are following the same pattern of development: factories are set in the feedlots and rely increasingly on an undocumented Mexican workforce that is paid far less and worked much harder and more dangerously than the unionized Euro-American workforce of earlier generations.

The home of pork processing in the nation was traditionally Iowa, but this is no longer the case. As we will discuss in the next chapter, the pork industry has shifted away from production employing White union workers in Des Moines and Sioux City to the South where primarily non-unionized Mexican immigrant laborers are employed. The pork industry has followed the meat-packing industry and shifted slaughter and packing operations to rural communities; the remaining pork plants in Iowa are increasingly to be found in small towns. Immigrants who are recruited to work in the industry are finding themselves relocating to some of the most desolate and isolated regions of the rural Midwest where once only cows roamed the open ranges. Wages have been severely reduced, but the biggest cost-cutting measures have been the elimination of fringe benefits and pension plans.

Marshalltown, Iowa, has held on to its Swift and Company pork processing plant, but its labor force has shifted markedly. "In 2001, approximately three thousand Latino residents came from the same rancho in Michoacán, Mexico—Villachuato" (Grey and Woodrick 2005, 144). The transnational connections between the two small communities transcend the movement of residents between the two locales. Villachuato is a typical example of radical agrarian reform in Mexico. During the Revolution, some haciendas were disbanded, and communal landholdings, called *ejidos*, were put in their place in the hope that *campesinos* (farmers) would be able to return to self-sustaining agriculture. Water that once freely flowed through the village was diverted by a major dam project to meet the needs of the growing Mexico City population and several large agribusiness projects. Over the years, given the increasing inability to maintain subsistence standards with the loss of its water, the village has turned to migradollars for survival and future well-being. Never content with basic survival, however, the community has funneled $25,000 in remittances to rebuild the town church. The most interesting interconnection between Villachuato and Marshalltown came in response to a series of INS raids that led to the deportation of several hundred undocumented Swift meat-packing plant workers. As Grey and Woodrick (2005, 145, 149) note: "In the summer of 2001, we took the Marshalltown mayor and police chief to see and experience the sending communities of Latino migrants, including Villachuato. In February 2002, we took six other leaders on the same visit.... [T]he Marshalltown leaders have used the Villachuato visits to inform their efforts back home."

In Northeast Indiana, the two major industries bringing Mexican immigrants into what was once thought of as Amish country are the burgeoning recreational vehicle (RV) production industry and one of the largest duck processors in the nation. A recently opened Walmart distribution center has also followed suit in recruiting predominately Mexican labor. Millard and Chapa (2004) conducted a community study of Ligonier, Indiana, to document the increasing demographic and social presence of Latinos there as well as the derogatory views of Mexican newcomers held by some local White residents. A newspaper analysis by Crane and Millard (in Millard and Chapa 2004, 196–203) exposes these stereotypes, such as in this story headlined "Mexican Situation": "More complaints about the presence of Mexicans in public space began to find their way to the mayor's desk and onto the editorial page. One woman (unidentified) wrote, 'I can't take my grandkids to the park and I don't like to go to the stores in Ligonier because of the illegals' always saying things about white people in Spanish'" (*Ligonier Advance Leader*, September 22, 1994, cited in Millard and Chapa 2004, 198). The newspaper reporter unfortunately did not inquire into the woman's Spanish comprehension level to verify if the so-called illegals did talk about Whites behind their backs. However, her comments match the long-standing nativist response to non-English speakers: that they are to be avoided because they elicit fear in US citizens.

Ligonier is in Noble County, where 554 Latinos resided in 1990; within 10 years, there was a 481 per cent increase to 3,220 Latino residents in 2000, representing 33 per cent of the city's population. There is an assumed, though rarely empirically proven, rural-to-urban migration trend as immigrants decide to escape the discriminatory treatment they receive in the rural hinterlands for larger cities with well-established Mexican neighborhoods, such as South Bend, Indianapolis, and Fort

Wayne. The Latino population in urban Indiana certainly exceeds its rural counterparts. With nearly 12,000 Latino residents, Fort Wayne in Allen County far surpasses all surrounding counties combined.

Midwest Urban Destinations: Connecting Past and Present

Mexicans migrating to Fort Wayne, the second largest city in Indiana, followed many of the same patterns that brought their countrymen to urban Midwest centers such as Detroit and Chicago. Track work on the railroads eventually led to hopes of year-round employment in factory production. Rather than in the automobile and meat-packing industries, the Fort Wayne Mexican population found gainful employment with large factories affiliated with General Electric (GE) in the 1910s and 1920s and then with International Harvester in the 1940s.

Mexican migration to Fort Wayne has also followed moderately strict lines of segregation (see Mize 2003). In the 1980s, International Harvester relocated to a rural town in Ohio to lower labor costs, and General Electric eventually moved all of its factory operations to *maquiladoras* along the US-Mexico border. Today, Latinos are filling the buffer zone between the African American and White populations on the south side of the city. Following Gary, Fort Wayne is the second most Black–White segregated city in Indiana; nearly three-quarters of the African American population would have to move to White neighborhoods to achieve an integrated city.

Given the heavy concentration of Latinos in primarily two tracts, the community is considerably isolated in a low-rent, high-density area with very few amenities such as grocery stores, banks, or shopping malls. Yet signs of immigrant entrepreneurship are on the horizon. There are small, locally owned businesses that cater to Mexican residents: a store specializing in CDs *en español*, two clothing stores—one in a former convenience store—a *zapatería* or shoe store specializing in Mexican cowboy boots, and a Mexican grocery store. There is a dance hall on the southern outskirts of town and a restaurant, Mi Pueblo 4, which serves both the Mexican immigrant clientele as well as White and Mexican American residents. The restaurant, a mini-chain started by Juan Flores over 20 years ago in Franklin, has five other locations in Indiana communities with a serviceable Mexican population. A translation services firm operates in response to the needs of a monolingual Spanish-speaking community and hosts an annual Latinos Count summit to educate the community and eradicate many of the persistent stereotypes about Latinos.

Despite the signs of progress, the Mexican community is on the receiving end of very negative treatment. St. Paul's Catholic Church was the only one to offer mass in Spanish, but it was recently closed by the diocese. The strong commitment to the Church was evident in ways that no other Fort Wayne parish approached. Annual commemorations of *Las Posadas* (the nine-day celebrations leading up to Christmas) brought parishioners into the streets in full regalia to celebrate the birth of Jesus and document Joseph and Mary's path to Bethlehem in their search for lodging. Other street processions in commemoration of the Stations of the Cross and a courtyard altar honoring *La Virgen de Guadalupe* brought visible signs of Mexican Catholicism to the city. The consolidation of St. Paul's with a working-class White parish brought to the surface the latent views some White Catholics held about their Mexican counterparts, as was made clear in nativist talk of "those people taking over our church." It also followed a well-established pattern of the South Bend-Fort Wayne Diocese closing down well-attended Mexican churches and keeping often poorly attended, middle-class White parishes intact. The result is to cast the religious community in Fort Wayne as neither particularly tolerant nor welcoming to Mexican Catholics. Clearly, race and class still matter in a town where in 2005 the Latino population consisted of 16,438 residents or 7.4 per cent of the population.

Industrial recruitment in Fort Wayne, Ligonier, Gary, East Chicago, Indiana Harbor, Indianapolis, and many small towns and suburbs too numerous to mention is the reason why Indiana's Latino population has increased by 221 per cent over the past 24 years (see Table 7.2). Demographers Suro and Singer (2002) identify Indianapolis as one of 18 Latino hypergrowth metro areas. Over 20 years, the city's Latino population has increased 338 per cent to 42,994 people, comprising 3 per cent of the population.

Other urban destinations in the Midwest are seeing similar growth trends among the Latino and specifically the Mexican population. The entire Midwest has witnessed a 135 per cent increase in its Mexican population (nearly 2.9 million); the state of Illinois alone is now home to over 1.3 million Mexican-origin residents. The Chicago metropolitan area is definitely the nexus with the second-largest concentration of Mexican residents in the US after Los Angeles (De Genova 2005, 4). One cannot minimize the role that racial segregation plays in the maintenance of Mexican and Latino neighborhoods. For years, South Chicago's Little Village

Table 7.2: *Demographic Distribution of Mexicans by Midwestern State*

	2004	2000	1990	Per cent Increase 1990–2004
US	25,894,763	20,320,095	13,495,938	92
Midwest Region	2,875,771	2,323,546	1,225,214	135
Illinois	1,361,997	1,119,312	623,688	118
Indiana	214,553	148,918	66,736	221
Iowa	84,044	60,559	24,386	245
Kansas	191,318*	146,603	75,798	152
Kentucky	47,527	31,000	8,692	447
Michigan	260,030	218,627	138,312	88
Minnesota	119,358	94,445	34,691	244
Missouri	99,936	76,884	38,274	161
Nebraska	96,251	70,477	29,665	224
North Dakota	5,159	4,269	2,878	79
Ohio	106,858	89,871	57,815	85
Oklahoma	174,865	131,822	63,226	177
South Dakota	8,946	6,315	3,438	160
Wisconsin	167,607	124,444	57,615	191

*Lower and Upper Bounds and Total Latino population suggest the 2004 figure is a severe underestimation so 2005 figures used.
Source: US Census 1990; US Census 2000, Summary File 3; US Census 2005.

(La Villita) was viewed, alongside Pilsen, as the Mexican heart of Chicago; Back of the Yards is also exclusively Mexican. Since steel-mill days, South Chicago is also predominately Mexican along with its sister community across the state line of East Chicago, Indiana. Of course, the meat-packing plants and steel mills are now vacant buildings, as most operations slowed in the 1950s and completely ceased by the 1970s. Because these communities served as gateways for the Mexican immigrant influx, their lack of an economic base has not deterred subsequent generations from settling in these traditionally Mexican neighborhoods.

Table 7.3: *Immigrant Mexican Occupations in Chicago Food Service Industry*

Occupation	2000 %	RI
Chefs and head cooks	26.8	2.43
Cooks	36.8	3.78
1st Line supervisors/managers	24.3	3.01
Waiters and waitresses	14.5	2.14
Food preparation workers	28.6	2.81
Dining room and cafeteria attendants	39.4	4.71
Dishwashers	58.6	4.68

Source: Hancock (2007) citing US Census 2000, 1% PUMS sample; *Chicago Tribune*, February 26, 2006: 1.

Koval and his Depaul University colleagues have defined the "New Chicago" in terms of economic restructuring and immigrant gateways. Though manufacturing has not completely abandoned the city, declining industries have been replaced by service-sector employment where Mexicans tend to predominate. Using the Index of Representation (RI) to calculate niche concentration (any number over one represents an over-representation of particular immigrant groups than their proportional representation), Koval notes: "Nearly 75 percent of male and female Mexican immigrants in the labor force are found in four industries and over half in but two…. Manufacturing, food service, grounds maintenance, and construction jobs permeate the Mexican occupational landscape—all blue collar jobs" (Koval *et al.* 2006, 201–2). Ongoing research by Hancock (2007) and Koval (2006) finds that in the restaurant industry, Mexican immigrants are able to translate niche employment into occupational mobility. Though RI concentrations are highest for Mexican immigrants in the lowest rung of the industry (dishwashers and busers), nearly 27 per cent of head cooks and chefs are Mexican immigrants (see Table 7.3).

Long considered to be the most important "port of entry" neighborhood for newly arrived Mexican migrants, the Near West Side (Hull House) neighborhood, where Mexican migrants first settled because of its proximity to the railroad yards, was ultimately decimated by "urban renewal projects associated with the construction of expressways and the

University of Illinois Chicago campus during the 1950s and 1960s.... Much of its Mexican community, however, was mostly displaced to the adjacent Lower West Side community area, immediately to the south and southwest, better known as Pilsen, or later, as *La Dieciocho* (the Eighteenth Street Barrio)" (De Genova 2005, 118).

To the north, Humboldt Park was the main home to the city's Puerto Rican population. Latino Chicagoans are segregated into three discrete pockets of the city: what was once the Puerto Rican–dominated Humboldt area in the city's near northwest side, the lower-westside communities of Pilsen and La Villita, and the South Chicago eastside neighborhood that spreads over the border to the Indiana cities of East Chicago and Indiana Harbor. In all three areas, anywhere from 75 to 98 per cent of the residents are Latino.

> Between 1970 and 1980, in the historically most significant neighborhoods of Puerto Rican concentration on Chicago's Near Northwest Side (Humboldt Park, West Town, and Logan Square), the Mexican population nearly quadrupled.... As of US Census 2000, Mexicans had become the majority among Latinos in *all* of the historically Puerto Rican neighborhoods on the North Side, as well as in the adjacent areas of more recent Puerto Rican resettlement. (De Genova 2005, 119; emphasis in original)

In 2005, Latinos comprised 28.8 per cent of Chicago's population and with the significant African American population (38.6 per cent) and other non-White groups, Whites comprised only 38.6 per cent of the city. The 778,000 Mexicans in Chicago were nearly equaled by the number of Mexicans who reside in Chicago's suburbs of Cicero, Rosement, Waukegan, Elgin, Addison, Aurora, and Chicago Heights, which were all between 25 to 50 per cent Mexican.

> Chicago, once the port of entry for Latino immigrants, has seen many newcomers immigrate directly to the suburbs. As a result, Latinos in suburban Chicago increased from 291,653 in 1990 to 651,473 in 2000. For example, in the city of Elgin, forty miles from Chicago, the Latino population grew from 28% in 1998 to 34% in 2000. Cicero, a city once comprised of a population predominately Italian and Eastern European, grew from 37% Latino in 1990 to 77% [in 2000]. (Parra 2004, 15)

Cicero's 66,000 Latinos are most often concentrated on the east side even though they comprise three-quarters of the population, showing that the intense segregation within Chicago's city limits tends to be replicated in its suburbs as well. The dividing lines and resultant separation between Cicero's Latinos and non-Latinos is clearly mapped: the major dividing streets and other barriers keep the highest concentration of Whites in the far southwest and the highest concentration of Latinos in the upper northeast. Martinez (2009, 3) notes that the recent housing bust and foreclosure crisis are particularly pronounced in Chicago's Latino neighborhoods, which "experienced reductions in values between 17 and 50 percent [between] 2003–09."

The patterns of residential segregation are not as pronounced in neighboring urban areas, but they are nevertheless quite prominent. Longstanding Mexican destinations such as Milwaukee and Detroit place their Mexican residents in the same neighborhoods that they occupied before the repatriation program. The railroad houses and tanning factories of Milwaukee, industries that brought Mexicans to the city in 1917 and 1923, were located on the city's south side. In 2000, Detroit's Latino population was concentrated in the exact same four city blocks that were vacated 70 years earlier. Though neither city has rates approaching 100 per cent, the contemporary segregation patterns identify the restriction of Mexican residents to particular sections of the city.

Closer to Chicago, the nearby communities of Gary, Indiana Harbor, and East Chicago also find high Latino concentrations in a handful of neighborhoods. Gary is the second most Black–White segregated city in the nation (following Detroit) and from 1970 to 1999 held the dubious title of the most segregated US city. The Latino population in Gary is much smaller (5,065) than the smaller communities of Indiana Harbor and East Chicago (16,728 or 51 per cent of the total population) and thus is more diffuse. The largest steel-mill employers of Mexican workers were located west of Gary and today host a Latino community that encircles the remaining White community.

Conclusion

Mexicans in the Midwest have a long history of settlement that informs the present-day migration and settlement patterns. The massive recruitment and intermittent expulsion of Mexican residents follow patterns of economic expansion and contraction. From season to season, Mexican workers have been forced to be extremely mobile in seeking gainful employment. Even work in urban centers has followed cycles that result in unsteady employment patterns. The repatriation program during the Great Depression only magnified a certain view of Mexican laborers as disposable bodies. The old maxim of "last hired, first fired" has been a reality for many Mexicans seeking to eke out an existence in communities that segregate them to low-income, ethnically homogenous neighborhoods.

Today, Mexicans continue to migrate not only to traditional Midwest destinations but also new ones that correspond with the economic restructuring of the meat-packing industry. Exponential Latino population increases in small-town Nebraska, Kansas, Oklahoma, and Iowa are directly related to the relocation of factories to the feedlots. The three largest meat-packing corporations monopolize the industry and are acting in concert to employ a predominately Mexican immigrant workforce, often undocumented, in small cow towns for low wages and few benefits in non-unionized, and increasingly dangerous, working conditions.

The urban and suburban destinations are also receiving large numbers of Mexican immigrants with Chicago still serving as the Mexican immigrant gateway. But an equal number of Mexicans are selecting the surrounding suburbs as their first and final destination rather than the earlier rural-to-urban migrations or later urban-to-suburban upwardly mobile patterns. Mexicans have been in the Midwest for well over 100 years, and the latest generations are putting down roots and standing up for their rights in ways that challenge the status quo of race and class relations. The immigrant rights movement is alive and well in Garden City, Kansas, and Lexington, Nebraska, as the 2006 marches and May Day boycotts demonstrate. Chicago hosted one of the largest pro-immigrant rallies in the nation and is currently home to the new sanctuary movement for undocumented immigrants, thanks to the tireless efforts of organizers such as Emma Lozano and the *Sin Fronteras* mutual aid society. "As of 2002, there were more than 160 Mexican hometown associations and seven state federations — Durango, Guanajuato, Guerrero, Jalisco, Michoacán, San Luis Potosí, and Zacatecas — organized in the Chicago metropolitan area" (De Genova 2005, 4). As the SEIU and Teamster locals in Chicago and the Toledo-based FLOC reconceptualize their organizing base in terms of immigrant and civil rights, the potentialities for collaboration with transnational hometown associations signals that the immigrant rights movement may find its strongest foothold in Chicago and the Midwest.

At the same time, the conservative anti-immigrant backlash, which has had a head of steam in the Southwest for over 20 years, is beginning to foment. Evidence of this includes the Minutemen vigilante group holding its 2006 annual convention in Chicago and the all-too-frequent INS-ICE raids on meat-packing plants that rarely punish employers for knowingly hiring undocumented workers but swiftly pass judgment on those deemed illegal by deporting workers who are required to authenticate every document in their possession on the spot. In the next chapter, we will discuss how these demographic and economic trends are redefining the South, Northeast, and Pacific Northwest.

Notes

1. This vignette of Robert Salinas, a pseudonym, is excerpted and adapted from Fink 1998, 146–50.
2. Direct accounts of the raid can be found at http://thesanctuary.soapblox.net/showDiary.do?diaryId=269.
3. Fortune 500 rankings were consulted and can be found at http://money.cnn.com/magazines/fortune/fortune500/.

Chapter Eight

Mexican Labor in the Hinterlands

In 1995, while working in Wisconsin on a National Cancer Institute investigation of the long-term effects of pesticide exposure in migrant farmworker communities, Mize interviewed Don Américo.[1] In his fifties, Don Américo stated that he was from Rio Grande Valley in South Texas. His car's "lone star" bumper sticker, Texas license plates, and "Don't Mess With Texas" t-shirt led the research team to not question his origins. He said he had lost his driver's license and was always paid in cash (minus a fee) since he could not get a check cashed in the small town where he was interviewed while taking a break from cutting Christmas trees. After interviews with his family members, it became unclear if he was a documented immigrant, although he had spent most of his 50 years as a migrant worker and all his children were born in the US and were thus citizens. He had lived his entire life in Spanish-speaking farmworker communities, mostly in migrant housing camps, but spent less than three months per year in his winter home in South Texas. Since adolescence, Don Américo had followed migrant streams to find work. His earliest travels brought him to Florida to pick watermelons during the time of the Bracero Program. With the exception of one year he missed due to a foot injury, he and his extended family, now including his grandchildren, traveled either the East Coast or Midwest migrant streams to earn no more than about $5,000 per worker per season. They are now collectively home-owners in Texas—their acre-sized plot had four trailers at last count—but they cannot afford to stay home for any extended period as they need to work to pay their basic expenses. A trailblazer, Don Américo was probably among the first Mexicans to pick Florida watermelons in the late 1950s, but today his experiences are shared daily by many others throughout the hinterlands of the US Northeast, South, and Northwest.

The largest percentage increases of Mexican in-migrants over the past 10 to 15 years have not occurred where the Mexican population has been concentrated historically. The phenomenon of rapid Latino population growth is often referred to as "Latinization." Part demographic fact, part media-hyped panic, the geographic dispersion of Mexican immigrant laborers is a response to changes in the US economy and reproduces a very long pattern of moving to where the jobs are. For reasons still not fully understood, the agricultural migrant streams that in a previous generation brought Puerto Rican, West Indian, White Appalachian, and African American workers up and down the Eastern seaboard have become increasingly dominated by Mexicans and Central Americans. Predominately White or Black–White cities are transformed by newcomers who are bilingual, bicultural, and binational and who do not fit easily into binary race relations in the Southern and Northeastern US. In predominately Latino communities that less than ten years ago were mainly Puerto Rican, Dominican, or Cuban, residents are noticing a Mexican presence.

In urban industrial sectors, factory jobs are dwindling and relocating as corporations shift manufacturing operations abroad or to right-to-work[2] Southern states to minimize labor costs. Mexican immigrants, perennial sources of cheap labor, are being heavily recruited to work in carpet factories in Dalton, Georgia; poultry plants in North Carolina and the "New" South; and in construction, service, landscaping, and other informal temporary jobs. In the South and Northeast, the rise of Latino day laborers (predominately Mexican and Central American) reveals the scarcity in gainful job opportunities and underscores fears of White residents who view their communities as under siege rather than as recognizing the change as one more chapter in the long history of immigration that links the fates of newcomers with not-so-new residents.

This chapter focuses on illustrative case studies of particular communities in the South, Northeast, and Northwest to more fully document the processes of the US consumption of Mexican labor.[3] With the heavy concentration of H-2A workers in North Carolina, the recent labor agreement between the North Carolina Growers' Association and FLOC offers a glimmer of hope in the context of very antagonistic and exploitative labor relations. We also examine the Latino hypergrowth of the metropolitan South, demographic changes of communities large and small, and the effects of economic restructuring on Mexican in-migration rates. In the Northeast, shifts in the rural, suburban, and urban areas are evident in New York state. As more Latinos, predominately of Mexican origin, make non-metropolitan New York their home, the region offers a glimpse into the early stages of Latino incorporation.

Historical Antecedents of the Latinization of the Hinterlands

The three regions of the hinterlands have incorporated Mexican labor in distinct ways. In the Northwest (Washington, Oregon, Idaho, and Montana), Mexican labor was used to build the railway system as well as to pick the crops that fed not just the region but the nation. The South and Northeast are much more interconnected by overlapping migrant streams. A story of ethnic succession informs the current preference for Mexican immigrant workers. Finally, the economic restructuring of the industrial economy in the rural South, in part following the distribution network model of Arkansas-based Walmart, is partially responsible for the recent Mexican influx to the New South.

Today, Mexican immigrants are most prominently located in the agricultural communities of Eastern Washington state, Oregon, and Southwestern Idaho. The region's historical reliance on migrant labor for agriculture rivals the Midwest's sugar beet stream, but the first sizeable migration of Mexicans to the area was a result of the railroad industry. Tens of thousands of Mexicans were brought into agricultural communities in Washington, Oregon, Idaho, and Montana during the Bracero Program to pick strawberries, hops, sugar beets, potatoes, apples, peas, and cranberries, in addition to shepherding the region's livestock. A migrant stream through the Imperial Valley of California, which predated the Bracero Program, brought Mexican Americans and Mexican immigrants into the Yakima Valley of Washington. The Mexican population in the metropolitan areas of the Northwest has grown intensely in recent years as a logical outgrowth of previous settlement patterns.

As we highlighted in Chapter 1, migrant streams that connected Mexican Americans (particularly from the Imperial Valley of California but also South Texas) and Mexican immigrants to the Northwest were institutionalized by the Bracero Program, particularly during its war phase. Table 8.1 shows that there were more than 50,000 Braceros contracted to work in the Northwest, evenly distributed among Idaho, Montana, Oregon, and Washington. Gamboa documents the experiences of Braceros in the Northwest where they were subjected to harsh working and living conditions. Northwest growers were notorious for opposing special concessions like free housing and often housed Braceros in military-issue canvas tents.

Table 8.1: *Braceros Contracted in the Hinterlands by State and Region, 1942–47, 1952*

	Workers Contracted (1942–47)	Workers Contracted (1952)	Workers Employed (December 31, 1952)
South in Total	410	30,247	517
Arkansas	0	28,363	500
Georgia	0	596	0
Louisiana	0	822	17
Mississippi	0	60	0
North Carolina	410	0	0
Tennessee	0	406	0
Northwest in Total	**51,891**	**4,951**	**93**
Idaho	11,088	326	1
Montana	12,767	1,841	0
Oregon	13,007	823	91
Washington	15,029	1,961	1
Total for Both Regions	**52,301**	**35,198**	**610**

Source: Adapted from Rasmussen 1951 and Lyon 1954.

When the Mexican workers were not quartered in tent camps, they were placed in makeshift shelters where conditions were as bad if not worse. In Idaho, an abandoned Civilian Conservation Corps camp was used to accommodate the Mexican men. The Oregon State Extension Service had the choice of placing the braceros at either the Hillsboro High School or the fairgrounds and opted for the latter. In Washington, farmers placed army cots against the walls of the main grandstand at the Whatcom County fairgrounds.... In some communities, farmers obtained permission to erect tents at the city ball park. (Gamboa 2000, 94)

Braceros actively resisted these injustices by striking and walking out at rates seen in no other part of the country. "Of all the problems associated with the Bracero Program in the Pacific Northwest, work stoppages or strikes were the most alarming to farmers. Unlike their counterparts in other parts of the country, Braceros in the Northwest exhibited little reluctance to stop work" (Gamboa 2000, 75).

To this day, the largest concentrations of Mexican-origin residents in the Northwest are in the agricultural communities that originally housed Braceros. In Southwest Idaho, the Mexican communities of Caldwell, Payette, Nampa, and Twin Falls (to the east) are legacies of the original Bracero labor camps. The Washington communities of Walla Walla, Yakima, Sunnyside, Toppenish, Grandview, Wenatchee, and Granger have large and thriving Mexican populations with first-, second-, third-, and even fourth-generation residents. The Oregon communities of Milton-Freewater, Medford, Hood River, Bend, Klamath Falls, Ontario, and Nyssa were also major Bracero destinations that continue to serve as Mexican destinations.

The railroad Bracero Program also introduced Mexican laborers to the South and the Northeast. Agricultural streams in these regions were affected by the Bracero Program to a small degree, but they tended to be localized to first Arkansas cotton growers and later North Carolina farmers. Though the program did not expand beyond the Southwest until mid-1943, the lines connecting the New England states and Florida to the West were the first to receive a few thousand Mexican Braceros. "Early in 1944 ... the Pennsylvania [railway], an important road bridging the East and Midwest, was allowed 3,200 Braceros authorized to work in Pennsylvania, New York, New Jersey, and Delaware" (Driscoll 1999, 144). Two other Eastern rail lines, the New York Central and the New York, New Haven and Hartford, were allotted 500 and 300 Braceros respectively.

Though very few Mexican immigrants came to the Northeast, their presence on the rail lines often led to other employment opportunities in agriculture, construction, and steel. Paul Schuster Taylor's 1931 magisterial *Mexican Labor in the United States* focuses on traditional receiving and sending areas in Colorado and Texas but also on Mexican communities as far east as Chicago-Calumet and Bethlehem, Pennsylvania. The Bethlehem Steel Corporation actively and aggressively recruited Mexican immigrants to its Pennsylvania plant in addition to employing Mexican steel workers in its Los Angeles factory and most points in between. For Mexican workers, this resulted in "[s]mall outpost colonies of two hundred, four hundred, or perhaps more; each are scattered through the principal steel centers as far east as Ohio, Pennsylvania, New York and New Jersey" (Taylor 1983, 7).

State interventionism and direct labor recruitment introduced Mexican laborers into the East Coast migrant stream. Cotton growers in Arkansas employed sharecroppers until the Bracero Program was introduced around the time the Korean War ended, as they realized that mechanization was on the horizon and harvesting by hand would soon be obsolete. As is clear in Table 8.1, the Arkansas strategy was evident; employing short-term Bracero labor to harvest the last bolls of cotton by hand severed ties with an earlier production model and eased the transition to mechanization. Working conditions were brutal. The main handling facility for Braceros was located in Jerome where Japanese internment victims were housed during World War II. As we documented in Chapter 1, work and life were conducted on a mass basis with a regularly routinized schedule of daily activities. Don Crecencio, interviewed in 2005, describes how picking cotton was very hard work for very little pay:

> Well then, we would enter and they would give each of us two sacks. More or less 80 pounds would fit in each sack. And from there, they would take us to the field. The fields were huge. It was the type of cotton that they called *chapo*. Then they would take us and tell each of us to select two rows [of cotton fields]. In only one attempt [collectively], we would complete a whole field like of 50 acres. What would we do? We would do nothing. Why? Because we would only earn more or less in a week we would earn like $150–$200, per week. So in the whole season that we were there, the weeks would not always be the same. Sometimes we would come out with $100, sometimes $80. It was a small amount that we would earn. It was 45 days. We suffered because frankly it was very little to send [home], right? Then we expected to complete the contract of 45 days and then return back. Then when the contract was complete we would be taken back to Mexico again. We would return to our homes again. Can you imagine? That money was very little. (Interview, 2005)

Arkansas was the only Southern state to employ Mexican cotton pickers; like Texan cotton growers, they sought to replace a heterogeneous workforce with exclusively Mexican immigrants.

Unlike in the Northwest, the expectation that Mexican immigrants would meet the labor needs of agribusiness became prominent in the South and Northeast only in the 1990s, a decade that witnessed a major surge in Latinization. For destinations in the Southern US, the Mexican influx was newer because the Bracero program was not heavily utilized by growers there. The reason for this can be traced back to Florida and the

Caribbean. In 1952, the US passed legislation overhauling the nation's immigration laws. A little-known provision inserted at the behest of East Coast growers created the H-2 temporary visa program. Florida's sugar corporations, particularly US Sugar, the last corporation to mechanize production, had a long history of labor violations. Indicted on several occasions in the twentieth century for employing slave labor, during World War II the companies off-shored their labor demands and heavily recruited Jamaican, Haitian, Puerto Rican, and other Caribbean islanders. The US government facilitated this relationship by creating a temporary visa contract between the government and grower on a per-worker basis. Growers gained several advantages: contracts could be negotiated in their favor; they could pre-select their workforce; and they could use deportation as a means of control in the fields (see DeWind, Seidl, and Shenk 1979). Individual work contracts tied the visa holders to a specific employer; protests, work stoppages, or the failure to achieve a certain quota could result in deportation. Through the 1970s an estimated 20,000 H-2 workers per year found employment in Florida sugarcane fields. In this way, Caribbean H-2 workers followed the established East Coast migrant stream and replaced white and black sharecroppers as the preferred labor source.

H-2 Worker

Most US citizens have no idea that the H-2 program exists unless they have heard reggae musician Mutabaruka's song:

> I am an H-2 worker
> Coming from the island of Jamaica
> I am an H-2 worker cutting cane in Florida
> Working so hard in the burning sun
> Wondering if slavery really done
> I'm working, working, working on the cane field
> Still working, working, working for your meager dollar bill
> So don't bite the hands that feed you
> I have dreams like you too
> Don't treat me like I'm a slave here
> Just get me a wage that is fair.

This gifted and socially aware Jamaican musician understands US immigration policy better than the US population at large.

Source: Mutabaruka, *The Ultimate Collection*, Shanachie Records 1996; printed with permission.

Temporary workers were nominally represented by the British West Indies Central Labor Organization (BWICLO). "Although BWICLO liaison officers are supposed to enforce the contract and look out for workers' interests on the mainland, none of these duties is written into the contract. The contract does not create any grievance procedure for workers to follow if their rights are abused, and BWICLO is not required to take any remedial action on the workers' behalf" (DeWind, Seidl, and Shenk 1979, 391). As a result, workers were severely abused over several decades. In 1986, IRCA was passed and not only upheld the temporary visa program but expanded it to several other occupational sectors. Under the renamed H-2A Program, growers could still gain access to a steady stream of temporary labor if they were willing to meet the bureaucratic requirements, which included providing free and adequate housing. Code inspectors were quite thorough in upholding these conditions. As a result, H-2A farm labor camps often offered better housing than that hitherto available to migrants. Growers also had to adhere to an adverse-effect wage rate[4] and ensure that working conditions did not deter domestic interest in these jobs. Interviews with the Department of Labor and lawyers from the US Sugar Corporation estimate that in 1992 there were 19,000 H-2A laborers, primarily Jamaican and Haitian workers, on the East Coast. From 1982 to 1991, Florida's sugarcane producers employed 10,000 H-2A workers per year, but mechanization has led to a steady decline and a now non-existent labor demand. The H-2A program brought 4,300 sugar workers to Florida, 1,145 sheepherders to Montana, and 2,800 apple pickers to New York.

The increasing reliance on Mexican labor has resulted in a redrawing of the migrant stream map with the development of Mexican migrant streams to new areas of the US that currently employ migrant labor. Workers in the established migrant streams travel from Mexico through the border states of California, Arizona, New Mexico, and Texas, to the Pacific Coast, Mountain States, Upper Midwest, or the Atlantic Coast. A number of agricultural communities in California and South Texas also send migrant workers along these same routes, but it is primarily Mexicans directly from Mexico who now occupy the Ozark/Appalachian streams as well as the Pacific, Atlantic, and Midwest streams.

The process has been accelerated and institutionalized by renewed grower use of the H-2A program. The latest available data come from 2003 and show that agricultural firms in all 50 states employ H-2A labor. In 2002, there were 42,000 visas issued, and that increased to 45,000 in 2003.

Tobacco is the largest single crop that employs H-2A workers, with tobacco workers primarily in North Carolina, Kentucky, and Virginia constituting 35 per cent of all H-2A visas. Though the US Department of Labor does not readily publish relevant data, it is widely acknowledged by scholars and labor activists that Mexican workers are the main visa recipients. The Global Workers Justice Alliance estimates 88 per cent of H-2A workers are Mexican (40,283 of 46,432 visa holders) according to their analysis of 2006 Department of Labor data.[5]

Rural, Suburban, and Urban Mexican In-Migration Trends

Mexican immigrants are settling in rural, suburban, and urban communities in the hinterlands. Earlier generations of immigrants often moved into the center cities of urban metropoles while subsequent generations moved to the suburbs. Today, although some Mexican immigrants settle in urban locales, equal numbers move directly from Mexico to suburbs or to midsize metropolitan areas. The Brookings Institution published a study in 2002 that identified metropolitan areas that witnessed a 300 per cent or more increase in their Latino population.[6] Defined as hyper-growth cities, with rates of growth ranging from 1,180 to 346 per cent, 11 of the 18 cities—in order Raleigh, Atlanta, Greensboro, Charlotte, Orlando, Nashville, Fort Lauderdale, Sarasota, Greenville, West Palm Beach, and Washington, DC[7]—were located in the Southern states of North Carolina, Georgia, Florida, Tennessee, South Carolina, and the District of Columbia. In the South, Northeast, and Northwest regions, from 1990 to 2004 the Mexican population increased by 361, 238, and 177 per cent respectively (see Table 8.2). Based on the disaggregated data, the growth rates of Latino populations are highly associated with Mexican growth rates, but they are not synonymous.

In the rural hinterlands, Mexican immigrants constitute the bulk of those identified by the Census as Latinos. A substantial Central American population is also migrating in response to structural shifts in the rural economy. Similar patterns of hypergrowth are documented in rural communities as well.

According to employment figures and informal surveys of county economies, a significant proportion of employment in high-growth Hispanic counties [Latino population growth exceeding 150 per cent and at least 1,000 persons, 1990–2000] stems from poultry processing (40 counties), beef and pork

Table 8.2: *Demographic Distribution of Mexicans by Region and State, 1990–2004*

	2004	2000	1990	Per cent Increase
US Total	25,894,763	20,320,095	13,495,938	92
South Total	1,956,142	1,382,517	424,668	361
Alabama	66,798	43,490	9,509	602
Arkansas	96,232	60,487	12,496	670
District of Columbia	5,001	4,978	2,981	68
Florida	465,706	356,243	161,499	188
Georgia	390,672	270,038	49,182	694
Kentucky	47,527	31,000	8,692	447
Louisiana	31,442	31,783	23,452	34
Maryland	61,7343	8,865	18,434	235
Mississippi	27,573	21,302	6,718	310
Missouri	99,936	76,884	38,274	161
North Carolina	358,648	242,515	32,670	997
South Carolina	73,485	51,714	11,028	566
Tennessee	115,319	75,963	13,879	731
Virginia	110,522	72,934	33,044	234
West Virginia	5,547	· 4,321	2,810	97
Northeast Total	602,012	478,071	178,079	238
Connecticut	41,802	23,002	8,393	398
Delaware	21,775	12,539	3,083	606
Maine	3,071	2,748	2,153	43
Massachusetts	18,614	21,937	12,703	47
New Hampshire	6,518	4,483	2,362	176
New Jersey	116,479	101,068	28,759	305
New York	315,265	251,206	93,244	238
Pennsylvania	70,176	54,305	24,220	190
Rhode Island	6,932	5,618	2,437	184
Vermont	1,380	1,165	725	90

	2004	2000	1990	Per cent Increase
US Total	25,894,763	20,320,095	13,495,938	92
Northwcst Total	810,897	625,765	293,071	177
Idaho	104,980	78,072	43,213	143
Montana	15,974	11,555	8,362	91
Oregon	271,916	212,025	85,632	218
Washington	418,027	324,113	155,864	168

Source: US Census 1990; US Census 2000, Summary File 3; and US Census 2005.

processing (25 counties), other manufacturing such as furniture and textiles (23 counties), and high-amenity resort areas that attract low-wage service workers (10 counties). (Kandel and Cromartie 2004, 14)

The restructuring of the meat industry has particularly impacted rural communities of the South. Nowhere is the connection between US consumption and Mexican labor more directly evident than in the poultry industry. Chicken is a very direct link between changing US consumer tastes and the hands that turn a live chicken into a processed chicken by-product. Large poultry monopolies, advertising campaigns based on branding, the land-grant university[8] and poultry science's assistance in making new processed chicken products to appeal to and increase the share of consumer tastes, and dieticians' characterization of chicken as "the healthy meat" are interrelated factors that have shifted the American diet away from artery-clogging, heart-stopping beef and directly to the lean chicken breast. As Striffler (2005, 30) notes, processed chicken is often less healthy than red meat, but the public perception that equates chicken consumption with healthy eating has vastly expanded poultry production. According to Kandel: "Chicken production has for many years been concentrated in the rural Southeast: in 1993, the four leading poultry-producing States were Arkansas, Georgia, Alabama, and North Carolina.... In the Southeast, for instance, a spike in the rural Hispanic population during the 1990s is clearly linked to a growing Hispanic representation in the poultry-processing industry" (2006, 13–14). There is a direct relationship between poultry production counties and Latino growth counties with substantial direct overlap or adjacent county correspondence.

Today, poultry plants are located in the Delmarva Peninsula of Virginia and near the state borders of North Carolina, Tennessee, Arkansas, Mississippi, Alabama, Missouri, and Kentucky (the last two are technically not Southern states, but their rural economies are similar to the South). The turkey capital of the US is North Carolina. Mexican immigrants have come to Northern Georgia, the self-proclaimed poultry capital of the world, since the 1970s. However, mass migration did not commence until the 1990s; as one supervisor notes, "if there weren't Hispanic workers, nobody in America would be eating chicken" (Guthey 2001, 61). The deleterious working conditions of the meat-packing industry are replicated in the poultry industry. "For example, jobs at Tyson Foods, the industry leader, are so dangerous, strenuous, and low paying that the turnover is around 75 per cent annually. Further, in 1999 Tyson was named one of the '10 Worst Corporations of the Year' by the *Corporate Crime Register*, because of seven worker deaths, fines from the Occupational Safety and Health Administration (OSHA), and other violations including child labor" (Striffler 2005, 8). Yet Mexican workers are relocating to the rural South primarily to meet US consumers' fondness for chicken. Though pay rates exceed those for agricultural work, dangerous working conditions often offset these gains. High turnover and other economic opportunities available in nearby cities suggest that it is difficult to foresee an end to the Latino influx.

We now turn to four places that have experienced significant demographic transitions in each of the hinterland regions. Dalton in Georgia, North Carolina, New York, and the Yakima Valley of Washington will serve as our case studies on the processes of Latinization.

Carpets and Chickens: Dalton, Georgia

One of the most explosive growth areas for Latino in-migration is the historic South. In the recently published *The Columbia History of Latinos in the United States Since 1960*, the chapter on Mexicans begins not in the Southwest but in Dalton, Georgia:

> In September 1999, in the small town of Dalton, Georgia, local citizens were treated to an unusual sight as hundreds, and eventually more than 2,000, of Latinos lined the city streets for a parade commemorating *el dieciseis de sep-*

tiembre— Mexican Independence Day... with street merchants peddling tacos, *pan dulce* (sweet bread), *raspadas* (snow cones), and other Mexican delicacies, and other vendors hawking miniature Mexican flags, T-shirts, and bumper stickers proclaiming love for Zacatecas, Jalisco, and Guanajuato, the celebration provided dramatic proof of just how much Latin American immigration has transformed American society over the past 20 years. (Gutierrez 2004, 43)

The first Mexican migrants came to the area in the 1970s to work in the poultry processing industry (Engstrom 2001). In 1990, the Latino population of Whitfield County was 3.2 per cent, but local school enrollment data for the academic year 1998–99 show the Latino school-aged population at 42 per cent (cited in Hernández-León and Zúñiga 2000). Census 2000 estimates of the Latino population show that 40 per cent of Dalton's residents self-identify as Latino.[9] Although poultry factories still employ a sizeable Mexican population, many prefer the carpet industry and self-employment. In the carpet factories, "observations conducted on the shop floor revealed that immigrants are overwhelmingly employed in labor-intensive stages of the carpet manufacturing process" (Hernández-León and Zúñiga 2000, 58). As these authors discovered,

> Poultry provides for many immigrants the entry into the local labor market. Thus, getting a job in the carpet industry represents a first successful move up the employment ladder. Besides wage labor, Mexicans in [Dalton] have been able to make inroads in the small-business sector. There are about seventy-two businesses owned by Mexicans. Immigrants own grocery stores, butcher and tortilla shops, taxi and other types of transportation companies, and insurance agencies. Although these businesses are heavily concentrated in the immigrant and ethnic economy, a few of them have begun to provide services to White and African-American consumers. These small enterprises have also played a role in revitalizing rundown and abandoned commercial areas. (Hernández-León and Zúñiga 2000, 58)

Mexican immigrants come to Dalton primarily because of the relatively higher wages and abundant job opportunities. Race relations in the city are complicated by their presence. The city's slave past and Jim Crow segregation pushed out many of the city's African American residents when the textile and carpet mills enforced a Whites-only employment policy. The shift of the carpet industry to predominately Mexican labor began by direct recruitment, but subsequent social networks have led to a signifi-cant increase in the overall population. White workers were rarely dis-placed and most often experienced upward mobility or switched to other employers as a result of the Mexican influx.

Tobacco and Pork: The Hypergrowth State of North Carolina

One of the few Southern states to employ Bracero labor, North Carolina has experienced the largest percentage increase of any US state in the Mexican and Latino population over the past 25 years. The economic restructuring of this right-to-work state has fueled much of the migra-tion, but Mexican immigrants have also expanded their opportunities by selecting urban destinations with high-growth industries. The historical origins of this "new" destination are rooted in the agricultural and poul-try industries. The transformation of labor relations in the tobacco indus-try, the state's largest agricultural product, from a sharecropper model to exclusively employing Mexican H-2A visa holders and undocumented workers reflects larger shifts in the state's demographic composition. The poultry and, increasingly, pork industries have also come to rely almost exclusively on Mexican labor and as a result have transformed small town North Carolina. Finally, in the urban metropolitan areas like Raleigh-Durham, Charlotte, Greensboro, and Fayetteville, the Mexican population is finding its niche in many sectors of the high-tech new economy.

From 1942 to 1947, North Carolina growers employed 410 Braceros and in effect initiated the migrant stream from Mexico to the agricultural South. Mize interviewed Don Liberio, a former Bracero, who recounted his experiences working in North Carolina in 1947:

> In North Carolina, we were picking green beans. We also picked potatoes. But there were too many men in the fields, and thus not enough work. In potatoes and green beans, we earned 40 cents per bushel, or about $8 per week, after deductions. After the contract ended, we had to pay transportation home. In North Carolina, we often complained and stopped work because of the rotten food. There was a man, he was protesting and complaining about the food. The next day he was gone, nobody told us what happened to him and we didn't ask. Later we heard that they killed him. (Interview, 1997)

Many stories abounded of Braceros who were killed to collect the insurance money or to punish recalcitrant agitators, but Mize uncovered no evidence to prove them. Quite likely, it was the message itself that mattered, as growers could use fear to keep workers in line with the message that "if you strike, you take your life into your own hands." Don Liberio recalled several contract violations by potato and green-bean farmers. He reported that the food served in the camp was occasionally rancid. If the workers united to complain, the quality of food would temporarily improve, only to return to spoiled servings.

Contemporary working and living conditions for H-2A workers in North Carolina are not markedly different from the Bracero experience of the 1940s. Ruben Martinez's *Crossing Over* (2001) details the experiences of Mexican migrants in this latest era of Latinization. His visit to North Carolina brought him into contact with the Mexican temporary workers who cultivate the state's lucrative tobacco crops.

> In the tobacco fields of North Carolina, for example, the picking is now done by Mexicans, many of whom possess H2-A [sic] work visas permitting them to take short-term seasonal jobs in agriculture. Mexican American labor organizers are active in the area, yet working conditions are often poor and housing not far removed, geographically and qualitatively, from the plantation days. The farms are frequently located in remote areas where the workers are put up in "labor camps." At one place I saw, the men slept in long, one-storey, tar-papered buildings with no insulation and prison-issue cots. The outhouses were splattered with feces and swarming with flies. Forty workers were being served by four latrines, two showers, two sinks, and one water fountain. (Martinez 2001, 285)

In rural North Carolina, the exponential increase of Mexican migrants to the area can be partially attributed to the Latinization of the tobacco industry. In 2002, approximately 9,000 H-2A guest-workers were employed in tobacco cultivation in that state while an additional 2,372 workers were employed on Kentucky tobacco farms and 2,291 workers on Virginia tobacco farms (US Department of Labor 2003b), making the tobacco industry the largest single employer of H-2A agricultural workers in the nation. From 1990 to 2000, the North Carolina Latino population increased at a rate of 394 per cent (Johnson-Webb 2003, 53). More impressively, the 25-year Mexican growth rate is closer to 1,000 per cent. Research findings compiled by the Center on Globalization, Governance, and Competitiveness at Duke University show that counties that rely on tobacco as their main cash crop are the same counties where the Mexican population lives.[10]

East Carolina University Professor David Griffith argues that it was US immigration policy (particularly the H-2A program and the SAW legalization program) that led to the large-scale migration of Mexicans to the state in the 1990s. "With legalization of large numbers of Special Agricultural Workers (SAWs), many Mexicans familiar with North Carolina's labor markets, now free to move between the United States and Mexico, began facilitating travel and employment among new immigrants from their home communities" (Griffith 2005, 55–56).

The data from the most recent H-2A annual report available to the public is that in 2003 there were 14,822 tobacco workers out of 41,894 workers certified for employment by 6,608 employers.[11]

Even as temporary contract workers, Mexican immigrants have defied the odds and organized to demand their rights. As discussed in Chapter 3, the North Carolina Growers' Association is now under contract with FLOC, which acts as the contractually obligated collective representative of the state's H-2A workers. A FLOC-monitored grievance procedure yields daily complaints by workers who have returned to Monterrey, Mexico, and has resulted in a significant recuperation of back wages and evidence of contract violations.

The image of the temporary agricultural worker is almost always that of a single male. But in North Carolina's blue crab processing industry, the workers who are recruited for jobs are almost exclusively Mexican women. In Pamlico County, North Carolina, H-2B[12] Mexican workers have replaced African American women as the preferred labor source. Temporary workers began to be used in 1988 and "initially, the program [was] used by only three or four processors in Virginia, North Carolina, and Maryland, who together imported around 100 workers... [less than 10 years later,] together, the North Carolina processors imports between 1,000 and 1,200 workers... or around 10 times the number they imported originally" (Griffith 1995, 175). Employers in the industry pursued different pathways to the H-2B program. "One used the Virginia Employment Service, one learned of the program through a crab processor in Mexico, and the third worked with Del Al Associates, the largest contractor of H-2 workers in Mexico" (Griffith 2005, 66). In order to place controls over the workforce, rules barring pregnancy and attempts to control women's behavior beyond the confines of the workplace are customary informal practices.

The poultry and pork industries in North Carolina are also important players in the rural economy. North Carolina is the fifth largest poultry producer and the number one producer of turkeys in the US. "Among the largest counties for turkey production are the Southeast part of the state, most in the Cape Fear River watershed...[centered in] Duplin County, home to Carolina turkey, the largest turkey producer in the world and among the earliest in the state to recruit and house Mexican workers" (Griffith 2005, 64). According to Census data, Latinos are concentrated near turkey processing plants, and Duplin County has the largest Latino population, by percentage of total population, of any county in the state.

Combined, the top ten North Carolina counties employ more than 8,000 workers to process more than 420 million birds annually. Because the industry rule of thumb is to place processing plants within 25 miles of chicken production areas, these plants are located across the coastal plain, in the Appalachian foothills, and across the central piedmont. Many plants are inside small and medium-sized towns such as Siler City, Robersonville, and Wilkesboro, while others are near the large metropolitan areas of Raleigh and Charlotte, giving poultry workers access to urban occupations and factory work in other industries that have been, historically, important to North Carolina, primarily furniture and textiles (Griffith 2005, 64).

North Carolina is also the nation's second-largest producer of pork, behind Iowa. The single largest pork plant in the nation is in Tar Heel, North Carolina, and is owned by the Smithfield Corporation. At this recent site of ICE raids and mass firings due to workers' immigration status, Mexican workers and their allies have engaged in a wildcat strike to protest company policy. The UFCW has been organizing in the plants, but the Mexican workers' walkout took both the company and the union by surprise. Duplin County is home to a burgeoning pork-processing industry. The explosive growth in the industry directly impacts the number of Mexican immigrants moving to the area. From the Duke University data on North Carolina hog processing, we note how meat and poultry processing entails significant labor inputs while tending to livestock is much less labor-intensive.

It is not simply one industry that brings Mexicans to work in North Carolina, nor is it one region that can be viewed as the main destination. Numerically, the majority of Mexican immigrants reside in urban areas, particularly the Research Triangle Park (Chapel Hill, Raleigh, and Durham), but their arrival is often predicated on other industries and regions.

Johnson-Webb (2003, 52) states that the Latino population can be found "widely dispersed throughout the North Carolina economy" though they tend to predominate in low-wage sectors. Griffith (2005, 72) notes both the traditional occupations that employ Mexicans and their low-wage service industry employment in urban destinations (fast food customer service, hotel and travel industry cleaning, and office work). Another group of scholars more specifically note:

> Latinos/as are primarily moving into traditional and declining North Carolina manufacturing industries. These tend to be low wage industries. Meat Products, Knitting Mills, and Household Furniture are the top three destinations for Latinos/as entering the North Carolina Labor market. Within industries, the Latino/a labor force is primarily concentrated in Operative, Laborer and Service jobs. A detailed analysis of shifts in the ethnic composition of occupations in the top ten Latino/a industries suggests that generally Latinos/as are replacing African American or White workers who leave the worst jobs in those industries, rather than displacing them from the more desirable jobs in the industry. (Skaggs, Tomaskovic-Devey, and Leiter 2006)

Unfortunately, none of these scholars disaggregate the Latino category. Even though 66 per cent of the state's Latinos are Mexican, the socio-economic indicators allow scholars to see the glass half-empty or half-full as it relates to social mobility. Yet, as all scholars writing on the Latinization of North Carolina note, the heavily Mexican influx presents a complication to already uneasy race relations among Whites, Blacks, and Native Americans.

Mexicans in Latino and White New York

One region of the nation that Mexicans have traditionally not dominated numerically is the Northeast. Much more the Latino destination for Puerto Ricans, and later for Dominicans and immigrants from throughout Latin America, New York City is a global destination that serves as a barometer for larger migration patterns throughout the world. The increasing international migration directly to the surrounding suburbs of Long Island and Westchester County has resulted in clashes with the earlier generation of European immigrants who fled to the suburbs to escape the minority presence in the city—the so-called White flighters. Though the relative rates are comparatively small, an increasing Mexican presence in upstate New York has triggered backlashes in a rapidly declining and deteriorating rural context.

New York City has long served as an immigrant destination. Every great wave of immigration has funneled through the city and has shifted the composition of its population. Today, sociologists such as Saskia Sassen and Robert Courtney Smith describe the processes of transnationalism as it affects the "serving classes" who live in such global cities (Sassen 2005) and contemporary immigrants living simultaneously in two worlds (Smith 2006b).

Sassen (2005) makes a useful distinction between globalization from above and below. The home to the United Nations and the World Bank, New York City is defined from above in terms of its international financial markets, transnational corporations, and international governance regimes. Globalization from below accounts for its status as a city in which immigrants from all over the world occupy transnational networks and organizations that transcend nation-state borders. Increasingly a major Latin American destination, New York City relies on immigrants, particularly immigrant women, to fill the ranks of the serving classes. Sassen writes of the "localizations" of economic restructuring in global cities, leading to growth in low-wage jobs: "In research on New York and other [global] cities, it has been found that between 30 per cent and 50 per cent of the workers in the leading sectors are actually low-wage workers" (Sassen 2005, 205).

Mexicans are the fastest increasing Latino subgroup in New York City, and their relatively young age will translate into large growth rates well into the future. "In 2000 the Mexican-origin population in New York City, including both immigrants and native-born Mexican Americans, was 275,000 to 300,000, about half of whom were between the ages of twelve and twenty-four" (Smith 2006b, 20). "According to estimates by New York's Department of City Planning, in 2000 the city's 850,000 Puerto Ricans accounted for 38 per cent of the total Hispanic population, 615,000 Dominicans for 27 per cent, 200,000 Mexicans for 9 per cent, 125,000 Colombians and 125,000 Ecuadorians for 6 per cent each, and other Latin Americans for about 14 per cent" (Ricourt and Danta 2002, 4). Mexicans are the numerical minority in every neighborhood and borough where they tend to congregate. Sunset Park, Brooklyn, and El Barrio or Spanish Harlem have the highest concentrations of Mexicans, but all are majority Puerto Rican. Though their New York destinations vary, the sending areas in Mexico are strikingly uniform. Smith (2005, 224) finds that a single indigenous group in Mexico provides the vast majority of New York City's Mexican population as most come from "the Mixteca region, a cultural and ecological zone that includes the contiguous parts of three states, southern Puebla, northern Oaxaca, and eastern Guerrero. In 1992, the Mixteca accounted for two-thirds of the Mexican migrants to New York, with 47 per cent from Puebla alone." Pfeffer and Parra (2004) also find that the majority of Mexican immigrants to rural, upstate New York are from Puebla.

Nowhere is the marginalization and subsequent plight of Mexican immigrants more evident than in the experiences of day laborers who seek casual employment in construction, landscaping, cleaning, and home maintenance since most legitimate employment opportunities are difficult to secure without a driver's license, social security number, or a work visa. Day laborers are increasingly present in the Eastern US but unlike on the West Coast, they work not in major cities but in suburbs. Westchester County and Long Island are home to an undetermined number of Latino immigrants who patch together a living through this informal work arrangement. In Chapter 5 we discussed the contentious Long Island suburb of Farmingville and the efforts of the Workplace Project to defend the rights of day laborers there. One aspect of the Project's work that we did not address was its part in the successful passage of the Unpaid Wages Prohibition Act of 1997. "The act increased the maximum civil penalty the commissioner of labor can impose on the worst wage offenders from 50 per cent to 200 per cent of the amount owed and it raised the criminal penalty for repeat violating employers from a misdemeanor to a felony, doubling the maximum penalty to twenty thousand dollars" (Fine 2006, 172). Enforcement of the state act has been remiss under successive Republican gubernatorial administrations, but with the tireless efforts of day laborers and a committed core of activists, the Workplace Project has demonstrated that legal cases, worker centers, state bills, and worker rights education can all result in successful outcomes even in the face of vehement opposition. The National Day Labor Survey included responses from 2,660 day laborers who were selected from 264 hiring sites in 20 states and the District of Columbia. It concluded:

> Our findings reveal that the day-labor market is rife with violations of workers' rights. Day laborers are regularly denied payment for their work, many are subjected to demonstrably hazardous job sites, and most endure insults and abuses by employers. The growth of day-labor hiring sites combined with rising levels of workers' rights violations is a national trend that warrants attention

from policy makers at all levels of government. (Valenzuela *et al.* 2006, i, 22)

Recent data collected by Eberts and Merschrod (2004) and Pfeffer and Parra (2004) demonstrate a small but relevant increase of Latinos in non-metropolitan counties of the state. The Hudson and Champlain Valleys, as well as central and western rural regions, are the main receiving areas for migrant farmworkers. None of these counties have experienced the exponential growth of the non-metropolitan South and Midwest, nor do their numbers come close to approximating the Latino population in the New York City metropolitan area, but a population increase from nearly 0 to a high of 4 to 5 per cent is relevant and elicits reactions from local communities.

Mize is currently conducting research in upstate New York on the many rural communities that are experiencing a comparatively small influx of Latino and Mexican immigrants who are offsetting overall population declines. Agricultural labor is still the primary draw for Mexican H-2A workers to work in apple orchards as well as with other commodities such as cabbage, cranberries, truck crops, flowers, fruit, general farm, grain, hay, horticulture, logging, nursery, orchard, peaches, raspberries, sheep, squash, strawberries, tree pruning, and other vegetables. In 2002, there were 1,800 H-2A workers picking apples in New York.

Most agricultural workers finding employment in New York state are likely undocumented and beginning to settle permanently. As Pfeffer and Parra (2004) note, the New York migrant labor pool has been filled in succession by African Americans, Puerto Ricans, Haitians, Jamaicans (as late as 1995), and most recently Mexicans. Their interviews with social-service providers find that communities have difficulties grappling with a very small Latino influx. No Mexican community exceeds 5 per cent of a county's total population in upstate New York, but some community leaders have publicly expressed their dissatisfaction with what they characterize as the "Mexican invasion." Survey research conducted in the same agricultural communities found a much more tempered response. "Approximately half of non-immigrant residents consider that the number of outsiders in their communities is 'just about right,' and more than half consider immigrants 'neither an asset nor a burden.' In general, non-immigrant residents in the five communities are ambivalent about the presence of immigrants in their community. This sentiment is similar to that expressed by New Yorkers statewide" (Pfeffer and Parra 2004, 2). If upstate New York becomes a major new destination — although the economic woes of the region seem to preclude this possibility—we wonder if this current ambivalence will be sustained.

The Old and the New: Yakima Valley, Washington

Our final case brings us back to the Pacific Northwest. The Yakima Valley of Washington has been a traditional Mexican destination for the past 100 years. The current demographic shifts in Eastern Washington are extremely pronounced in the historical connections with the Pacific migrant stream and Bracero Program and the valley's Mexican immigrants of today. According to Census 2000 data, the distribution of the Latino population in Washington State is heavily concentrated in the agricultural counties, four of which are more than 30 per cent Latino and two almost 50 per cent Latino. It is precisely those towns—Toppenish (75.7 per cent Latino), Yakima (33.7 per cent), Granger (85.5 per cent), Sunnyside (73.1 per cent), Wapato (76.2), and Grandview (68 per cent)—that had housed Bracero camps where Mexicans now tend to predominate in permanent majority communities.

Unfortunately, the seasonal demands of agricultural work still require many of the region's residents to follow the migrant trail. Isabel Valle's *Fields of Toil* (1994) details the lives of Mexican migrants in the Northwest. Valle joined the Martinez family in their migrant circuit from Boardman, Oregon, to Pasco and Walla Walla, Washington, and back to their winter home in La Grulla, Texas. It is difficult to say where home is for the family. They have made this trip annually for the past 35 years to find work in onions, potatoes, tomatoes, apples, asparagus, and raspberries, in addition to odd jobs in construction and housecleaning. When they return to La Grulla, they rarely find any gainful employment and must stretch any earnings through the lean winters.

One way the family survives is through a group strategy of employing all able hands, regardless of age. They are not breaking any child labor laws, as each state makes its own regulations and most often holds agriculture to a lower standard than all other industries. A hold-over from the family farming days, lax child-labor laws most often place the children of migrants in the most precarious situations. In 1994 Washington's child-labor laws permitted long hours for child labor in the fields:

> The minimum age for most agricultural work is 14. Children 12 and 13 can work only during non-school weeks for hand harvesting or cultivating berries,

cucumbers, and spinach. Children ages 12 and 13 may only work eight hours a day 40 hours a week in non-school weeks, and begin no earlier than 5 a.m. and finish no later than 9 p.m. Children ages 14 and 15 may work up to 21 hours a week.... For minors 16 and 17, up to four hours a day of work before or after school is permitted, and up to 28 hours per week. When school is not in session, hours increase to 10 hours a day, 50 hours a week. (Valle 1994, 37)

Even if a family keeps to the letter of the law, we educators must wonder when school-aged children would possibly have time to study or even to have fun. Migrant families often find themselves in desperate circumstances, and yet they will forego a full family income to provide for their children's educational future. It is clear that the children's best interests are not considered when it comes to harvesting crops. Child-labor laws in the US, as of January 1, 2007, still exempt agriculture from meeting the rest of the economy's standards and allow 10- and 11-year-olds to work in agriculture (see US Department of Labor 2007). In 2008, the state of Washington's child-labor laws had remained unchanged since Valle's publication in 1994. In the final chapter, we will address this discrepancy that allows agribusiness to claim exceptional status under some of the most spurious of rationales.

Notes

1. A pseudonym.
2. Right-to-work states, mostly in the Southern and Western US, prohibit agreements by trade unions and employers that require union membership or union dues in order to hire a worker.
3. We should note that the Mexican population in Hawaii and Alaska is sizeable and important but beyond the scope of our analysis, given the dearth of research. In 2000, the Mexican population in Alaska numbered 13,334; in Hawaii, it was 19,820. In 2005, the population increased by 8 and 49 per cent respectively, to 14,442 in Alaska and 29,542 in Hawaii (US Census 2000, Summary File 2; US Census 2005).
4. Adverse-effect wage rates are the minimum wage rates that the US Department of Labor sets for wages paid to US and foreign workers by employers of H-2A visa holders.
5. See http://www.globalworkers.org/migrationdata_US.html#H2.
6. See http://www.brookings.edu/~/media/Files/rc/reports/2002/07demograph-ics_suro/surosinger.pdf.

7. The difficulty with interpreting the Brookings data is that the Latino population is so diverse that lumping them into one category elides differences within national origin groups and the collective and individual resources at their disposal that facilitates migration.

8. Land-grant universities were created by the Morill Acts of 1860 and 1890 when US federal lands were granted to states to create educational institutions.

9. Recent estimates suggest that the Latino population constitutes 40 per cent of Dalton's total population (with 20 per cent of the total population citing "some other race" and 60 per cent citing White as their racial identification). The vast majority of the "other" race is consistently found to be Latino, and if the remaining 20 per cent of Latinos (predominately Mexican) self-identify as White, then the White and Latino populations are roughly of equal size.

10. See http://www.soc.duke.edu/NC_GlobalEconomy/tobacco/overview.shtml.

11. The mean number of employees per farm is six, but this low number is misleading. The H-2A report lists all employers as individual requesters, although often requests for workers come from associations. An association, representing multiple employers, makes one request for a number of workers, although some of its members may not employ H-2A workers at all while others may share workers en masse. For instance, there were only 4,200 applications but 6,000 employers certified to employ temporary visa holders.

12. See Table 0.1 for explanation of classes of visa holders.

Chapter Nine

Mexican Labor *en la Frontera*

The border region, *la frontera*, is found in the US Southwestern states of California, Arizona, New Mexico, and Texas and in the border states of Northern Mexico — Baja California, Sonora, Chihuahua, Coahuila, Nuevo León, and Tamaulipas. The last 35 years have witnessed major changes in this area, including demographic shifts, economic restructuring, the physical and social construction of the border, and growing inequalities. To understand the contemporary realities of the US-Mexico border, we begin with a focus on the historical formation of the area.

The Historical Origins of the Border|*la Frontera*
The US-Mexico border has a history of contestation. This imaginary line in the sand has shifted several times over the past 200 years and has recently been increasingly fortified, with deadly consequences. When Mexico threw off the colonial shackles of the Spanish Empire in 1821, the land of New Spain and its far northern frontier became part of the sovereign United States of Mexico. The largest Mexican states were on this northern frontier, although they were populated much more sparsely than the population center of the Central plateau. The lands we currently associate with California, Arizona, New Mexico, Texas, and parts of Oklahoma, Kansas, Colorado, Utah, Nevada, and Wyoming were all claimed by the nascent Mexican nation-state. In the early 1800s, the US Monroe Doctrine threatened European nations that sought to extend their colonial reach to the Americas and put the US in the paternalistic role of protecting newly independent Latin American nation-states from European invaders.

Mexico had already experienced US colonization, first with the annexation of *Tejas* (Texas) in 1845 and eventually in the US-Mexico War of 1846–48, which forced the still-young Mexican government to cede nearly one-half of its territory. It also solidified the organization of the first "illegal aliens" in the area — the US citizens who made Mexico defend itself first in Texas and then in California. These filibusters—US soldiers and mercenaries who invaded the Spanish Americas to bring the region under US control—legitimated their attacks on Latin American state sovereignty with a much different doctrine, the ideology of Manifest Destiny (see Gonzalez 2000, 37–38). The ideology that the US was on a God-given mission to rule from sea to shining sea justified its shift from lowly colonized status to exalted colonizer. The US assumed this role both directly and indirectly in the Caribbean (Puerto Rico, US Virgin Islands, Cuba, and the Dominican Republic), the Pacific Islands (Hawaii, Guam, and several other islands), and Asia (particularly the Philippines).

What we now identify as the US-Mexico border was not solidified in its current demarcation until 1853 when the final piece of what is now Southern Arizona was brokered for the same amount of money that the US paid for all of the northern territories at the end of the US-Mexico War. The strategy of the US military was to force concessions directly from the federal government of Mexico by surrounding the Mexican capitol. The Treaty of Guadalupe-Hidalgo of 1848 clearly laid out the new boundaries between Mexico and the US. The Gadsen Purchase of 1853 was justified to ensure a straight southern railroad route from El Paso to the Pacific Ocean. It is certainly no coincidence that the land also contains the largest copper deposit in the world and a long history of gold, silver, iron, and copper mining.

The contested claims to this region and the interconnectedness that developed between the economies and people on both sides of the border deepened in the ensuing years. The border region of Northern Mexico has long been dependent on the markets of the US. Since 1858, the Mexican federal government has provided special concessions to Mexican companies that want to do export business with the US. A *zona libre*, or free trade zone, was established in the immediate border region of Tamaulipas and Chihuahua in 1858 (Sanchez 1993) and was expanded by dictator Porfirio Díaz to the entire US-Mexico border in 1885. This allowed the US to collect duties on exported goods until the zone was struck down in 1905. In the early 1930s the Mexican government officially designated free trade border zones to boost the Mexican border economies ravaged by the Depression and the end of US Prohibition. Manufacturing, mineral extraction, textiles, and smelting plants were all developed with the aid of the Mexican government's policy shift in favor of Northern Mexico's "special status" as a US trading partner.

From the US government perspective, the only thing worth regulating was the flow of goods across the border, so customs agents regulated the flow of trade from Mexico. The flow of people was not addressed until the establishment of the US Border Patrol in 1924 by the last of the quota acts — the Johnson-Reed Immigration Act. Until that point, most immigration laws were aimed at restricting Southern and Eastern European, as well as Asian, immigration to the US. Under the auspices of the Monroe Doctrine, with the US as self-professed "great father of the new world," the nations of the Western Hemisphere were exempt from quotas. Literacy tests and head taxes were selectively applied to bar some Mexican entries, but in the early years the Border Patrol mainly served to alienate and humiliate potential Mexican immigrants. At the time, the Ku Klux Klan was prevalent in El Paso, and many border agents were members. The increasing use of racial violence to control the Mexican population reached its most fevered pitch in Texas with the officially sanctioned actions of the Texas Rangers. Working more as a paramilitary and terrorist force than in their stated role as law enforcement officers, the Texas Rangers pursued citizens of Mexican origin and often resorted to lynching to enforce Jim Crow-style segregation. According to Tim Dunn (1996), Border Patrol agents were directly recruited from the ranks of the former Texas Rangers so that it was often difficult to distinguish between Ku Klux Klan, Ranger, and Border Patrol members, as they were often one and the same. Contemporary economics, politics, vigilantism, and culture were shaped by this history of US-Mexican relations in the borderlands.

The Demographics of the Border Region

In 1990, an estimated 9 million people resided in the border region. The population was concentrated in two sets of sister cities: San Diego, California/Tijuana, Baja California and El Paso, Texas/Cuidad Juárez, Chihuahua where an estimated 3,153,830 people, or 35 per cent of the total border population reside. According to Ham-Chande and Weeks (1992), the San Diego metropolitan area encompasses nearly one-half of the total US border population. The US-Mexico Border Health Commission estimated that the border population had grown to over 12 million by 2000.[1]

This large population along the border is a relatively new phenomenon. For instance, in 1900 Tijuana had a population of only 242 people while San Diego's population numbered nearly 18,000. As historian Oscar J. Martinez (1975a) notes, the regional economies and populations of the border towns have tended to follow boom-and-bust cycles. Since the border has been heavily dependent on extractive industries, regional economies fluctuated with mineral prices, trade relations between Mexico and the US, the market value of agricultural commodities, and the relative global supply of raw materials. US Prohibition also provided a stimulus for demographic growth in Mexico's border towns, which capitalized on the lack of sanctions on serving alcohol. A number of nightclubs, bars, resorts, racetracks, and gambling halls were built in Tijuana and Cuidad Juárez. Agua Caliente in Tijuana entertained patrons with cockfighting, horse racing, dog racing, gambling, theatrical performances, nightclubs, and golf. Hollywood entertainers made their way to this popular hot spot during the days of Prohibition.

One of the unique phenomena defining the US-Mexico border region is the rise of sister cities on both sides. Where California meets Baja California, the sister cities of San Diego/Tijuana and Calexico/Mexicali come together. On the border of Arizona and Sonora, one finds the sister cities of Nogales/Nogales, Yuma/San Luis Colorado, and Douglas/Agua Prieta. Along the Texas-Mexico border, a number of sister cities have developed: El Paso/Cuidad Juárez, Del Rio/Cuidad Acuña, Eagle Pass/Piedras Negras, Laredo/Nuevo Laredo, McAllen/Reynosa, and Brownsville/Matamoros. Mexico's federal government's disinvestment in rural development also increased pressures to develop an export-based, urban manufacturing economy along the border.

Economic Restructuring of the Border Region: Industrialization and Urbanization

Like the sister cities, a number of twin or sister *maquiladoras* have developed along the border. The *maquilas del norte* are part of the much larger global economic trend that utilizes cheap labor from underdeveloped nations to assemble (and sometimes produce) goods at low costs. In the US, sister plants were built to facilitate the shipping and distribution of goods produced and assembled in Mexico, where a number of foreign-owned assembly plants located operations along the border after the Mexican government initiated the Border Industrialization Program of 1965. In some ways, that program was developed to fill the void left by the termination of the Bracero Program (see Kiser and Kiser 1979).

The Border Industrialization Program extended the notion of the northern border region as a free trade zone. It was designed to encourage US companies to send raw materials and components to the Mexican *maquiladoras* for assembly. Finished goods would be returned to the US and sold through US distribution plants. As early as 1969, US companies such as RCA, Motorola, Hughes Aircraft, Litton, and General Electric all had assembly operations in the border industrial zone. In that same year, 72 US corporations established assembly plants in Mexico's border region. Primarily concentrated in Cuidad Juárez and Tijuana, the plants were a major impetus in encouraging internal migrants to settle permanently in these cities. As more US corporations established operations in Mexican state- and federal government-funded industrial parks, urban populations increased to keep pace with the labor needs of the *maquiladoras*. In 1974, the number of US plants rose to 655. In 1990, there were almost 1,500 *maquiladoras* with almost 450,000 employees. The establishment of assembly plants in Mexico by US and other TNCs relates to global economic shifts in labor and capital. Today, the workforce exceeds 1 million, and there are between 2,000 and 4,000 plants, owned by TNCs or their suppliers, illustrating the increasing global division of labor and accompanying strategies of capital flight to low-wage nations.

NAFTA was ratified in 1993 by Mexico, Canada, and the US to develop a tariff-free trade bloc. Using the *maquiladoras* as the main source of cheap labor, assembly plants were established and expanded to capitalize on the labor of predominately Mexican women. In 1975, nearly 80 per cent of all *maquila* "operatives" were female (Sklar 1989); this figure has consistently gone down to 69 per cent in 1985 and 62 per cent in 1990. The *maquila* industry is still segregated by gender, and depending on the job task and industrial section, Mexican women are found in the lowest paid and most hazardous job positions. They occupy at least three-quarters of the positions in the service sector, food processing, assembly line work, and smoldering activities (Peña 1997, 258).

Fronteras, Lineas, O Paredes: Contemporary Constructions of the Border

As the late Chicana scholar-activist Gloria Anzaldúa (1987, 2–3) characterized the US-Mexico border:

> 1,950 mile-long open wound
> dividing a *pueblo*, a culture,

running down the length of my body,
staking fence rods in my flesh,
splits me   splits me
me raja   *me raja*
This is my home
this thin edge of
barbwire.

The border is much more than the line on a map that divides two nations; it has a symbolic, political, physical, and militarized presence. From the strictly political definition that emerged at the end of the US-Mexico War, the border is now marked by newly erected walls, fences, and entry inspection stations. The physical construction has been accompanied by a more deadly militarization of the entire region. As we have seen before (see Chapter 2), the US Border Patrol has employed an LIC policy along the border. At the same time, increasing military enforcement has a corollary in citizens' vigilante groups, such as the Minutemen and American Patrol. As a result, the border has become a much more dangerous place. The long history of treating Mexican laborers as disposable has perhaps its most deadly manifestation in the murders of hundreds of women *maquiladora* workers in Juárez (frequently referred to as femicides) and in the deaths of thousands of immigrants who cross the border at the most treacherous unguarded crossing points.

The symbolic representation of the border has shifted depending on US-Mexican relations. The best way to visualize it historically is as an imaginary line in the sand. As Rodríguez (1997, 223) notes: "nation-state boundaries are social constructions. They do not exist independent of our volition.... Nation-state borders exist primarily because state governments agree, voluntarily or through coercion, that they delimit political divisions. Solemn treaties formalize international boundaries, but it is the daily reproduction of ideas and myths that socially construct borders." The Rio Grande (referred to as the Rio Bravo on the Mexican side) provided the major symbol for undocumented border crossers in the 1970s and 1980s before a wall was built out of steel landing strips and erected to separate the major sister cities. The river is the source for the favored term of denigration for undocumented Mexicans, "wetback," as people have to wade through it to cross into the US.

ICE/INS Border Ops

A series of campaigns from 1993 to the present has resulted in physically demarcating the line in the sand or the rivers that symbolically mark the border between Mexico and the US. They go by military names: Operation Blockade and Operation Hold-the-Line in El Paso, Operation Gatekeeper in San Diego, and Operation Guardian — "Light up the Border" campaign — in Douglas and Nogales, Arizona. In El Paso, 450 agents manned vehicles along the 20-mile stretch of the border to prevent undocumented crossings. While this operation was almost completely successful, it also displaced those undocumented border commuters who crossed from Ciudad Juárez every day to provide essential service work in El Paso. They had to divert their crossing strategies to more isolated and dangerous parts of the border. In the end, undocumented daily border crossers who comprised El Paso's low-wage service sector were the most affected by Operation Hold-the-Line.

Another defining characteristic of the contemporary US-Mexico border region is, as we saw in Chapter 5, its increasing militarization. The military equipment used to patrol the border (helicopters, night-vision equipment, electronic intrusion-detection ground sensors), the operational tactics and strategies of border enforcement (combining police, military, and paramilitary forces), and the overall aim of social control of a targeted civilian population all embody the LIC doctrine that the US military put into action in Vietnam, Somalia, Libya, Kuwait, Panama, Iraq, and Grenada.

Andreas (2000) argues that boundary enforcement along the US-Mexico border during the 1990s stemmed from political factors and pressures to gain control of the region. He asserts that enforcement is less about curtailing the flow of drugs and undocumented migration as it is about setting the symbolic territorial boundaries of the nation-state since the state has in the past failed to implement immigration policies that would deter the movement of undocumented immigrants along the boundary. Romero and Serag investigated the joint operation of the Border Patrol and Chandler Police Department to target working-class Chicano neighborhoods in the Phoenix metropolitan area. In what has come to be known as the Chandler Round-Up, the detainment and inspection of papers of those who looked like "illegals" or were of Mexican ancestry certainly represents racial profiling. It also deployed class profiling, by targeting neighborhoods slated for redevelopment and by unannounced house-to-house visits and by stopping pedestrians in public shopping areas, on residential streets, and at bus stops (Romero and Serag 2005). In 2010, this informal practice became the law of the land with the passage of Arizona's SB1070 immigrant profiling law.

As the undocumented are criminalized upon entering the US, the border has become much more dangerous. With increased enforcement, immigrants have been forced to cross in the least defended and thus most treacherous and dangerous stretches. Researchers Eschbach, Hagan, and Rodríguez (2004) estimate that with the increased border militarization nearly 5,000 immigrants died on the US side of the border from 1985 to 2002. In San Diego, the American Friends Service Committee (a Quaker organization) has focused on immigrant rights in the California-Mexico border region. In addition to numerous direct action activities, they make daily updates to a banner that tallies the number of immigrants who have lost their lives attempting to cross the border. The banner is visible to drivers on Interstate 5 who drive by the Coronado Bridge and Chicano Park (where the world's largest display of public murals chronicles the Chicano experience in San Diego) on their daily commute to downtown jobs. This public critique of border militarization has created a link between Chicano activists who took over the park 34 years ago to keep the city from placing a police station in the heart of Barrio Logan and today's immigrants who deal daily with the increased threats associated with undocumented border crossing.

The presence of citizen's militias, and other self-proclaimed defenders of "America," exacerbates the paramilitary and hypermilitarized situation along the border. The American Patrol and Minutemen Project are both self-declared vigilante groups that have determined that federal immigration policy is a failure; they have taken the law into their own hands to detain suspected undocumented immigrants. The militias have garnered significant media attention but in an actual combat situation are roughly as effective as a group of paint-ball enthusiasts. Nevertheless, their anti-immigrant rhetoric and actions have provided a legitimating context for extremely xenophobic legislation such as Sensenbrenner Bill HR 4437, which would have made it a felony to be undocumented or assist an undocumented immigrant. The bill passed the House by a vote of 239 to 182 but could not be reconciled with a stalled Senate immigration bill, and so its measures have not been enacted into law. The Minutemen also emboldened Republican representatives to present bills that called for mass deportations of "illegals." As a result, some of the largest demonstrations in the history of the nation have been organized in most major cities to support immigrant rights, denounce HR 4437, and remove the media spotlight from vigilante approaches to immigration reform.

In March 2010, the governor of Arizona signed SB1070 into law. Dubbed the "Support Our Law Enforcement and Safe Neighborhoods Act," it requires law enforcement to check the papers of any person suspected of being in the state illegally by empowering them to "lawfully stop any person who is operating a motor vehicle if the officer has reasonable suspicion to believe the person is in violation of any civil traffic law." Some critics fear the act will lead to racial profiling; on closer read it is clear the act does mandate racial profiling and provides a how-to manual for police on how to profile those who look like immigrants.[2]

Though it seems that the criminalization of undocumented immigrants will not be entertained by the Senate, and in lieu of comprehensive immigration reform, both the Senate and House passed the 2006 "Secure Fence Act" to erect a 700-mile fence along the US-Mexico border. "The Secure Fence Act authorizes the construction of at least two layers of reinforced fencing around the border town of Tecate, Calif., and a huge expanse stretching from Calexico, Calif., to Douglas, Ariz.—virtually the entire length of Arizona's border with Mexico. Another expanse would stretch over much of the southern border of New Mexico, with another section winding through Texas, from Del Rio to Eagle Pass, and from Laredo to Brownsville" (Weisman 2006). To make the symbolic commitment to "stemming the tide" one month before the 2006 midterm elections, the act received substantial bipartisan support as neither party wanted to be viewed by voters as soft on illegal immigration deterrence.

The symbolic relevance of the border cannot be understated. For the mass media and politicians, it represents a dividing line that must be fortified to keep undesirables out. For immigrants, it is a barrier that is increasingly dangerous and deadly. For those living on either side, it has become an inconvenient crossing point (see Simpson 2006). The rhetoric of the Minutemen is legitimized by equally xenophobic spin machines like Fox News, Lou Dobbs, and the always vitriolic Pat Buchanan. The symbolic representation of the border as a wall or fence in need of further fortification only serves to place the problems associated with illegal immigration as a burden on those deemed illegal. Lost in the equation are the employers who are illegally employing workers without papers and government officials who criminalize immigrants for their own political gain.

Disposable Labor and Gendering Border Work

The lives of Mexican citizens compared to US citizens point to the very real differences between the two nations. The level of inequality is demonstrated by a few recent statistics published by the San Diego Association of Governments (SANDAG) and Mexico's National Commission on Minimum Wages (*Comisión Nacional de los Salarios Mínimos*—CNSM). First, when data are collected by US agencies on the labor force, the assumption is that wage labor does not begin until 18 years of age or after high-school completion. When the Mexican government collects statistics on labor force participation, they begin with those aged 12. Second, the federally mandated, minimum-wage differential is representative of the inequalities between the two nations. In the US, the minimum wage is currently $7.25 per *hour*. In Mexico, the conversion of pesos into US dollars puts the comparative wage from Mexico at $5 per *day*. We used data from SANDAG (1992, 13), US Federal Reserve (1999), and CNSM (2006) to understand both the inflationary tendencies of the peso and the exchange value in US dollars. The US equivalent of Mexican daily minimum wages has varied between $2.43 and $4.59. The short-lived increase in real wage values, related to the introduction of the newly devalued peso, were undercut in 1995 when wages dipped to $2.43, the lowest value in the last 20 years. The 2006 wage equivalent of $4.44 per day is a stark reminder of the vast inequalities between US and Mexican workers.

According to Muñoz Rios, "In December 2000, with the minimum wage, one could purchase 21.8% of the basic family foodbasket, but this percentage returned to 16.9% in the end of 2005. In contrast with statements of the Secretary of Labor and the National Commission on Minimum Wages (CNSM) which say that there are very few people who have this wage, workers who obtain the minimum salary in the country represent 26.6 per cent of the national total, or in other words, one in three." The inability to meet basic sustenance requirements for the vast majority of Mexican cities has only been exacerbated by International Monetary Fund and Mexican state-sponsored neoliberal reforms and displacements associated with NAFTA. "According to [UNAM calculations], from the devaluation of December 1994 until August 2002, the minimum salary in Mexico could only cover 27.7 per cent of the basic family foodbasket, and one needed four minimum wages to cover the full cost ..." (Muñoz Rios 2006).

In terms of educational inequities, the relatively high drop-out rate of students living in US border towns cannot compare to the barriers facing the population in Mexico. For example, of the Mexican citizens aged 15 or older living in Baja California, 44.9 per cent have no education beyond grade school (SANDAG 1992, 8). In the US border states, the percentage of the population who have graduated from high school is between 75 and 85 per cent. In predominately Latino or minority school districts, the high-school completion rate drops to only 50 per cent, but again these numbers pale in comparison to the lack of educational opportunities in Mexico. Out of these vast inequalities, there has emerged both a redefinition of identities and border cultures as well as new migration patterns. Inequalities between the overdeveloped US and underdeveloped Mexico point to larger global trends in the absolute immiseration of the world's population.

Around the globe every day, more than 30,000 children under the age of five die of starvation or completely curable diseases, adding up to some 10 million every year — one every three seconds. More than 1 billion of the world's population subsist on incomes less than $1.00 per day. The richest fifth of the world's population control 85 per cent of the globe's wealth, leaving little more than 1 per cent for the poorest fifth. In Mexico the 24 wealthiest families have more money than the 24 million poorest (Lipsitz 2001, 9).

Globalization, most authors concede, is a contradictory process. On one hand, it is about the free flow of capital and commodities over increasingly irrelevant nation-state boundaries, rewriting the rules of labor relations, gender relations, environmental laws, and the role of the nation-state in both the underdeveloped and overdeveloped world. On the other hand, in the global justice movement, workers come together to form labor unions and other forms of resistance (in cross-border social movements such as the Zapatistas), current migration trends are transnationalizing, and social identities are developing that transcend static nation-state allegiances. Along the US-Mexico border, it becomes clear that the global workplace has been engendered and that organized resistance to exploitation by TNCs is probably more successful and sustained in Mexico than it is in the US. The possibilities for transnational labor organizing are discussed below.

Where globalization, inequality, and gender come together most clearly is where the over- and underprivileged worlds collide. The US-Mexico border region and migrant life are the focus of two recent documentaries. *Performing the Border* by Ursula Biemann (1999), focusing on the sister cities of El Paso/Cuidad Juárez, provides a visually and aurally powerful elaboration of both the social-discursive construction and the militarization of the border. The words of women activists, journalists, prostitutes, and *maquiladora* laborers are coupled with images of environmental degradation, hard work for little pay, and deplorable living conditions. Working women in the *maquiladoras* and migrants bear the burden of the costs of Mexican modernization for US consumption. Direct testimonies demonstrate the sociological imagination in action and provide first-person accounts of how the concentration of capital in the North and the concentration of cheap labor in the South negatively impact the lives of Mexican women. Whether it involves *maquiladora* laborers, sex workers, immigrants, domestics, or laborers in the tourism industry, the gendered construction of border relations reveals larger power relations between the US and Mexico.

Señorita Extraviada (2001), by filmmaker and actress Lourdes Portillo, examines the murders of over 500 female *maquiladora* workers in the Cuidad Juárez/El Paso border region in the context of a complete lack of law enforcement, governmental, or industry concern. Nominated for an Oscar in 2003, it spawned a concerted reaction on the part of law enforcement officials in the US and a recent conference at the University of California Los Angeles on "The *Maquiladora* Murders," as well as a fictionalized account of the murders written by Alicia Gaspar de Alba (2005). The documentary details Portillo's two-year search for the truth behind the murder of *maquiladora* women and why they are so often viewed as disposable bodies. The marginalization of gendered labor in the *maquiladoras* coupled with a lack of state enforcement of the human rights of poor Mexican citizens (on both sides of the border) are implicated in these murders.

As we have seen earlier in this chapter and in Chapter 2, the overall effect of the criminalization of undocumented immigrants is that entry into the US has become much more dangerous. The nearly 5,000 immigrants who have died on the US side of the border from 1985 to 2002 should serve as just cause for moral outrage and condemnation. However, the actions of the Minutemen and their right-wing supporters in government have rendered these deaths nearly invisible as they blame the immigrants for crossing. The public discourse never includes the fact that employers who willingly employ undocumented workers (the reason why Mexican immigrants risk life and limb to come to the US in the first place) are also breaking the law and are as responsible for directly or indirectly recruiting workers to break the law to seek work in the US.

Finally, the prevalence of "commuter" migrants who live in either Mexico or the US and work and shop *en el otro lado* (on the other side) has not been fully examined by researchers. Recent estimates are that nearly 160,000 Mexican workers commute to jobs in the US each day. A Target department store in Chula Vista, California (South San Diego), estimates that 80 per cent of its customers live in Mexico (Herzog 1996). Studies should be conducted on US citizens who work in Mexico or shop in pharmacies and other local businesses that offer items not readily found in the US.

Maquilas del Norte: Distribution Centers and the NAFTA Circuit of Commodities

When US supporters of NAFTA were pressing for its passage, their main argument was job creation along the US side of the border. The US border region was touted as the growth corridor of the post-NAFTA trade and distribution economy. Supporters also assumed that the loss of factory jobs in the Rust Belt (Midwest and Northeastern cities) was a trend that had presumably run its course through the 1970s and 1980s. They rarely acknowledged that the remaining Rust Belt factory jobs would stand on even more precarious ground with the enactment of NAFTA. Yet this result was already set in motion.

In the post-NAFTA era, the border region is being reshaped by a circuit of commodities that crisscrosses the border to maximize profits by reducing costs of labor and duties. The assembly of commodities occurs in the Mexican border region where disposable female labor is most easily exploitable. The distribution of commodities occurs in the US to both avoid tariffs and duties while employing a minimum wage and temporary workforce to handle the shipping of goods. Mize embarked on a research study in 1998 to examine employment practices in the sister distribution centers in San Diego to the assembly plants in Mexico.[3] He worked in a warehouse, filling orders for an educational supply company. Many school teachers probably have little idea that one of their favorite educational supply catalogs can offer comparatively affordable educational learning aids, curricula, and supplies because of the female workers in a Tecate, Mexico *maquiladora* who work to assemble those products for approximately $8.00 a day, 10 hours per day, 6 days a week. In the distribution center, workers were sporadically employed and paid just above the US minimum wage with no fringe benefits.

When Mize's research was conducted, the industrial park, which was home to the educational supply company, was empty of all but that company, a windshield repair shop, and a well-known shipping company.[4] Located within the City of San Diego's Foreign Trade Zone, where a very convoluted and complex designation allows companies to import and export goods through the zone without adhering to US Customs duties, the company employed a fairly simple supply chain. A US supplier provided basic materials for number cards, wall organizers, and other displays, which were shipped to Tecate where the materials were assembled into final products and then shipped back to the San Diego distribution center where teachers' orders were filled and sent for delivery. The industrial park was built with city and county tax dollars — through tax abatements, designation of foreign trade-zone status, and land cessions — to encourage distribution development.

When looking at the various provisions in NAFTA, one would think that an industry with so much governmental regulation would adhere to fair labor practices. However, the labor process operated contrary to wage and hour laws in particularly unethical ways that are increasingly endemic to temporary work. In the distribution center, work was organized according to the number of orders taken the previous day. Around the beginning of each school year or during the holiday season, a group of maybe five order pullers and five shippers filled in excess of 1,000 orders. For temporary workers, such as Mize, the variation often meant that in any given week it was not known how many days they would be offered work. Because work was dependent wholly on the number of orders received, the work day varied between four and 13 hours. In California, state law requires workers be paid overtime for any work performed beyond eight hours per day. The company "reinterpreted" this so that work in excess of 40 hours per week would be subject to overtime pay, but the number of hours worked per day in excess of eight hours would not be considered eligible for overtime. Hours were recorded with the temporary agency, so they too were aware of this illegal practice. Invariably, long days on Monday through Wednesday would mean that work would not be available for temporary workers on Thursday or Friday to ensure that they were never paid overtime for any week's worth of work.

The number of orders also dictated pace of work, so all warehouse employees, temporary and full-time, learned to pace themselves to stretch out a short order day to maximize hours worked. On the other hand, workers were not allowed to leave (the threat of not being asked to return was the main method used) until all orders had been filled. During the holiday season, fellow workers told Mize they were working until midnight and coming in at 6 a.m. the next day to fill orders. It must be remembered that no worker, temporary or full-time, was eligible for health or other fringe benefits and that the workers were paid barely above the California state mandated minimum wage of $5.75. Full-time employees were employed for only 35 hours per week so they would not be eligible for benefits, and the foreman was on salary so he could always manage a workforce without being eligible for overtime himself.

The previous year, in 1997, Mize harvested crops in the Central Valley of California as part of his dissertation research on the US-Mexico Bracero Program. He picked, packed, and loaded grapes to gain a better understanding of how agricultural work affected one, both physically and mentally. It is probably obvious that the physical effects of stoop labor are particularly harsh, but Mize was surprised at the degree of control placed on workers in terms of intimidation to control the work-flow. The crew boss and farm labor contractor are the two direct managers of agricultural laborers, and the organization of work is very much akin to the dark satanic mills that Marx (1976 [1867]) chronicled in "The Working Day" chapter of *Capital, Volume One*. Workers were controlled, according to Marx, by coercion, threats, and intimidation. Mize found that agribusiness labor was not markedly different in terms of social control (see Mize 2006, 2004). For example, when preparing grapes for transport, Mize made the mistake of using a broken pallet to start stacking grape boxes. The farm labor contractor in charge of the work crew used the occasion to berate all of the employees present, sparing no Spanish expletive, to ensure that his workers, or "*pendejos estúpidos*" (stupid jerks), would not make the same mistake again. To control the pace and accuracy of his bilingual workforce, the foremen gave tongue-lashings, demonstrating mastery of both English and Spanish expletives.

Mize found that the labor process of these distribution centers did not vary greatly from what he saw in the agricultural fields of the Central Valley. The labor process and sources of control were much the same to be sure, but the seasonal nature of employment was also very similar. The demand for workers fluctuated over time; harvest time in the fields was not only as busy as the fall rush at the educational supply house but also the holiday rush in other distribution centers in South San Diego that rely on temporary workers. A large battery corporation hired seasonal workers during the holiday rush so shoppers could be sure their presents would have batteries included. The difference between the fields and the distribution centers was the use of temporary agencies rather than the farm labor contractor. For instance, the full-time foreman at the battery distribution center was Filipino, so the vast majority of employees at the battery *maquila* were Tagalog speakers. The job foreman in the educational supply house was of Mexican origin (he grew up in the fields where his dad was a crew boss) and spoke English and Spanish. As a result, all of the temporary agency employees sent his way were either bilingual Latinos or monolingual Anglos.

In the educational supply company, the organization of work was gendered according to job task. The company's San Diego headquarters consisted of an office and a warehouse. The office contained all managers, secretaries, receptionists, and customer service representatives. The managers were all male. Their secretaries as well as receptionists, order takers, and customer service agents were female. In the warehouse, all of the workers were male. Two times a year, the full-time staff and a few of the temporary agency employees were required to work on a Saturday to conduct an inventory count in the Tecate *maquiladora*. The warehouse full-timers stated they had to do inventory twice a year due to their sexist and nationalist assumptions that female Mexican workers could not count. The inventory count shed light onto the possibilities and limits of cross-border unities and organizing. All of the full-time warehouse employees were either sons of Mexican immigrants or second-generation Mexican Americans. Most grew up in South San Diego, Chula Vista, or San Ysidro, which are cities less than five miles from the border. The perceptions of "*el otro lado*" (the other side) expressed by the predominately young, male Mexican Americans reinforced nearly every stereotype of Mexicans as dirty, lazy, or stupid and thus deserving of only $5 per day and easily controlled by employers.

Working in the US distribution centers often requires at most a high-school diploma or equivalent. Many counter-culture Chicano youth, derisively referred to as *vatos* or *cholos*, find few other employment options. Their working conditions are often extensions of inferior schooling conditions. Filling the bottom end of the labor market might encourage them to seek out counterparts to build alliances and resist those conditions. Yet, even in the same company that employed exploitative practices on both sides of the border, the Mexican American male distribution workers most often naturalized the differences between themselves and their Mexican female counterparts in terms of gendering relations (assembly is women's work), nationalizing working conditions (Mexicans deserve to work in substandard workplaces for little pay), and claiming a slice of superiority at the expense of those below them on the wage scale.

The question we pose is this: given these assumptions about their co-workers, how ready are Mexican American workers for a transborder, post-nationalist political project of economic equality, racial fairness, and non-nativist relations? In 1998, Mize was not particularly hopeful. The non-unionized labor force was clearly not in a place where they might be able to exert pressure from both sides of the border for better working conditions, work schedules that adhered to California law, and a cross-border solidarity that would bring together Mexican and Mexican American workers. In 2006, the entire picture changed with the immigrant rights movement so strongly and publicly calling for recognition of their contributions to the US economy. The groundswell of support for immigrants to come out of the shadows and claim their rights is undeniable. What protestors recognized is an economy that increasingly relies upon Mexican immigrant labor to service consumers' basic needs.

The story of the distribution *maquila* should serve as a reminder that Mexican solidarity is never to be assumed. It requires as much work to bring the people together in common cause as it does to keep them apart. Clearly, it is in the interests of *maquiladora* owners to have workers on both sides of the sister plants see their lives and collective fates as disconnected and to accentuate differences based on nation, gender, and other factors. A key lesson to be taken from the nationwide immigrant rights movement is that the possibilities for cross-border organizing and transnational mobilizations from below are not only necessary but fully realizable. In the next chapter, we will discuss the relevance of cross-border organizing in the context of the North American consumption of Mexican land and labor in Mexico.

Notes

1. See "Border region," http://www.borderhealth.org/border_region.php (accessed May 17, 2010).
2. See Arizona State Bill 1070, http://www.azleg.gov/legtext/49leg/2r/bills/sb1070s.pdf (accessed May 17, 2010).
3. This section is based on Mize's employment through temporary employment agencies. In San Diego, Mize was hired for about six months to work for municipal and private water companies, a *maquiladora* distribution center for

a K-12 educational supply company, and other one-day jobs that unfortunately escape his memory. Mize kept a fieldnotes journal on the work experiences in the distribution center and with the water companies.

4. In the last five years, industrial development along the US border has expanded tremendously. The Otay Mesa border crossing on I-905 (the easternmost checkpoint between Tijuana and San Diego) is now the busiest industrial land port of entry along the US-Mexico border, and several large distribution centers have located in the Foreign Trade Zone.

Chapter Ten

Mexican Labor in Mexico: The Impact of NAFTA from *Chiapas* to *Turismo*

In the face of NAFTA and the neoliberal policies that paved its way, popular responses and survival strategies have differed across geographic regions. In this chapter, we focus on the Zapatista uprising in Chiapas, cross-border indigenous organizing between the US and Oaxaca, and resistance to the infrastructure development of the Plan Puebla-Panamá as three examples of resistance to neoliberal restructuring.

With a Harvard education in government and political economy and an intimate knowledge of the Mexican political system, former Mexican president Carlos Salinas de Gortari was obsessed with modernizing Mexico's economy and bringing the country into the First World (Preston and Dillon 2004, 185). In 1988, he began pushing to implement neoliberal reforms that emphasized state withdrawal from the economic sphere and state facilitation of foreign investment and free trade (Levy and Bruhn 2001, 166). Salinas privatized state-owned corporations, liberalized trade, restructured government agencies, and promoted NAFTA. Under pressure from the World Bank to implement a structural adjustment loan, he removed agricultural credits and price supports, including supports for basic grains. At the same time, he devalued the peso, thereby raising prices of agricultural inputs—the seeds, fertilizers, and all other elements needed for farming. This meant food prices went up.

To further remove the state from the market, in 1989 the federal government dismantled the coffee marketing board, the *Instituto Mexicano del Café*. When the International Coffee Organization failed to fix production quotas in 1989, world coffee prices fell by 50 per cent (Stahler-Sholk 2000).[1] Seventy per cent of those affected were small producers who farmed less than two hectares and who suffered an average of 70 per cent drop in income. Thousands were caught in a cycle of debt and had to abandon production. "We had to practically give away our coffee because there was no price for it," said a farmer from the northern region of Chiapas (Harvey 1998, 177–78).

In 1992, Salinas's administration reformed Article 27 of the Constitution to modify the Agrarian Law and communal land or *ejido* structure. Since significant percentages of the land in Southern Mexico is *ejido* and communal property (Instituto de Geografía 1986), some feared these lands would be sold, privatized, or concentrated in a few hands, and rural communities could be destroyed. In Chiapas, *campesino* organizations mobilized mass protests and workshops to oppose the reforms (Harvey 1998, 189).

By 1997, the neoliberal model had replaced the Import Substitution Industrialization (ISI) mode of development. Since the 1940s, along with ISI, the Mexican development model had relied on rural farmers to produce cheap food that essentially subsidized the growth of urban industry, manufacturing, and services (Bartra 1985, 22). Under the neoliberal model, the state withdrew from supporting production for national markets but facilitated foreign investment, free trade, and production for global markets (Levy and Bruhn 2001, 166).

As the Mexican government shifted its allegiance to the global economy, the government's political and social role was eroded. To ameliorate NAFTA's effects, Salinas created social programs such as the national solidarity program, PRONASOL, and a direct rural subsidy program, PROCAMPO. PROCAMPO served mainly as a palliative to favor political allies because the payments found their way back to merchants and intermediaries (Harvey 1998, 183). These programs became known for their irrelevance. For example, many rural towns received basketball courts, an expenditure that clearly did not address their critical needs.

NAFTA and the Rural Crisis in Mexico

To prepare for NAFTA, the Mexican government decided to restructure the economy so as to neglect and thereby displace rural indigenous people. Yet Mexico's rural population and subsistence farmers continue to fill an important social need. The country's population shifted from 35 million inhabitants, half rural and half urban in 1960, to 24 million in rural areas and 75 million in cities in 2000. That means one-quarter of Mexicans live in towns of less than 2,500 inhabitants, and one-fifth of the economically active population works in agriculture or livestock. Today, nine out of ten Mexican farmers produce for self-consumption to varying extents. Four out of ten sell their surplus in the market or sell cash crops. However, farm incomes are extremely skewed. Of 4.5 million farms, 1.5 million are privately owned, and of these 15,000 large business owners earn 50 per cent of the value of agricultural production. The remaining 3 million are held in the "social sector" as *ejidos* or communal lands. Less than one-third can survive on their farm income, and more than one-half of these farmers earn most of their income from other sources (Bartra 2004, 22).

For Mexico's small rural farmers, NAFTA has been a death sentence. Since its ratification, agricultural products enter the country without tariffs.[2] As a result, agriculture has slid from 7.3 per cent of Mexico's GDP in 1992 to 5 per cent in 2004 (Bartra 2004, 22). Mexico's already suffering small farmers, rural workers, and peasants have suffered even more. Critics had warned that the US would dump cheap corn into the Mexican market, and indeed US corn exports to Mexico have increased eighteen-fold, according to the US Department of Agriculture (Weinberg 2004, 52). Imports of grain from the US increased by 73 per cent and 76 per cent for corn (Bartra 2004, 24). The crisis hit low- and medium-yield farmers in the south and central Mexican states, as well as high-tech farmers with high production costs in Sinaloa and other northern states. Peasant farmers in Chiapas suffered disproportionately because they produced more corn for national markets than any other state (Stahler-Sholk 2000).

Although prices for Mexican corn have dropped, farmers continue to produce it. In south-southeastern Mexico, "traditional" production has matched and even surpassed pre-NAFTA levels (Tepeyac 2002, 5). Why would farmers defy the law of supply and demand? First and foremost, they lack other options. Second, production may have grown due to increased yields. Third, corn is considered a safe crop; it is a staple used not only for food but in rituals, religious ceremonies, traditional nutrition, and healing. Finally, crops that could substitute for corn are also expensive (Henriques and Patel 2004, 5).

Even so, while the price of corn has fallen, the price of corn in the form of the tortilla has not decreased. In fact, it has increased 279 per cent (Henriques and Patel 2004, 6) for two reasons. First, tortilla prices were subsidized until 1996. After subsidies were cut, manufacturers transferred increased costs to consumers. Secondly, two large companies monopolize the tortilla market. GIMSA and MINSA account for 70 per cent and 27 per cent of the market respectively (Henriques and Patel 2004, 6). In spite of the increase in corn production in some parts of Mexico, concerns remain that low-cost imports and genetically modified corn will eventually displace Mexican farmers and replace local varieties.

Far from improving Mexico's economic situation, NAFTA prevented the government from safeguarding against speculation and threatened rural livelihoods, which caused the 1994 financial crisis.[3] While NAFTA has meant suffering for many Mexicans, neoliberal policies have generated diverse responses and survival strategies. In Chiapas, NAFTA was the last straw for small farmers and indigenous and displaced people. It served as an opportune moment for the emergence of the Zapatista movement, which had been building for more than 10 years. Many people had only recently begun to migrate from Chiapas to the US, but the coming of NAFTA accelerated migration from Oaxaca, especially among indigenous people. Migrants have found diverse ways to remain politically active in Oaxaca with cross-border organizing rooted in indigenous forms of organization and collective work.

Chiapas: The Zapatista Uprising

On New Year's Eve 1994, some Mexicans welcomed NAFTA, hoping it would mark Mexico's achievement of First World status. That night thousands of indigenous people emerged from the mountains and the Lacandon Jungle, wrested control over municipal governments in Chiapas, and declared war on the state's armed forces. They called themselves Zapatistas after 1910 revolutionary peasant leader Emiliano Zapata. Their first declaration, read at the San Cristóbal municipal palace, was "¡Basta ya!" — for indigenous people, 500 years of oppression "was enough!" The Zapatistas condemned NAFTA, denounced the reforms in Article 27 that opened *ejidos* to the market, and protested free market policies that ended price guarantees for corn, beans, and coffee. While the Zapatistas were by no means a serious long-term threat for civil stability, they threatened the ideological underpinnings that cemented the elite Mexican and North American alliance. They embodied the brutal effects of free trade in Mexico, bringing to light those neglected and excluded from the global economy that elites preferred to forget.

The Mexican Armed Forces responded to the uprising with brutal attacks on indigenous communities in Chiapas. In turn, the Zapatistas spread their demands. Accounts of the repression on Internet lists run by networks of human rights organizations challenged the media blackout that colluded with the country's free-trading elites. By January 10, the Mexican stock market had plunged. Demonstrators throughout the country and around the world denounced the government repression.

In 1995, a Chase Manhattan Bank report called for the Mexican government to "eliminate the Zapatistas" (Roett 1995). In February, the army invaded Zapatista-controlled areas, moving 60,000 troops to Chiapas and displacing 20,000 *campesinos*. In December 1995 the government was forced to default on its loan payments to the International Monetary Fund. The Mexican peso fell to half its value. The Fund's US$50 billion bailout for speculators did not reverse the crisis for workers. By spring 1995, the army began counter-insurgency warfare to isolate the insurgents, and the state government began funding paramilitary groups. The *Ejército Zapatista de Liberación Nacional* (Zapatista Army of National Liberation, or EZLN) and the government signed the San Andrés Accords, agreeing to a program of land reform, indigenous autonomy, and cultural rights. But the talks failed by August because government representatives refused to consider the Zapatista proposals and had no acceptable alternatives to offer. The Zapatistas called for international observers to discuss and organize caravans, peace camps, referenda, meetings, and election observations.

While NAFTA proponents may not have intended to kill indigenous people, military and paramilitary strategies after the uprising have been deadly. Forty-five Zapatista supporters were massacred in the community of Acteal on December 22, 1997, as they prayed and fasted for peace. Rape and threats of rape have been used to control indigenous women who make up an estimated 30 per cent of the insurgents (Stephen 2000, 835). The EZLN, the Catholic diocese, networks of women's and *campesino* organizations, and concerned citizens continued organizing for peace and human rights.

In spite of the government's military strategy, the Zapatista insurgents have inspired independent organizations to support their demands, including non-governmental and grassroots organizations rooted in liberation theology, women's organizing, indigenous and small farmers' issues, development, and human rights organizations. The Zapatistas' call to "create a world where many worlds fit" and their proposal of autonomy to resist neoliberalism resonate with civil society and inspire organizing far beyond Mexico. The Zapatistas explicitly began to form national and international networks with the "Intergalactic Encounter" held in the

Lacandon Jungle in July 1996. The emergence of the EZLN reactivated Chicano Movement veterans (Zepeda 2006), as well as solidarity networks that had in the past supported the Cuban, Salvadoran, and Nicaraguan revolutions (Leyva-Solano and Sonnleitner 2000). The networks' goals were to oppose neoliberalism, create new modes of solidarity, and advance new politics of building autonomy in their localities.

In August 2003, the Zapatistas took a new step toward deeper autonomy from the Mexican state by creating the *Juntas de Buen Gobierno* (JBGs, or Good Government Councils). The JBGs deepen grassroots democracy and build autonomous governance by teaching new leaders through rotating leadership, mediating between Zapatista communities and civil society, creating local justice tribunals, and building culturally appropriate autonomous schools (Speed and Forbis 2005). The JBGs assert the right to make decisions about their territory and about economic and environmental policies. They resist "neoliberal laws" that threaten to privatize natural resources (Harvey 2005b). Continuing with the posture established earlier by the Zapatista communities, JBGs reject government programs and services and struggle to sustain themselves economically. They support health care, education, and organic agriculture with networks of *promotores*, or community workers. Many communities combine subsistence farming and cooperative production with barter for other goods. In 2005, the EZLN issued the Sixth Declaration of the Lacandon Jungle, articulating a more direct anti-capitalist position and calling for sympathizers to join them in working for political and economic transformation (Harvey 2005a). With the "Other Campaign," they traveled around the country holding discussions and popular education workshops to build networks of sympathizers who share their program of identifying alternatives to neoliberalism. Even with networks of supporters, the Zapatista communities' survival is precarious. Extreme poverty, marginalization, and state and paramilitary violence push some to give up autonomy and accept government programs, or even to migrate for work.

Oaxaca, Migration, and Cross-Border Indigenous Organizations

Migrants from Mexico have come to the US for well over 100 years. For most of that century, central-western Mexico was the home for most. Traditional sending states included Zacatecas, Jalisco, Guanajuato, Durango, and Michoacán. In smaller numbers, indigenous Mixtecs and Zapotecs from Oaxaca have migrated within Mexico and to the US from 1942–64 during the Bracero Program (Escala-Rabadán, Rivera-Salgado, and Rodriguez 2006). Many remote communities were incorporated by the mid-1950s. In the 1980s, migration patterns changed significantly when migrants from the traditional states of origin were joined by states farther south, including Puebla, Guerrero, Oaxaca, and most recently Chiapas.

After NAFTA, up to 2 million Mexican farmers have migrated to the slums of Mexico City, other cities in Mexico, or the US. Legal immigration to the US increased by 55 per cent under NAFTA, and illegal immigration is thought to have increased by a similar proportion (Weinberg 2004, 52). "NAFTA has forced a lot of small farmers out of rural southern Mexico.... They can no longer survive," said Schell, an attorney with the Farmworkers Justice Project (Rivera-Lyles 2004). The terrible drop in coffee prices has forced many people to leave the Mixteca region in Oaxaca, the sierra of Guerrero, the Soconusco in Chiapas, and Central Veracruz. In this section, we will focus on NAFTA's impacts on migration from Oaxaca.

Even before NAFTA, there was significant migration from the state of Oaxaca. During the first half of the twentieth century, many Oaxacans migrated within Mexico for seasonal, wage, or contract labor. Many remained within the central and southern regions of the country. Factors favoring internal migration included agricultural policy that favored irrigation directed to large-scale operations rather than smaller farms, price controls on corn that reduced its market value from the late 1950s to the early 1970s, and job opportunities in Mexican cities (Cohen 2001).

Until the 1970s, Oaxacans were a relatively small percentage of migrants to the US, comprising 0.6 to 1 per cent of the total migrant population in California (Koch 1989). However, by the late 1980s, 8.2 per cent of migrants were from new regions farther south, including Oaxaca, Guerrero, Puebla, and Morelos (Bustamante *et al.* 1998). In the 1980s, it was estimated that some 80 per cent of Oaxaca's municipalities were sending migrants to Mexico City and the US (Embriz 1993). Many intended to stay away for short periods and migrated cyclically for work, yet the increasing border controls made circular migration much more difficult.

The experiences of a rural Oaxacan village called Santa Ana suggests that migration occurs in stages, and decisions about migration are made by households in the context of changing domestic structures and community participation. Communities like Santa Ana may lose business and political leaders as people migrate. They may become dependent upon income from goods and services rather than investing money in their own economic development (Cohen 2001). Alternatively, some migrants maintain political participation in their home communities and contribute significantly.

Many of the migrants from Southern Mexico are indigenous, and some have begun to create binational, community-based indigenous organizations. These differ from the HTAs that we referred to in Chapter 4 that were developed by mainly mestizo migrants from west-central Mexico (Jalisco, Michoacán, Guanajuato, and Zacatecas) (Rivera-Salgado 1999). In comparison, HTAs are at times less politicized, less formal, and often intended to finance public works projects. The cross-border indigenous organizations, on the other hand, focus on social and political justice in their Oaxacan home communities and in communities of residence in the US.

In 1991, the *Frente Indígena de Organizaciones Binacionales* (FIOB or the Binational Front of Indigenous Organizations), a coalition of HTAs, joined forces for the first time as "indigenous peoples." They brought together the *Tlacotepense* Civic Committee and six Californian associations of Zapotec and Mixtec migrants: *Comité Cívico Popular Mixteco, Organización de Pueblo Explotado y Oprimido, Comité Tlacolulense en Los Angeles, Organización Pro-Ayuda a Macuiltianguis, Asociación Cívica Benito Juárez,* and *Organización Regional de Oaxaca*. The Zapotec migrants' *Organización Regional Oaxaqueña* organized the July festival of *Guelaguetza*, an indigenous cultural celebration, in Los Angeles. The FIOB organized to coordinate the transnational protest campaign that commemorated Five Centuries of Resistance with protests of the celebrations of the discovery/conquest of America.

What is new about these organizations is that migrants maintain political participation in their communities of origin, and the economic development projects they promote engage both the people who migrate and those who remain. Their political participation is rooted in a strong identification with home communities, and they adapt indigenous forms of organization and political participation to their new contexts as migrants. These include leadership by popular assembly and collective volunteer work or *tequio*. Adapting traditional forms to the migrant context depends on the community's autonomy (Rivera-Salgado 1999). The efforts of migrants, both in the US and in Mexico, as a recent article in *La Jornada* noted, mean that Mexicans and other immigrants in the US are leading what could be described as a "democratizing movement in the country that loves to describe itself as the biggest democracy in the world" (Cason and Brooks 2002).

Impacts of NAFTA on Urban Areas

The impact of NAFTA on urban Mexico was similarly harsh for urban dwellers and went well beyond the pressures of rural-to-urban migration from a displaced countryside. The monster that is NAFTA relies on an economic logic that pits nation against nation in selling their citizens' labor to the lowest bidder. In the race to the bottom, lesser-developed nations compete for fewer and fewer manufacturing and assembly opportunities provided by TNCs.

The industrial triangle of Mexico (Mexico City, Guadalajara, and Monterrey) developed primarily to provide exports for US consumers. All Mexican industries have undergone bouts of serious competition with other nations of the Pacific Rim, but nowhere are the effects more clearly felt than in Mexico's textile industry.

As late as 2000, Mexico was the largest exporter of apparel to the US (Gereffi 2005). Table 10.1 demonstrates how global competition over the past five years has dramatically reduced the value of exports from Mexico to the US. As China entered into the World Trade Organization, with relative wages that are almost one-fifth the value of Mexican minimum wages, the result has been an off-shoring of multinational apparel companies from relatively high-wage nations like Mexico to even cheaper wage structures operating in China and Southeast Asia. The value of Mexico's exported apparel has shrunk from 13.6 per cent of the total exports to 9.6 per cent over the last five years. At the same time, the industry has gone from an $8.7 billion industry to a $7 billion industry while China now accounts for nearly 30 per cent of US apparel exports and was on track to clear $20 billion in 2000.

Mexico's development project is in serious jeopardy, and the dreams of NAFTA-supported industrial parks and "Textile Cities" are becoming nightmares. The industrial park located near Mexico City in Heujotzingo was dubbed "Textile City" as the Fox administration supported the state government of Puebla in assisting an investment group on a major infrastructure project there. Yet, before plants could even be built, most of the investors had backed out in the face of global competition for textile jobs. "Since 2000, Mexico has shed more than a quarter of a million industry jobs, nearly one-third of its textile and apparel employment" (Dickerson 2005). In Puebla, a textile capital of production since the 1800s, the lack of urban opportunities and the economic restructuring of the rural agrarian society have led to a major influx of Poblano immigrants to New York (Pfeffer and Parra 2004; Smith 2006b; see also Chapter 8 in this book).

Table 10.1: *Mexico and China Apparel Exports to the US, 2000–05*

	Export Value (US $mil)		% of Total	
Year	Mexico	China	Mexico	China
2000	8,731	8,486	13.6	13.2
2001	8,128	8,866	12.7	13.9
2002	7,733	9,565	12.1	15.0
2003	7,199	11,381	10.6	16.7
2004	6,945	13,607	9.6	18.8
2005	3,776	11,660	9.6	29.6

Source: Adapted from Gereffi 2005, 18.

Marginality and the "Informal Sector"

Structural adjustment has been particularly hard on the poor (Beneria 1996). Cities concentrated wealth *and* poverty (Vite Pérez and Martínez 2001) so that those who were excluded from the system of production and consumption became increasingly confined to ghettos where they did low-wage or informal work. What have been the effects of neoliberal social policies on the poorest of the poor? In this section, we examine the history of urban marginality in Mexico and highlight policies of macro-economics, labor, social programs, and land that have exacerbated conditions for the urban poor.

Closings of some of the less productive industries meant at least 800,000 workers were laid off throughout the 1980s (Hellman 1999, 8). At the same time, wages for those who still had jobs sank miserably. Between 1980 and 1991, real manufacturing wages fell by 23 per cent in Mexico, and the value of the minimum wage fell by 57 per cent in Mexico City (Gilbert 1994, 73). Meanwhile, the distribution of income inequality widened considerably. By 1986, nearly two-thirds of urban households earned less than the official minimum wage, and even official unemployment statistics showed that joblessness had doubled (Hellman 1997, 3).

Economic adjustment, culminating in NAFTA, has exacerbated urban poverty and exclusion that may lead to mobilization and organizing for change. From 1982 to 1986, official and real wages fell, and those who could not find formal jobs engaged in informal labor. Throughout the

1980s, real wages deteriorated, and unemployment rose (González de la Rocha 2006, 77–78).

Since NAFTA, even with economic growth (as measured by GDP), jobs have not grown as promised. From mid-1999 to mid-2000, although the GDP grew by 7.61 per cent, there was a net loss of jobs. Further, most existing jobs (61.6 per cent) have no benefits. In 1993, 36.9 per cent of formal waged workers did not receive the benefits required by law, such as social security, an extra end-of-the-year payment, or vacation. In 2000, this percentage rose to 39.4 per cent. The absolute number of workers earning less than the legal minimum wage increased. Furthermore, the national average minimum wage lost nearly one-quarter of its purchasing power (22.93 per cent) from 1994 to 2000 (Arroyo-Picard 2003, 74–77).

Corroborating political-economic evidence, ethnographers show that NAFTA's effects have been to exacerbate conditions for the poor in Mexico. In *Across the Wire* (1993) and *By the Lake of Sleeping Children* (1996), journalist Luis Alberto Urrea portrays the lives of the *olvidados*, or forgotten ones, garbage pickers in the Tijuana dump, who survive on refuse. He describes their crushing poverty, desperation, insanity, violence, and squalor. The title of the book *By the Lake of Sleeping Children* refers to the "cemetery" for all those who do not survive, many of whom do not reach adulthood. The push for free trade and anti-immigration legislation, e.g., NAFTA and Proposition 187, underlies the increasing horrors in the border region where orphans and dump dwellers eke out their survival amid missionaries, tourists, and coyotes.

In *Mexican Lives* (1999), Judith Hellman interviewed 60 people between 1990 and 1993 about how economic changes had affected their daily lives. She identified people who took part in collective strategies to resolve their economic problems as well as those who just relied on themselves and their families. The 15 profiles in her book show the diversity of the impacts of the economic changes on a range of people, from the very wealthy to the very poor. Even for those with more stable employment, economic changes obligated many to work longer hours. For schoolteachers, the "triple shift" became the standard workday. Teachers would work for six hours in one school in the morning, race across town to another school for a second shift, and then to a third job at night (Hellman 1997). Adelita, who worked for six years in the *maquiladoras*, explained, "when I was sewing all day, my back ached, my kidneys ached, and my feet swelled up for lack of circulation" (Hellman 1999, 165). She came to Tijuana to escape a violent, alcoholic husband and began crossing the border daily without legal papers to clean houses in San Diego. In Tijuana, the *colonia* where she lived was on a hillside that lacked water, electricity, paved roads, and sewer pipes. In the rainy season, the stream spread human waste and chemicals into the streets (Hellman 1999, 163).

Peña (1997) counters the incredibly pessimistic picture of the life that Mexican citizens face on a daily basis by demonstrating how a shared social space in the informal sector can provide the basis for solidarity building and organizing. Focusing on the trash dumps of Cuidad Juárez, Peña interviews the *pependores*, or informal trash recyclers, who have banded together to better their abysmal living conditions in sustainable ways.

Economic pressures intensify the struggle for survival. Rural crisis intensifies pressures on urban areas. NAFTA's promise to improve conditions for Mexicans has proven untenable. Rather, neoliberal policies concentrate wealth *and* poverty in cities, while impoverishing the countryside. Corn imports from the US make it harder for Mexican farmers to survive in farming. Yet the promise of jobs in the *maquiladora* sector is deceptive. As we saw in Chapter 9, *maquiladoras* exploit laborers, using gender and sexuality to divide them. Brutal labor exploitation, violence, and desperation characterize border cities, squatter settlements, and "irregular" barrios. Even workers with formal jobs feel pressure to work harder and longer hours, most often without benefits.

The Plan Puebla-Panamá: A New Infrastructure Plan for the Twenty-First Century

In 2001, the Fox government channeled its concerns about poverty into an ambitious, $20 billion development plan, known as the Plan Puebla-Panamá (PPP), to attract public investment to the most marginalized areas of Southern Mexico. With support from the Inter-American Development Bank (IDB), and with Central American business and government leaders, this large-scale infrastructure and industrial development program proposed poverty alleviation, human development, ecological protection, and tourism projects from central Mexico to Panamá. In spite of the PPP's rhetoric, preliminary budget information suggests that 90 per cent of its funding will go toward transportation and energy interconnection (Call 2002).

The PPP authors are conscious that the proposal requires a massive displacement of people from rural areas in the region (Castro-Soto 2001). In their language, such population movement is an "opportunity" to "concentrate population in urban nodes" (Presedencia de la República 2001).

According to the Mexican National Population Council, between 2000 and 2025 the population of south-southeastern Mexico might grow by 25 per cent, almost 7 million more than the current population, to reach a total of 34.4 million. In that same time period, rural populations of the south-southeast region could be reduced to only 2 million inhabitants. Currently, there are approximately 27.5 million people in the region, 58.7 per cent of which is urban (Banco Interamericano de Desarollo 2002). If what its authors project holds true, the PPP would require the gradual displacement, over the next two decades, of 9.3 million people from rural areas in this region. Such an exodus would occur through urbanization and migration. The PPP projects that the states of Veracruz, Chiapas, and Oaxaca would have the greatest reduction in rural populations (Castro-Soto 2001).

If 2 million people could be displaced as a result of NAFTA (Harvey 1998, 181), the PPP threatens to accelerate the displacement of the remaining maize and bean producers, *ejidatarios*, and *comuneros* to other forms of livelihood. In combination, NAFTA and the PPP are forcing many people in Southern Mexico to migrate, either within Mexico or to the US, and to convert from rural to urban lifestyles. For many indigenous peoples, this is not a simple change of profession, but a cultural transformation, and one that is not often without trauma.[4]

Citizen resistance has derailed several PPP initiatives (Call 2003; Pickard 2003). The budget for the PPP has been cut, and IDB officials have expressed concerns about the Mexican government's commitment (Call 2003). Since China joined the World Trade Organization, 600 *maquiludoras* have left Mexico for better opportunities in Asia, deflating the plans for a free trade zone. From June 2001 to June 2002, 250,000 workers were left without jobs (Pickard 2003). Policy-makers may attempt to implement the same policies with less publicity so as to provoke less public controversy.

Tourism in Mexico

The various types of tourist destinations in Mexico reveal the centrality of Mexican workers in providing the labor, spaces, and resources for US tourist gazes, performances, and consumption. Néstor García Canclini (1995) situates the role of tourist consumption within the hybrid cultural realm of museum displays and US tourist conspicuous consumption practices in Tijuana. But border towns and archeological sites represent just two of several forms that Mexican tourist destinations assume. The images that are often invoked when North Americans think of Mexico as a tourist destination range from Club Med to border town, from urban Mexico City to pre-Columbian pyramids. We identify the following types of tourist destinations that have come to predominate in Mexican tourism: 1) beach resorts, 2) border towns, 3) urban attractions, and 4) archeological sites. By far beach resorts are the largest draw for international tourists.

Tourist Consumption

In Mexico, tourism is the third largest source of foreign income, behind oil revenues and remittances. At the point of interaction between tourists and hospitality employees, the exploitation of Mexican land and labor for US consumption becomes most apparent. "It must be remembered that the US is Mexico's main international market for tourism services, providing 87 per cent of all international tourists which penetrate beyond the border zone and practically all of those who stay within the border strip" (OECD 2001, 19). We view tourist gazes and performances as embedded in social relations that require usurpation of land and labor, which leads to the displacement and exploitation of those who live in tourist destinations (Swords and Mize 2008).

Aspects of Tourism in Mexico as a % of GDP, 1993–98

Transport services	29.2
Restaurants and bars	24.8
Hotels and lodging	12.7
Commerce	12.3
Handicrafts	11.4
Miscellaneous	9.6

Source: OECD 2001.

Beach Resorts

In many ways, the development focus shift to tourism is evidenced by the new beach destinations that are most often frequented by tourists. In the 1970s, Acapulco was the favored destination for both air travelers and cruise ship passengers. The 1980s saw Puerto Vallarta assume predominance, and currently Cancún and Los Cabos cater to resort or ecotourist sensibilities, respectively. As the Pacific-side hotels age and the Caribbean becomes the choice of cruise ship companies, the Gulf Coast of Mexico has taken the lead. Currently envisioned by the Mexican government as a *megaproyecto*, or megaproject, the resort cities of Cancún and Playa del Carmen, the state of Quintana Roo, and the Yucatán peninsula are currently being slotted as the major growth areas for tourism development. Gladstone identifies positive and negative outcomes of tourism to the Third World, but it is difficult to see how the positive aspects can possibly outweigh the negatives. "Throughout the Third World, in both rural and urban areas, local residents are displaced by land grabbers, real estate speculators, state authorities, and others involved in the provisioning of international tourist space" (Gladstone 2005, 53–54).

Nearly one-third of current international tourists to Mexico are choosing the Cancún and Playa del Carmen beach resorts as their destination. As a result, local communities are increasingly displaced by large resort projects, and local employment options are severely limited to the worst-paying, most degrading jobs because higher-wage, higher-status jobs require a facility with English, computer experience, higher levels of education often requiring college degrees, and customer service experience. As real estate speculators make land too expensive for locals to afford, government-supported infrastructure initiatives leave poor communities either behind walls of shame or entirely displaced from the region. Land is privatized and commodified for the purposes of US tourist consumption. Those most negatively impacted are the most marginal communities. When considering international tourism to Mexico, the Organization for Economic Co-operation and Development (OECD) finds that:

> Cancún receives 22 per cent of arrivals, and if one adds neighboring Playa del Carmen the figure goes up to more than 30 per cent.... The following four most important destinations in this respect (Puerto Vallarta, Acapulco, Los Cabos, and Cozumel) account for a further 25 per cent of international arrivals, so that over three-quarters of arrivals are concentrated in seven destinations, six of which are beach destinations. (OECD 2001, 21)

It is the generally accepted hospitality staples of food, lodging, and transport that comprise the major drivers of the Mexican tourism economy. "Restaurant and hotel workers in the Mexican resort of Cancún also express misgivings about serving tourists from the US, with one hotel worker asserting, 'The gringos expect to be treated like kings and queens when they travel to Mexico on vacation, but we are not their subjects'" (Gladstone 2005, 77). The Gulf Coast destinations are the largest single destination draw; increasingly, the preferred Pacific beach resorts of 20 years ago are being reduced from upscale beach resorts to party towns.

Border Towns

The Mexican border towns have always seemed to typify this party orientation in the eyes of US consumers. Hollywood movies such as Peter Bogdanovich's *The Last Picture Show, Fandango* (starring Kevin Costner), and *Losin' It* (starring Tom Cruise) very crassly capture US views of Mexican border towns. Though the plots and timeframes may differ, the basic premise of Hollywood border town movies goes like this: the search for a "good time" impels young White American boys to the border. Their hedonism often leads to drunken bar fights that disrupt their main purpose, which is to lose their virginity in bordellos. Problems arise when clashes with *la policía* result in jail time, bribery, or trickery. Tension arises as the boys try to get back over the border; having learned their lesson, they are ready again to pay heed to US norms of delayed gratification, Protestant work ethic, and "civilized" behavior.[5] What they see in the main streets of border towns is often a façade:

> In reality [the zebras on Avenida Revolución] they are painted burros. They are there so that North American tourists can be photographed with a landscape behind them in which images from various regions of Mexico are crowded together: volcanoes, Aztec figures, cacti, the eagle with the serpent. "Faced with the lack of other types of things, as there are in the south where there are pyramids, there is none of that here…as if something had to be invented for the gringos," [said one Tijuana resident in an interview]. (Garciá Canclini 1995, 236)

The border towns, beyond their media representations, are created to facilitate tourist consumption. They become the way stations for cheap pharmaceuticals, handicrafts available at the lowest bartered rate, and in general every type of "cheap stuff" that US dollars can buy.

Urban Destinations

The third type of Mexican tourist locale is the urban destinations, which display the colonial and indigenous past. The major metropolitan areas of

Guadalajara, Queretaro, Monterrey, and San Luis Potosí have captured a small share of North American tourist attention by packaging their cities primarily as relics of the past: ornate colonial buildings that housed Spanish soldiers and bureaucrats, stunning Catholic cathedrals on plazas built on both the backs and homelands of indigenous laborers, and museums designed to sanitize the ugly past of Spanish colonial conquest and indigenous subjugation.

This is never clearer than in the nation's capital, Mexico City. Its central plaza (*El Zócalo*) contains the national cathedral, the most extravagant colonial buildings, national museums, and the pre-Columbian ruins of *El Templo Mayor* that was destroyed and built over by the Spanish to ensure that Mexican beliefs in Tenochtitlán would be supplanted by the authority of the Catholic Church. Construction crews uncovered the temple ruins in 1978 and in the process unearthed much of what Spanish conquistadors, soldiers, friars, priests, and bureaucrats had attempted to bury for the last 500 years. In the heart of Mexico City, the tourist can connect to both the indigenous and colonial past with a prime view of the temple from the cathedral.

Archeological Sites

The creation of an indigenous past for contemporary tourist consumption is most directly evidenced at the various pre-Columbian cities that are a major draw for tourists: *El Templo Mayor* (Aztec), Teotihuacán (Toltec), and Chichén Itzá (Mayan and Toltec). Much of the archeological history is on display in the National Museum of Anthropology in Mexico City. Garciá Canclini (1995, 120) notes that "… [w]ithout neglecting aesthetic veneration, [the National Museum] resorts to the *monumentalization and nationalist ritualization* of culture" (emphasis in the original). The sense of Mexican national culture is invented in this tourist destination, designed more for Mexican citizens than travelers to instill an idea of what it means to be Mexican and to represent the historical origins of the Mexican people in a particular way.

The long-term and irrevocable destruction that hordes of tourists inflict on relics of the past are currently being weighed against the short-term monetary rewards that correspond with greater numbers of tourists visiting archeological sites. From the Great Wall of China to the Great Pyramids of Giza, officials are closing off portions of the sites to tourists because of the destruction wrought by the sheer numbers of visitors. At this point,

Mexico's archeological sites have no long-term survival plan. Rather, they are geared toward short-term economic benefits. Thus tourism is linked to destruction in a myriad of social, cultural, and ecological ways.

Ecotourism

The latest trend in what is often self-referentially defined as environmentally friendly tourist practices is called "ecotourism," which posits that international travel should be sustainable and part of a larger purpose of experiential education. This form of tourism is fraught with contradictions, but it is becoming increasingly attractive to both tourists and the large hotel chain industries. "Ecotourism is a sustainable form of natural resource-based tourism that focuses primarily on experiencing and learning about nature, and which is ethically managed to be low-impact, non-consumptive, and locally oriented (control, benefits, and scale). It typically occurs in natural areas, and should contribute to the conservation or preservation of such areas" (Fennell 1999, 43).

The reality of tourist consumption means that the more popular ecotourism is, the less sustainable and increasingly high impact it becomes. Currently, two of the more popular ecotourist destinations are the whale-watching excursions in the Baja Peninsula of Northwestern Mexico and the rainforest safaris in the southern Yucatán Peninsula. Both governmental agencies and NGOs have established "biospheres" to capitalize on protected natural lands in order to market them as eco-friendly. The Sea of Cortés Biosphere, Sian Ka'an Biosphere, Baja California Peninsula, Chihuahua's Copper Canyon, and the six national parks in Chiapas are the main destinations for tourists who maintain their travels should be sustainable. These ecotourist regions are often next to indigenous communities, where the well-intentioned "post-tourist" appears to deny the usual tourist demand for natives to "play Indian." But eco-tourist consumption practices may not be much different from mass tourism in terms of the roles that indigenous people are expected to play as they perform for the tourist gaze. Given the long history of European colonialism, any form of Northern tourism to Southern destinations cannot escape the sense that Northerners are consuming the Southern Other.

Data compiled by the OECD show that ecotourism is not a major contributor to the tourism economy. The selling of goods (souvenirs and handicrafts) actually keeps pace with lodging services. "The share of tourism in total GDP was 8.9% in 2000 according to preliminary figures, up from 8.1% in 1993.... More than half of the gross value added of hotels and restaurants (51.4%) is explained by tourism demand, as is 28.6% of transport activities and 18.6% of all leisure activities" (OECD 2001, 2).

Mexico is the eighth most popular worldwide destination as measured by the number of international tourist arrivals, but it does not rank in the top ten in terms of tourism income. For the sake of comparison, let us look at tourism in Mexico and Canada in 2004. That year, Mexico had over 20 million international tourists, and those visitors spent $10.7 billion during their travel. Canada had fewer visitors (19 million) but generated more dollars ($12.8 billion). Thus, the cheaper cost of visiting Mexico means that more tourists generate fewer dollars in Mexico than in Canada. Clearly, tourist destinations, including beach resorts, border towns, urban attractions, and archeological sites, are places in which elites accumulate wealth as tourists consume Mexican labor and resources.

Conclusion

Rather than modernizing Mexico, the neoliberal policies of the 1990s have made survival difficult for *campesinos* and indigenous people and have also exacerbated conditions for the urban poor and for those who migrate to Mexican cities. Social assistance programs, such as PRONASOL and PROGRESA (the Education, Health, and Nutrition Program), target the extremely poor, but to the extent they pacify those hit by economic adjustments, they reduce the likelihood of organizing for economic rights. The "regularization" of urban settlements can also serve as a tool for demobilizing urban movements. Even so, collective survival strategies persist.

In Southern Mexico, we see a contrast between Oaxacans, who were already involved in transnational migration, and Chiapans, who only recently have begun to migrate outside of Mexico in large numbers. In both cases, people migrate and resist policies that threaten their livelihoods and collective cultural existence by working to exercise political and economic rights. The Zapatistas challenge free trade policies, declaring rights to inclusion and autonomy. Indigenous Oaxacans take part in cross-border forms of organizing, pushing for social and political changes in their hometowns and in the US.

The PPP proposes displacing hundreds of thousands, if not millions, of rural people from Southern Mexico, either to urban areas in Mexico or to the

US. This plan too provokes resistance and has generated networked organizing around development alternatives that focus on collective rights to territory and resources. Tourist development paints an image of Mexico as paradise, which belies the privatization and commodification of Mexican land and the exploitation of already vulnerable communities for consumption by tourists. As neoliberal policies facilitate wealth accumulation by dispossessing and exploiting Mexicans, people resist and propose alternative forms of development.

By taking a hemispheric perspective, this chapter shows that US consumption drives the exploitation of land and labor, even outside US territory. Further, this chapter requires a new perspective in our inquiry about the experiences of Mexican workers in the US. That is, we must ask how we can expect Mexicans *not* to migrate when lawmakers and industries in both Mexico and the US promote displacement of rural workers, promote tourism and *maquiladoras*, and neglect the needs of poor and indigenous peoples.

Notes

1. Opposition from the Reagan administration forced the collapse of the International Coffee Agreement, a pact between coffee producing and consuming nations that guaranteed relatively high prices (Collier 2001).
2. Tariffs on corn, beans, and powdered milk were phased out over ten years (Bartra 2004).
3. NAFTA's Article 1109 demands that all payments transferred between the countries be made "in an unrestricted manner and without delay." This prohibits regulation on capital flight. Article 2104 permits restrictions on transfers when there are serious difficulties in managing the balance of payments but stipulates that these restrictions be linked to International Monetary Fund provisions (Arroyo-Picard 2003).
4. Within *ejidos* and communal lands, displacement and migration affect different people differently. Some communities affected by highway projects are involved in land conflicts, which may affect decision-making and possible compensations for their lands (Tepeyac 2002). Women are targeted as labor for *maquiladoras,* in which working conditions and labor rights have not been consistently respected (Tepeyac 2002, 16). Migration is experienced differently by those who migrate and those who stay behind, including men, women, the elderly, young people, and indigenous peoples.

5. The main exceptions to this genre of border representations are Gregory Nava's *El Norte* and Richard "Cheech" Marin's *Born in East L.A.* Nava dramatizes the difficulties of border crossings and the precarious nature of undocumented immigration. But it is Marin's comedy that directly takes on Hollywood representations and subverts them by presenting an elderly White couple in an RV as drug smugglers, the Tijuana residents as real people with lives outside of the tourist industry rather than objects to be consumed, and border crossing as an act of transgression against a racist *migra* (Border Patrol) and US public.

Chapter Eleven

Mexican Labor in Canada: From Temporary Workers to Precarious Labor

When anthropologist Catherine Colby interviewed an Oaxacan man working on a tobacco farm in Southern Ontario, he shared the effects of a tractor accident he had during a working day: "My side hurt for weeks. I thought I broke some ribs. My boss told me to take a day in bed. So I worked again, even though I was hurt. I didn't want to cause problems because I need to come back next year. I have five children at home" (Colby 1997, 6). Reminiscent of the stories told by former workers of the US-Mexico Bracero Program (discussed in Chapter 1), the untreated injury was a direct result of the temporary labor system. Workers are often powerless to protect their own bodies in the face of a web of labor controls that force the calculus of complacency, desperation, and acquiescence to trump personal safety and caring for one's health.

When NAFTA was ratified in 1994, it facilitated the unencumbered flow of goods and capital by building upon existing corporate and financial linkages among firms in the US, Mexico, and Canada. Never mentioned in the final accord was the issue of the flow of labor among the three nations. The hemispheric erasure of borders—at least for markets, commodities, and corporations—seemed to cease when it came to labor migration. Rather, increased enforcement along both the US-Mexico and US-Canada borders clearly marked nationalist convergence in the post-NAFTA era. The difficulty of crossing and the limited extensions of citizenship have created a huge undocumented migration issue in the US and a taxing of the legal mechanisms for securing entry and permanent residence in Canada, as evidenced by expanding temporary worker programs and increased refugee asylum claims and denials (see García 2006, 154–55).

Mexican Migration to Canada in the NAFTA Era

Compared to the US, the number of Mexican immigrants who move and settle in Canada is minor in terms of absolute numbers as well as percentage of the total Canadian population. Referring to Mexican immigrants, "Canadian immigrant admissions numbered 15,567, or only 1.6 per cent of total legal admissions.... This compares with 11,446 in FY 2003" (Davy and Meyers 2005). In addition to their small numbers, Mexicans in Canada are neither concentrated spatially and occupationally, nor are they excluded from citizenship. As Goldring (1998) notes:

> Mexican immigrants represent a small proportion of immigrants in Canada (less than half a per cent); they have a relatively short history of migration to Canada; they tend to come from middle-and upper-middle class backgrounds; they do not live in segregated or concentrated enclaves; and the majority come as legal immigrants.

Goldring identifies four major groups of Mexican immigrants residing in Canada: middle- to upper-class professionals seeking advancement or promotion opportunities, middle-class immigrants with college degrees or technical training, Mennonites who are historically connected to both nations, and holiday spouses. The first two groups are eligible for citizenship as economic class entrants because of the particular skills or specialized knowledge they bring to Canada. The major difference between them is social class and linguistic proficiency in French and English, but they share a sense of Canada offering better opportunities for themselves and their children.

The Mexican Mennonite migration is most often a return migration to Mennonite communities in Southern Ontario in response to economic difficulties precipitated by severe drought in Chihuahua and Durango. The original southward migration was in response to offers by Mexican President Alvaro Obregón in 1922 that land would be sold to the religious community, who would be allowed to retain its customs and practices — something increasingly difficult in Canada with military conscription and compulsory education. By 1940, there were 5,838 Canadian-born persons in Mexico, the majority of whom were Mennonites. Over the years some have returned to Canada as recruited labor. This trend appears to have accelerated in the mid-1980s and again in the early 1990s in response to economic difficulties in Mexico (Goldring 1998).

Holiday spouses relocate to Canada after marrying a Canadian citizen. The group varies but is predominately female, either students who decide to settle permanently or women who marry Canadian tourists.

The absolute numbers of Mexican immigrants are increasing slightly, according to official Canadian government statistics. The number of permanent immigrants from Mexico to Canada has been steadily increasing from 1,392 annual entrants in 1998 to 3,224 in 2007. The percentage of Mexican immigrants in comparison with all immigrant arrivals is less than 10 per cent of all immigrants arriving during that eight-year period. The rate of increase is more marked among potential refugees, who are defined as humanitarian entries, though again the numbers are quite small (from 1,057 in 1998 to 7,009 in 2007). Since 2005, most humanitarian entrants have been Mexican refugees (now approximately 24 per cent of all claimants by national origin). The largest number of entrants are temporary immigrants who enter via the Mexican Seasonal Agricultural Worker Program (SAWP; discussed below), new temporary restricted visas for jobs deemed unskilled, and the much less used NAFTA visas. In 2007, 17,665 temporary entrants from Mexico entered Canada on temporary worker arrangements with nearly 70 per cent as return migrants. Only the US sends more temporary migrants. The number of temporary migrants is consistently more than the other two classes of permanent and humanitarian combined (see Table 11.1).

The 1991 Census recorded 16,460 residents of whole (8,015) or partial (8,445) Mexican ethnic origin in Canada. Most resided in Ontario, British Columbia, and Quebec, followed by Alberta and Manitoba (Goldring 1998). By the 2006 Census, the Mexican population in Canada numbered 36,575, with 15,815 identifying exclusively as Mexican and 20,755 partially identifying as such, which represents only 0.1 per cent of the total population. The vast majority of permanent immigrants from Mexico to Canada are middle-class, educated professionals, though that profile is slowly diversifying in spite of Canadian immigration policy that favors highly skilled, well-educated migrants. Alarcón (2007, 251) notes that the number of skilled permanent immigrants from Mexico is minimal (less than 1 per cent) but that Mexico is a prominent supplier of temporary, most often non-professional, migrants (closer to 13 per cent in 2002).

Shared among the NAFTA nations is a temporary visa program that facilitates preferential treatment in the temporary movement of intra-company transferees, business visitors, merchants, investors, and other

Table 11.1 *Mexican Migration to Canada, by Entrance Status, 1998–2007*

	1998	1999	2000	2001	2002	2003	2004	2005	2006	2007
Permanent	**1,392**	**1,723**	**1,658**	**1,939**	**1,919**	**1,738**	**2,245**	**2,851**	**2,830**	**3,224**
%	7.4	8.3	7.3	7.4	7.8	6.6	7.5	8.4	8.0	8.9
Temporary (total)	**6,993**	**8,119**	**10,013**	**11,322**	**11,520**	**11,288**	**11,663**	**12,945**	**14,662**	**17,665**
Initial entry	1,763	2,171	6,583	4,327	3,946	2,922	2,524	3,260	3,768	5,317
%	2.7	3.0	7.8	5.4	5.4	4.4	3.4	4.0	4.0	4.6
Re-entry	5,230	5,948	3,430	6,995	7,574	8,366	9,139	9,685	10,894	12,348
%	15.1	17.3	10.8	17.6	19.9	22.8	23.7	23.6	24.4	24.8
Humanitarian	**1,057**	**1,043**	**1,312**	**1,656**	**2,103**	**2,588**	**2,807**	**3,407**	**4,892**	**7,009**
%	4.3	2.8	3.5	3.7	6.1	8.0	10.8	16.8	20.8	24.0

Source: http://www.cic.gc.ca/english/pdf/pub/facts2007.pdf.

professionals. NAFTA visas (officially named TN or Trade NAFTA visas) are almost never used by Mexican professionals who might take up residence in Canada. In 2003, only 110 Mexican citizens utilized NAFTA visas to relocate in Canada. Conversely, the number of Trade NAFTA visa holders who moved from the US and Canada to Mexico was a combined 304,209 (see Alarcón 2007, 253).

Canadian immigration law clearly defines who is welcome. Temporary migrants, who arrive for specific work contract periods, predominate in terms of the Mexican population residing in Canada. Permanent migrants, those eligible for Canadian citizenship, are very much limited to professionals with high education levels. This category of "economic migrants" excludes working-class people, as working-class jobs are increasingly filled by temporary migrants (both internal and international). As much as the system is class-based, there is also a very long history of racial exclusion in Canadian immigration law that parallels US immigration law. To understand both the rise of temporary worker programs and the increasingly precarious status of recent immigrants, it is essential to begin with the push to exclude non-European immigrants in the making of the "Great White North."

Mexican Seasonal Agricultural Worker Program

The history of Canadian immigration law helps to explain why the Canadian government initiated temporary agricultural worker programs with Caribbean nations (former British colonies) in 1966 and with Mexico in 1974, affording temporary legal status to non-White migrants. Prior to important immigration reform in 1966, Canadian immigration policy explicitly restricted naturalization to European immigrants. Within the context of British imperialism, Canadian immigration law rested upon the twin commitment of keeping Canada White and distinguishing White British colonial rule from Black and Asian British colonial relations. In 1947, Prime Minister Mackenzie King declared in the House of Commons the right of the Canadian government to limit who could enter the nation to preserve "the character of our population."

> The policy of the government is to foster the growth of the population of Canada by encouraging migration.... With regard to the selection of immigrants much has been said about discrimination. I wish to make it quite clear that Canada is perfectly within her rights in selecting persons whom we regard

as desirable future citizens. It is not a "fundamental human right" of any alien to enter Canada. It is a privilege.... There will, I am sure, be general agreement with the view that the people of Canada do not wish, as a result of mass immigration, to make a fundamental alteration in the character of our population. (Quoted in Satzewich 1991, 123)

Canada's fellow Commonwealth members increasingly questioned these racist restrictions after World War II in response to the country's vocal, yet hypocritical, opposition to South Africa's apartheid state. In 1965, a White Paper called for an end to racist exclusions and quotas in immigration law (particularly by deeming the family sponsorship of new immigrants as a universal right, not one restricted to White Canadians) and proposed a new model of immigrant selection that would place a premium on highly educated, skilled, professional class, English and French speakers. "The 1965 White Paper and a reformed immigration act passed in 1966 that eliminated most overtly racist clauses paved the way for the recruitment of Jamaican workers (1966) and, during the course of the next ten years, the citizens of other Caribbean countries: Trinidad and Tobago and Barbados in 1968 and the Organization of Eastern Caribbean States... in 1976" (Preibisch and Binford 2007, 9).

The 1966 SAWP Act made Caribbean labor available, but temporary, and ultimately not connected to full citizenship. The long-held notion of Black Caribbeans as worthy laborers (with women doing domestic work and men doing agricultural labor) but not worthy citizens led to the establishment of the SAWP and a similar domestic temporary labor program. The Commonwealth connections make a certain sense in terms of the macrostructures that provided West Indian labor to Canada, but Mexico's inclusion is a bit more difficult to understand. A set of conjunctural factors, by the Canadian government as well as actions by Ontario growers, are crucial in explaining why Mexico was included in Canada's Caribbean foreign worker program.

From the immigration department's point of view, adding Mexico to the SAWP was an effort to control an unsanctioned migration stream that had gone out of control and that was undermining its claim that it could supply Ontario farmers with suitable supplies of labour. By formalizing the movement of migrant workers from Mexico to Canada, immigration officials hoped to reaffirm the program's legitimacy and re-establish the appearance of its ability to control migrant labour to Canada. At the same time, however, evidence suggests that regularizing this already existing migration flow also took into account employers' interests in having access to ever cheaper and more exploitable labour power (Satzewich 2007, 272).

Mexico's role in providing temporary labor predated the official 1974 inclusion of the country in the SAWP and certainly built upon the marginalization of Black Caribbean labor by Canadian growers, particularly in Ontario. As stated above, the increasing presence of Mexican Mennonites employed as temporary migrant labor was initiated by their recruitment by their Canadian counterparts starting in the 1970s to work seasonally in Ontario as a wage-cutting strategy *vis-à-vis* the use of legal temporary migrants from the Caribbean. This recruitment undercut mobilizations by workers who were becoming more aware of their workplace and wage rights and were striking for better conditions. Another aim was to reduce the bargaining power of the Caribbean governments that were negotiating on behalf of their citizens for better terms of employment. The Canadian government's decision to create a bilateral temporary worker arrangement with Mexico both sanctioned and regularized the flow that would eventually come to predominate.

Canada's SAWP operates much like the US-Mexico Bracero Program (see Chapter 1). The bilateral arrangements are established at the federal government level and require both growers and workers to certify via respective bureaucratic channels that they are eligible for the program. In Mexico, the same agency responsible for administering the Bracero Program is responsible for the SAWP. Prospective laborers must register in person at the offices of the *Secretaría de Trabajo y Provisión Social* in Mexico City. Applicants must also provide results of a medical examination, procured at their own expense, to ensure their health. As a result, the majority of participants are from the Federal District, Tlaxcala, Guanajuato, and Hidalgo (over 69 per cent in 1996, according to Basok 2002, 100). Similarly to the Bracero Program, the selection process places a premium on applicants with agricultural expertise, with additional preferences for married men with children, for those who do not own land, and for those who have completed military service. Barndt (2007, 193) notes: "Only since 1989 have women been included in the SAWP, brought to pick and pack fruit and vegetables during the four months of the harvest season or for longer production periods in the increasing number of greenhouse operations, where Canadian hydroponic tomato production has become internationally competitive.... While their numbers increased from 37 in 1989 to 359 in 2005, women still only account for less than 4 per cent of the total seasonal workforce."

However, there are clear worker benefits and guarantees built into the Canadian SAWP that were missing from the original Bracero Program: guaranteed local prevailing wages, guaranteed number of hours of employment, housing inspected prior to occupation, free transportation and housing, and enrollment upon arrival in the Canadian health care system (e.g., in Ontario the workers qualify for the provincial medical program, the Ontario Health Insurance Program) and the Pension Plan. Due to the small size of the program, SAWP allows for oversight, regulation, and compliance (Basok 2000).

In Canada, the program is administered by two federal non-profit service organizations: FARMS, the Federal Agricultural Research Management Services for Ontario and Nova Scotia; and FERME, *Fondation des Entreprises en Recrutement de Main-d'œuvre Agricole Étrangère* for Quebec, New Brunswick, and Prince Edward Island. FARMS and FERME handle requests for labor and certification, as well as overseeing the allocation of Mexican farmworkers to Canadian growers. The agricultural industries that employ temporary Mexican laborers are predominately vegetable farms, fruit orchards, and greenhouses. The greenhouse industry in Southern Ontario began with tomatoes destined for a large Heinz processing plant there that relies upon a huge supply of greenhouse tomatoes and is increasingly expanding its consumer lines to process other fruits and vegetables (see Basok 2002, 43). Declining in numbers but still present are tobacco growers as well as apiary, flower, ginseng, nursery, sod, and canning/food processing (see Table 11.2). In 2008, 8,475 Mexicans worked in those industries, even though 9,850 were requested by growers. This is up from 8,211 in 2007 and more than the figures for all Caribbean nations[1] combined of 7,507 working and 8,803 requested in 2008. Ontario is the main recipient of SAWP workers, but they are also employed in Alberta, Quebec, Manitoba, Nova Scotia, New Brunswick, and Prince Edward Island. Temporary workers are employed anywhere from three to ten months a year.[2]

Though clearly an improvement over US-Mexican relations during the Bracero Program, the SAWP still presents problems for temporary laborers. A report issued by the UFCW detailed the abuses endured by workers in 2005 in spite of stipulations in contracts that guarantee that mandatory health insurance, pension, and workers' compensation will be deducted from wages. Yet the ability to secure those benefits is practically non-existent

Table 11.2: *Mexican Seasonal Agricultural Worker Program, FARMS Statistics, 2007–08*

CROP	2007	2008	% Variance (Rounded)	Involved* 2007	Involved* 2008
Apples	1,758	1,739	-1	120	124
Canning/food processing	485	451	-7	13	12
Farmworker, bee	14	14	0	4	5
Farmworker, flowers	477	470	-1	34	43
Farmworker, fruit	3,464	3,423	-1	287	280
Farmworker, greenhouse	3,473	3,000	12	191	179
Farmworker, nursery	1,305	1,280	-2	62	66
Farmworker, sod	5	7	40	2	3
Farmworker, tobacco	2,098	1,397	-33	315	210
Farmworker, vegetable	4,403	4,553	3	363	370
Ginseng	553	702	27	52	65
TOTAL	**18,035**	**17,924**	**-1**	**1,411**	**1,343**

*Note: Vacancies filled by crop and number of employers involved.
Source: http://www.farmsontario.ca/Stat.htm.

for the majority of laborers. Rarely are workers able to collect what they pay into the system (e.g., by definition they do not qualify for Employment Insurance, as the program operates for the unemployed, and pensions are rarely collected). If workers have grievances, most often they express "reluctance to complain about poor or inadequate living and/or working conditions due to fear of repatriation. The workers do not believe they receive adequate support or help from their consular officials—and, in fact, have little trust in these officials" (UFCW 2006, 9).

The question of SAWP workers' captive or unfree status is seriously considered in the academic literature that turns a critical eye on the operations of the program. Basok (2002, 2000) and Satzewich (1991) refer to the situation as "unfree labor" due to the high degree of grower control over Mexican laborers. Since workers are tied to a single employer, threatened with repatriation or deportation if they organize complaints expressed through strikes or work stoppages, and are dependent for subsequent renewals on grower requests or call backs, the contracted benefits and worker protections are rarely utilized or received. Beyond the veneer of protections put in place by the Canadian government, a substantial amount of exploitation is present in the SAWP:

> ... the contractually sanctioned powers granted the employer, competition among source country governments, and the contradictions that permeate the liaison/consular official role conspire against contract workers, whether Mexican or Caribbean. The workers are not powerless and do not lack agency. But the use (or threat) of force—embodied in the annual evaluation, the three-year rule, arbitrary dismissal and so on—is usually enough to confine grievances to the margins, out of sight and hearing of their targets. (Binford 2009, 512)

Precariousness and Lack of Exceptionalism

Temporary migration to Canada, as formalized in the SAWP, is increasingly becoming the norm in the post-NAFTA era. Goldring, Berinstein, and Bernhaus refer to the "precarious status" of immigrants in relation to Canadian immigration law: "We use this term to capture the twin tendencies on the part of states of immigration to restrict routes to citizenship and make citizens increasingly individually responsible for their existence. The former involves making citizenship more exclusive, the latter is part of a broader process of reducing the welfare state and social citizenship" (2007, 9–10). The concept, first voiced in *Precarious Employment*, which describes the Canadian economy as marked by "forms of work characterized by limited social benefits and statutory entitlements, job insecurity, low wages, and high risks of ill-health" (Vosko 2006, 11), is designed to explore twenty-first-century manifestations of the economic restructuring that has reconfigured the global economy since the early 1970s. For Vosko, the idea of precariousness links the economic restructuring that loosened the guarantees of security in the labor market with how contingent employment relations and eviscerated government safety nets combine to impact the processes of social reproduction. Precariousness is a departure from welfare states dedicated to fulfilling a social contract with their citizens and represents the rise of neoliberal reforms that place the onus of survival (economic, health, civic, etc.) on the individual. It is not coincidental that the evisceration of the social contract arose concomitantly with the informalization of labor and temporary worker arrangements. It is also no coincidence that the Canadian state's commitment to multiculturalism as an overarching immigration policy arose at the same time that the state made it much more difficult to secure permanent status and the accompanying full rights of citizenship. Preibisch and Hermoso Santamaria (2006, 109) and Sharma (2006, 117) note that in 1973, 57 per cent of all immigrants entering Canada for employment were granted citizenship, whereas 20 years later, in 1993 this had decreased to 30 per cent. No longer a nation of permanent settlement, Canada is clearly opting for flexible workforces, as indicated by its temporary programs for agribusiness. There are currently more temporary than permanent immigrants residing in Canada.[3]

In addition to the growing utilization of temporary admissions for Canada's racialized in-migrant population, the full range of contemporary immigration policy is modeled on this construction of precarious status:

> Canadian immigration policy demonstrates two trends that suggest that the number of people with precarious immigrant status and documented illegality is going to grow. The chilly climate for refugee claimants may produce decreases in the overall number of applications.... More restrictive immigration policies may also have the unanticipated effect of increasing the number of people who overstay visas because other options for entering and remaining in Canada are narrowing. (Goldring, Berinstein, and Bernhaus 2007, 42)

The overall effect of limits on family sponsorship, refugee admissions, and the issuance of more temporary visas is that fewer immigrants are both eligible for public services and becoming Canadian citizens. As NAFTA displaces more of the rural population in Mexico, workers will eventually follow the commodities that freely flow among the three nations. Binford (2009, 505–6) notes that NAFTA makes conditions for food self-subsistence much more limited in Mexico, as more of the countryside is devoted to heavily subsidized export agriculture by TNCs. The costs associated with importing food (particularly corn and other staples) come at too great a price. Barndt (2007) traces the global commodity chain of the North American tomato to demonstrate how food on the tables of North American consumers is directly linked to the limited economic opportunities for survival in Mexico where more land is cultivated for export purposes rather than feeding its own people. She points out that transnational migration results in Mexicans working for cheap in the burgeoning tomato industry of Southern Ontario as perpetual temporary laborers with few options in terms of permanent citizenship and settlement.

The key point is not that there is a large "undocumented" problem but that immigration law is allowing people to reside only temporarily in Canada by placing the onus of regularizing status on individuals. This occurs by limiting the economic class of permanent migrants, denying refugee asylum cases, making family reunification more precarious, and, most importantly, throwing open the doors to temporary worker programs. Though temporary migrants are known to Canadian immigration officials, they are not finding pathways to becoming citizens. A report by the Alberta Federation of Labour (2007) identified this trend by noting: "The government dramatically expanded the list of occupations under which workers could come to Canada on temporary, restricted visas; the list now includes unskilled workers (e.g., fast food counter clerks), low skilled workers (line cooks at fast food restaurants), and skilled workers (trades people)."

Meat-Packing and Other Industries or Regions Employing Mexican Canadians

The economic restructuring trends noted in the Alberta Federation of Labour report are important for the future of Mexicans residing in Canada. Currently, in terms of their placement in the labor market, Mexicans in Canada are not concentrated in any particular occupational category. According to Table 11.3, the majority as of 1992 were students, spouses, or children who were not working at the time. The remaining 43 per cent of those working were listed as 2.7 per cent entrepreneurs and investors, 9.5 per cent professionals, 3.6 per cent clerical, 7.1 per cent sales and services, 6.3 per cent primary industries (agriculture), 2.5 per cent manufacturing and processing, 0.2 per cent construction, and 11.1 per cent not otherwise classified. Rather than large concentrations in particular occupations, Mexicans are evenly represented in most industries. More recent Census data on the Latin American population point to a slight increase in unskilled job concentration.

In 2006, the occupations where Latin Americans predominated included, in rank order: 1) sales and service; 2) business, finance, and administration; 3) trades, transport, and equipment operator, and 4) manufacturing (see Table 11.4; Statistics Canada 2006). Though this rank includes all Latin Americans, not solely Mexicans, the overall lack of concentration in any particular occupation and the inconsistency over the 18-year period mark a lack of labor market concentration. Industries that employed more than 10,000 Latin Americans included construction, man-

Table 11.3: *Mexicans in Canada by Occupation, 1992*

Job Classification	Per cent
Not working (children, students, spouses)	57.0
Working	43.0
Professionals	9.5
Sales and service	7.1
Primary industry (Agriculture)	6.3
Clerical	3.6
Entrepreneurs and Investors	2.7
Manufacturing	2.5
Construction	0.2
Other job, not classified	11.1

Source: Goldring 1998.

ufacturing, retail trade, administration and support, health care and social assistance, and accommodation and food services. It is the jobs associated with a restructured economy, dependent upon consumer demand, that are increasing as the main employment options for Mexican immigrants to Canada. Jobs in the precarious economy with few benefits, irregular employment, and low wages are now more likely to employ Mexicans than the professional occupations. This aligns with a statistical analysis of Canadian Census data by Kazimipur and Halli (2001, 1143) that finds the poverty rate of Latin American immigrants is over 38 per cent and that the rate for permanent residents of Latin American origin is even higher (39.5 per cent). There seems to be a significant racialized component to living in Canada over several generations that leads to more poverty rather than less (Black Caribbeans experience the largest increase between immigrant and resident poverty rates). With the overall poverty rate at 15.6 per cent, the differential impact of poverty on Latin American and Black Caribbean residents and immigrants only reinforces the precariousness of the contemporary Canadian economy.

Particular industries are susceptible to increased precariousness due to their labor practices and oligopolistic tendencies. The meat-packing

Table 11.4: *Latin American Residents In Canada by Industry and Occupation, 2006*

	Total	Male	Female
		Gender	
Total labor force 15 years and over by industry — North American Industry Classification System 2002	**175,570**	**93,500**	**82,075**
Industry — Not applicable	5,975	2,545	3,425
All industries	169,595	90,950	78,645
Agriculture, forestry, fishing, and hunting	3,635	3,000	635
Mining and oil and gas extraction	1,265	780	490
Utilities	535	330	205
Construction	11,840	10,800	1,040
Manufacturing	27,760	18,600	9,160
Wholesale trade	7,455	4,720	2,735
Retail trade	18,360	7,965	10,400
Transportation and warehousing	6,860	4,895	1,965
Information and cultural industries	4,185	2,305	1,885
Finance and insurance	5,880	2,365	3,515
Real estate and rental and leasing	2,460	1,425	1,035
Professional, scientific, and technical services	9,725	5,455	4,265
Management of companies and enterprises	210	100	110
Administrative and support, waste management, and remediation services	17,110	8,555	8,560
Educational services	7,295	2,900	4,395
Health care and social assistance	15,330	2,825	12,500
Arts, entertainment, and recreation	2,710	1,355	1,350
Accommodation and food services	13,850	6,580	7,280
Other services (except public administration)	8,745	3,995	4,755
Public administration	4,380	2,015	2,365
Total labor force 15 years and over by occupation — National Occupational Classification for Statistics 2006	**175,570**	**93,495**	**82,070**
Occupation — Not applicable	5,970	2,545	3,425

	Total	Gender Male	Female
All occupations	169,600	90,950	78,645
Management occupations	9,380	5,795	3,580
Business, finance, and administrative occupations	26,390	9,095	17,300
Natural and applied sciences and related occupations	11,245	8,665	2,580
Health occupations	7,015	1,620	5,390
Occupations in social science, education, government service, and religion	11,175	3,495	7,685
Occupations in art, culture, recreation, and sport	4,465	2,295	2,165
Sales and service occupations	53,145	22,400	30,740
Trades, transport and equipment operators, and related occupations	25,390	23,345	2,045
Occupations unique to primary industry	4,705	4,105	595
Occupations unique to processing, manufacturing, and utilities	16,710	10,145	6,560

Note: These figures are accurately reproduced from the 2006 Canadian Census. Any errors reside in the original document.
Source: Statistics Canada, 2006 Census of Population, Catalogue no. 97–564-XCB2006009.

industry in Canada is a prime example, even as some of the most profitable TNCs in the world maneuver to dominate the industry. The history of meat-packing in Canada is often recounted in terms of the Big Three — Canada Packers, Burns and Company, and Swift Canadian — as the oligopoly that dominated the industry. Increasingly, the story now includes US corporations (Tyson, Cargill, and IBP) operating as TNCs that dominate the industry worldwide. This corresponds with the burgeoning meat-packing industry in Brooks, Alberta, which follows the Iowa Beef Producers (IBP) model of controlling the entire commodity chain from farm to market in a vertical integration of the industry. "IBP in Brooks, Alberta, was the first in Canada to own, operate, and integrate the feed mill, feedlot, processing plant, and fabricating plant" (MacLachlan 2001, 330). Boxed beef, refrigerated rail cars, refrigerated tractor-trailers, and other technological changes enabled the largest companies to relocate operations in rural, often Western, Canada where packing plants could be built alongside feedlots. The old Big Three model of large packing plants in the major population centers of Eastern Canada has given way to industry restructuring in exactly the same way seen in the Midwestern and Southern US (see Chapters 7 and 8). This restructuring followed on the heels of buyouts and takeovers by US corporations (Cargill and IBP) that resulted in the shutting down of operations in the large Eastern cities (and the eventual demise of Canadian Packers and Burns) with replacement increasingly by US-controlled subsidiaries.

The largest producer of pork and poultry in Canada is now Olymel (majority owned by *Coopérative Fédérée de Québec*) with ten plants in Quebec and one in Red Deer, Alberta. Schneider Foods (once wholly owned by Smithfield Foods, the US-based pork processor but now controlled by Maple Leaf) operates large plants in Ontario, Manitoba, and Saskatchewan. Beef processing is dominated by three large firms squarely rooted in the US: Cargill Foods of High River, Alberta; Lakeside Packers of Brooks, Alberta (both controlled by Tyson Foods, the largest meat processor in the world); and Better Beef, once an independent packer in Guelph, Ontario, now controlled by Cargill. Beef processing in Alberta is increasingly a two-company affair as Cargill is the largest private corporation in the world and Tyson's recent acquisition of IBP is part of its attempt to corner the global meat-processing market.

The economic restructuring of ownership, a long-standing reliance upon internal migrants to provide labor for the industry, and increasingly monopolistic practices all point to a growing reliance on Mexican immigrant labor (either temporary or undocumented) as the industry seeks to undercut UFCW labor representation and the wage and safety protections currently extended to the predominately Asian and African immigrant workforce. If the SAWP is any indication of future trends, meat-packing in Canada is more likely to rely upon Mexican immigrants in the future.

Broadway's analysis of Brooks, Alberta, shows that refugees from Africa and Southeast Asia are the major sources of labor, most often as internal migrants to these remote packing towns, due to Canadian immigration law that favors highly educated, high human-capital migrants.

> In Alberta, Lakeside has been unable to recruit from a poorer southern neighbor [Mexico]; instead it has turned to Canada's population of Sub-Saharan

and Asian refugees. This difference is attributable to Canada's immigration policy which emphasizes recruiting highly skilled immigrants and, by default, the packers resort to hiring refugees. (Broadway 2007, 578)

As the industry seeks to replicate US business practices, it is highly unlikely that the rapid turnover in the pork, poultry, and beef plants will sustain the current practice of employing de-skilled internal migrants. Always turning an eye to a more exploitable labor pool, Cargill and Tyson will undoubtedly look to Canadian temporary visa programs and undocumented labor recruitment as they gain more control over the Canadian meat Industry.

Conclusion

Rather than passively accepting their increasingly precarious status, immigrants and their advocates have used various means to put pressure on the Canadian government to end differential treatment and create pathways to citizenship and full respect for human rights. Organizers and activists have provided support for immigrants, rallied on their behalf, and engaged in popular education campaigns to improve their working and living conditions. Much of the focus has been on the participants in the SAWP, as their lack of workplace and citizenship rights are particularly egregious. Unions, such as the UFCW, have created campaigns and provided services for SAWP workers. There are currently nine UFCW worker centers that provide basic services. "The centers offer a range of services to migrant workers, including assistance with social benefits, legal counseling, and translation. They also engage in raising workers' awareness of their rights" (Preibisch 2007, 110). The current UFCW campaign in Ontario, and to a lesser extent in Alberta, is designed to force provincial governments to recognize the rights of agricultural workers to form unions. The campaigns are building upon successful efforts to recognize health and safety protections, but the Ontario provincial government has defied court orders allowing workers to organize and is relying upon long-standing exemptions of worker rights in agriculture.

Additionally, the Agriculture Workers' Alliance (AWA), sponsored by the UFCW, is offering services to migrant workers through nine worker centers in British Columbia (Abbotsford, Kelowna, and Surrey), Manitoba (Portage la Prairie), Ontario (Bradford, Leamington, Simcoe, and Virgil) and Quebec (St. Rémi). It also gives support in person as well as via phone with Mexico and Jamaica and provides workers with education on their rights regarding health and safety, working conditions, provincial labor rights, wage protections, pensions, employment insurance, income tax, workers' compensation, health insurance, and translation services.

The UFCW works closely with Toronto-based migrant advocacy organizations such as *Justicia* for Migrant Workers (J4MW). The Global Justice Car Van Project was a joint effort between UFCW and J4MW to provide mobile services for SAWP workers in Ontario but was also designed to educate the Canadian public about the program and the abuses workers endure. The van project and worker centers are part of the UFCW's three-pronged campaign to use media, protests, and lawsuits to fight for health and safety enforcement in the fields of Alberta and for collective bargaining rights in Ontario. Agriculture is one of the most dangerous occupations in Canada with 10 to 15 deaths occurring annually and injuries too numerous to count.[4] In the "McGuinty's Plantation" campaign, the union has invoked United Nations Human Rights, International Labour Organization, Ontario Court of Appeals, and Canadian Supreme Court decisions to demonstrate that the current provincial premier, Dalton McGuinty, has been ignoring these rights (see also Preibisch and Raper 2007). Another campaign focuses on immigration reform. "Justice for Immigrants" calls for an end to scapegoating immigrants for the nation's economic woes and demands means to regularize immigrant status and more pathways toward citizenship, particularly for low-wage workers. All UFCW campaigns are couched in the language of human rights.

Other relevant campaigns include those run by the Canadian Farmworkers' Union (CFU) among Punjabi immigrants in British Columbia (particularly in the Fraser Valley) with a string of successful strikes leading to labor contracts in the 1980s. Teetering on the edge of survival, the CFU resurfaced in 2007, after the deaths of three migrant farmworkers who lost their lives due to shoddy transportation practices. The newly constituted union pressured the British Columbia government to enact transportation safety regulations that would have prevented the accident.

No One is Illegal! (NOII) is an activist organization committed to radical democratic reform in Canada's approach to immigration. "The No One is Illegal Campaign has two goals: to attain justice and victories for immigrants and refugees and to develop the communities' own capacity to attain dignity for themselves and their families" (Walia 2005). With chapters in

Vancouver, Montreal, Toronto, Victoria, and Halifax, NOII utilizes direct action tactics, webpages, public awareness events, direct refugee support, and multilingual community forums, as well as coordinating letter writing campaigns and facilitating workshops that are designed to challenge the neoliberal hegemony of the Canadian state. It views international migration as part and parcel of the rising inequalities that define globalization. NOII also links with First Nations' struggles for sovereignty in an explicitly multiracial, anti-capitalist style of networked politics. In contrast to NOII, ENLACE Community Link, Inc., operates as a cultural organization and assists migrants in their temporary adjustment to life in Canada. Primarily comprising of Mexicans who have settled in Toronto, the organization works to retain a sense of Mexican culture and avoids the politics of immigration that inform most other migrant-serving organizations.

The conditions for Mexicans residing in Canada are becoming more similar to those in the US as precariousness defines Canadian immigration law. These organizations are central to turning the tide away from precariousness and toward collective bargaining recognition, respect for human rights, and a reinstitution of the social contract for all residents of Canada, regardless of citizenship status.

Even in the NAFTA context, Canada's immigration and labor policies are significant because they demonstrate that a variety of models are possible. Historically, Canada promoted permanent migration by highly educated, skilled migrants and temporary migration for agricultural workers and service workers. While NAFTA has disrupted the Mexican economy, and Canadian policy has increasingly promoted temporary migration with precarious status, this history suggests that policy-makers and citizens can imagine alternatives.

Notes

1. Caribbean workers are predominately from Jamaica but also from Barbados, Trinidad and Tobago, and the Eastern Caribbean (Antigua and Barbuda, Dominica, Grenada, Montserrat, St. Kitts-Nevis, St. Lucia, St. Vincent, and Grenadines).
2. Colby (1997, 6) notes the following crops are harvested by SAWP workers: apples, ginseng, blueberries, cherries, grapes, peaches, pears, plums, prunes, raspberries, strawberries, asparagus, green beans, wax beans, beets, broccoli,

cabbage, carrots, cauliflower, celery, sweet corn, cucumber, lettuce, lima beans, onions, parsnips, green peas, peppers, potatoes, radishes, rutabagas, spinach, tomatoes, and tobacco.

3. See http://www.theglobeandmail.com/news/politics/leap-in-temporary-foreign-workers-will-hurt-canada-long-term-critics-say/article1568394/ (accessed May 19, 2010).

4. Stan Raper, the National Coordinator, Agriculture Workers, for UFCW, states in an interview: "twenty workers have died in Ontario each year for the last 15 or 20 years, not including lost limbs, lost time, lost fingers, lost or broken arms and legs" (Preisbisch and Raper 2007, 119).

Conclusion

As we have detailed in the previous chapters, Mexican immigrants have a long-standing relationship with US society, and the demographic shifts that make Latinos the largest minority group residing in the US drive that point home. After detailing the abuses suffered by workers and finding repeated evidence of the mistreatment of Mexicans as disposable laborers, it is clear that we must ask: what is to be done? Instead of justifying complacency by detailing the deleterious effects of economic and racial marginalization, we conclude with a range of possible action strategies. We believe social justice movements offer substantial hope for bettering social relations by ending the historical pattern of exploiting Mexican workers to satisfy the consumption desires of North Americans.

We fully acknowledge that the issues Mexicans face in the US are big issues necessitating big answers. Engaging in transformative politics requires building a movement to end the capitalist and racist system on a global scale. As a starting point, we talk about possible solutions or reforms that range from the pragmatic state of Mexican-US relations to anti-systemic global movements. We are concerned that envisioning new worlds through popular education, transformative social practices through grassroots participatory democracy, and transnational social movements is too often precluded by a discursive closure[1] on the topic of Mexican immigration that reduces all big issues to sets of binary options. Politics itself is too frequently defined by the non-representative political system or political talk shows, although it is clear that politics is all-pervasive.

We address the binary options that have been presented to this point and weigh in on the positions that may or may not move us closer to the end of capitalist inequalities and institutional racism. As we are considering directions for action, we recognize that in all of the major conversations on these topics, there are three main approaches to progressive social change: liberal adjustments, social democratic reforms, and transformative politics.[2]

Liberal adjustments make minor alterations that rarely address the fundamental causes of immigration dilemmas. They leave the transnational capitalist system intact, thus ensuring that Mexican immigrants will continue to be exploited as cheap labor. Social democratic reforms are, in a sense, nonreformist reforms (Gorz 1973) that seek fundamental transformations of the capitalist system through an engagement with policies and legal actions that play on the contradictions of the system to change the social order. The problem with social democratic reforms is that they all too often suggest that reforms have to be taken *for* the poor or racialized; they assume those deemed poor or racialized are not able to take action themselves. Transformative approaches get at the roots of the oppressive exploitative system. Rather than being passive agents, transformative subjects are active in reordering social relationships, diagnosing social inequalities, and mobilizing for a better way of socially organizing the world.

The discursive closure on US immigration law has precluded any serious discussion of real comprehensive immigration reform and of which actors should determine a fair, sane system. Even the most progressive of labor unions fall into choosing between either-or options to get a bill passed that eases some of the marginalization associated with undocumented immigration. We discuss potential solutions to the farmworker morass, as well as how to re-envision the notion of comprehensive immigration reform from social democratic and transformative perspectives. While the full demilitarization of the US-Mexico border and decriminalization of illegal immigration may seem like major steps, it must be noted that the militarized border as such has been in place for only 25 years. The border is not nearly as naturalized as is often assumed. Distinguishing between illegal and legal immigrants is also a recent phenomenon that is a direct result of the 1986 IRCA. Thinking beyond the "choices" offered to us by the mainstream media, such as more or less border enforcement and temporary worker programs or enacting harsher criminal penalties, is an essential precursor to pursuing transformative politics.

We close by discussing transnational strategies of democratic organizing and economic development, the immigrant organizing movement, and how mass pressure can be harnessed in a novel approach to labor movements. We examine network politics of movement organizing, legal reforms, and civil society transformations that recognize past injustices while impeding the future repetition of said injustices, and we consider how Mexican immigrant labor fits into the Zapatista idea for "new" worlds to be envisioned and enacted. The immigrant rights movement of 2006 should serve as testament to the notion that all hope is not lost and that even the most marginalized have the power to enact transformative social change when working in solidarity.

We end our analysis of reforms by detailing transformative political practices that are rooted in popular education approaches, which engage in social practices through grassroots participatory democracy and transnational social movements. We discuss the *Frente Indígena de Organizaciones Binacionales* (FIOB) as an example of how transnational organizing may employ testimonial-based truth commissions to mobilize Mexican laborers into networks of global anti-systemic movements.

Beyond the Current Immigration Reform Debate

The binary choices mapped onto the immigration debate severely constrain the realm of possible solutions. In addition, the central dilemmas that immigrants face are deemed non-issues, as immigration is constantly reduced to a cost-benefit analysis for US consumption. Part of the impasse should be directly attributed to the extremely vitriolic discourse originating in the far Right. Discursive closure is in some ways secured when the debate is reduced to countering the backlash of nativists and reclaiming the moral ground against criminalization, nativism, and vigilantism by identifying their proponents' xenophobic, racist, and hate-filled motivations. Much of the liberal response to immigration issues is taking conservative politicians to task for their hate-mongering and attempting to refocus the debate on immigration within its racialized context. The point of anti-immigrant rhetoric is to dehumanize immigrants and reduce the complexity of immigration to fear and a division of "us vs. them." Immigrants become an abstract threat, a foreign or alien force constructed as invaders and destroyers. Vigilante groups and their politically appointed spokesmen — the Minutemen, Pat Buchanan, James Sensenbrenner, Brian Bilbray, Saxby Chambliss, Tom Tancredo, Richard Lamm, and Bill Owens, among others — absorb entirely too much of the energies of immigrant advocacy groups. Liberal adjustments necessitate taking nativists head-on for their racist actions, which make clear that their support base is easily distracted from the wars in Iraq and Afghanistan and the deteriorating economy by bashing immigrants. Liberal approaches to immigrant rights are bound up with US foreign policy and its oil empire building, which simultaneously decimate the domestic economy by allowing for monopolization, capital flight, and tax breaks for the rich.

Specific bills for comprehensive immigration reform are currently being debated, but the scope of the issue is nowhere acknowledged nor addressed by piecemeal attempts at gains for particular groups meeting very specific criteria. The proposed DREAM Act (Development, Relief, and Education for Alien Minors) has been introduced in every session since 2005. It would permit certain immigrant students who have grown up in the US to become eligible for citizenship if they go to college or serve in the US military and would eliminate the IIRIRA provision that penalizes states that provide in-state tuition without regard to immigration status. The bill assumes that about 60,000 of the 2.8 million students who graduate from high schools each year are undocumented and are not able to pursue higher education. The goal is to extend the reach of the judgment in *Plyler v. Doe*[3] by making higher education available to undocumented children and moving the political rhetoric and policy discussion beyond restriction and retribution by providing one, albeit quite limited and narrow, pathway toward legalization of citizenship status. Without the DREAM Act, the policy debate will remain one-sided in favor of restriction and criminalization. Using the plight of immigrant children to defuse the rhetoric of nativists is an important strategy in making US immigration policy conform to the spirit of protecting human rights.

In Chapter 8, we mentioned the child-labor laws that the agricultural industry can use to compel farmworker families to subject children to long hours of paid work. Because it has never been required to meet minimum wage standards, the agricultural industry where most immigrant labor is consumed features both the lowest wages paid in any formal industry and systematic abuses of largely symbolic laws that mandate potable water, latrines within a certain distance of work, pesticide postings, and delayed entry into the fields after spraying. The simplest liberal adjustment is to make agriculture meet the legal requirements that all other employers in the US must meet. Growers use the exceptionalism claim to regularly seek exemptions from labor regulations:

[A]griculture as an exceptional system of production argues that characteristics of agricultural production distinguish it so greatly from other economic sectors and production processes that efforts to analyze it using industrial categories prove fruitless. Factors such as the perishability of the product, the time gap between the principal production activities (e.g., planting, cultivating, and harvesting), the relative immobility of agricultural firms, and the greater uncertainties brought on by plant biology and weather have historically been used by agricultural interests as an argument against their inclusion under generic policies, such as coverage under the stipulations of the National Labor Relations Act. (Thomas 1992, 12–13)

The only state that guarantees the right to collective bargaining for agricultural workers is California. The establishment of the Agricultural Labor Relations Board (ALRB) was a result of years of struggle by the UFW to force growers to meet the basic requirements of recognizing unions as legitimate collective bargaining representatives. The ALRB is very limited in scope and does not enforce or investigate wage or workplace infractions. The Republican state administrations of Wilson, Deukmejian, and Schwarzenegger have used their ALRB appointment power to remove most of its regulatory will; as a result, the agency tends to follow agribusiness's reluctance to deal with a collective bargaining agent.

Often, over the years, pro-grower interests in the state congress have ensured that the ALRB has not received a budget appropriation sufficient to fully conduct its business. A very simple reform would be to restore its full funding so that it can exercise its regulatory power. This would free it from the control of agribusiness and thus extend first collective bargaining and then all labor rights to agricultural workers. A basic liberal adjustment at the national level would pressure the US Congress to seriously consider why this agribusiness exceptionalism has been allowed to continue and at the very least give farmworkers the same rights as workers in every other industry.

The attempts at discursive closure on the contemporary immigration policy debate have limited it to the signifier of comprehensive reform that consists of punishment, militarization, temporary worker programs, and some legalization. The point of transformative politics is to blast open discursive closures and shift the terms of the debate to those deemed non-actors while pursuing solutions considered outside the realm of possibility. Substantive comprehensive immigration reform requires a consideration of one group that has rarely been consulted in the history of immigration law: the immigrants themselves. Policy should be designed less around the labor needs of corporations; it should begin with the premise that workers deserve to be treated and paid with dignity and have the right to live wherever they choose. Marginalizing immigrant workers only serves to increase the dangers associated with a hypercriminalized, hypermilitarized enforcement system. US citizens who do not want immigrants in their communities might be surprised to know that many prefer to maintain home connections and often consider returning home only to be deterred by a border that is increasingly dangerous to cross and a homeland with fewer and fewer employment opportunities available for even a subsistence living. Creating easier pathways toward dual citizenship and—first and foremost—respecting the rights of immigrants would not only represent a marked shift in how immigration policy is conceived but would also introduce a measure of reality in terms of how immigrants view their economic situation, why they select the destinations they do, and what are their long-term goals. It would be a right step toward global citizenship where the freedoms enjoyed solely by TNCs would be finally enjoyed by transnational migrants.

The key to a sane immigration policy is to remove illegality. The National Day Labor Organizing Network captures this approach in their social democratic policy advocacy.[4] "We day laborers declare ourselves in favor of a legalization process that leads to citizenship and to active civic participation. We demand unconditional legalization for everyone." Compared to the deleterious effects of the free flow of capital, decriminalizing the movement of labor seems fairly innocuous. If most people want to control the flow of labor in some way, a reformer might advocate for an H-2A or temporary worker program under the condition that collective bargaining guarantees and stringent enforcement were preconditions for employment. H-2A workers could be represented by the UFW and FLOC (as is already the case with Global Horizons and the North Carolina Growers Association), H-2B workers represented by SEIU or UNITE-HERE depending on their job classification, and specialty H-1B workers could be represented by the Communication Workers of America or a more closely connected trade union. Temporary immigration could then be legally mapped onto immigrant-preferred circular migration patterns that would allow people to not just survive but potentially thrive on binational living arrangements with pathways toward dual citizenship. Immigration policy needs to be considered from the perspective of immigrants and not designed to allow corporations to skimp on immigrants' human rights to turn wider profit margins.

"Mr. Gorbachev, tear down this wall," were the words uttered by President Ronald Reagan during his 1987 visit to Berlin. Ironically, while Reagan was challenging the Iron Curtain in Europe, the US was building its own wall to deter Mexican immigrants from entering the country. From the 1954 Operation Wetback to Gatekeeper or Hold-the-Line, the increasing militarization of the border has led to lost lives, increased costs associated with clandestine crossings, and entry points shifted to more dangerous locations. Yet undocumented immigration is at an all-time high. If the purpose of building walls and employing more border guards is to stop the flow of illegal immigration, then clearly these actions are complete and utter failures. When considering the demilitarization of the border, we recognize the symbiotic relationship between the US and Mexico as well as their sister cities. We then hopefully begin to recognize the long-standing flows of immigrants from the South and can conceive of a transnational social movement that is centered on the experiences of Mexican immigrant workers.

The European Union, with nations such as Germany, which holds much stricter criteria for citizenship, has in many ways solved its internal migration issue by fully opening up borders not only for commerce but also for people. Emigrating from Africa, Latin America, or Asia is still fraught with difficulties, but a more expansive view of the right to movement is espoused within the continent. The US could adopt this social democratic reform and offer a much more substantive challenge to the status quo if the open borders to free trade were expanded to include open borders for workers' movement. No political leader has expressed such a plan because discursive closure precludes any serious discussion about immigration expressed as a "freedom" or "right." This unfortunate hypocrisy points to the maxim that "those who own the pen write the rules." As corporations insert more elected officials into their back pockets, the only freedoms to be seriously defended are free markets or free enterprise, which are the antipathies of freedom in the first place. A transformative politics approach to immigration reform would necessitate fundamental changes in the root causes of what impels people to move—land reform, abolishment of capital and wage labor, decision-making models no longer based on the imperatives of the market, and participatory democratic decision-making in development options at the local and global levels.

Transnational Organizing and Development Strategies

Social democratic reforms apply directly to transnational approaches to immigrant organizing. It is the "new" labor movement, worker centers, and hometown associations that are pushing the limits of discursive closure to open the terms and introduce new actors into what has traditionally been a very closed debate. In terms of their mildest adjustments, they offer a strategy that is, in effect, choosing between the "evil of two lessers." They can lead to alternative forms of development through migradollars and organizing to improve immigrants' standards of living. At their most transformative, worker centers, unions, and HTAs can employ popular education approaches to construct and mobilize around alternative forms of organizing society.

HTAs represent both the ingenuity of Mexican immigrants as well as their willingness to view their own individual family's lives as interconnected with broader communities who share a sense of linked fates. As the second largest source of foreign revenue, remittances from recent Mexican emigrants are crucial for both the local and national Mexican economy. The concern is that once the Fox administration officially recognizes the serious financial contribution of HTAs, the democratic decision-making aspects may be quickly thwarted by bureaucratic controls. HTAs are crucial players in local development strategies primarily due to grassroots control over their collective resources. An ideal adjustment would be that HTA remittances could be bolstered and supported by US employers in a matching system similar to that of the Mexican government. If US employers refuse to increase immigrant workers' wages, a mandatory matching system for binational workers would facilitate a more just redistribution of resources and partially privilege the needs of immigrants *vis-à-vis* employers. Yet, it is most important to remove the cronyism in Mexican government regulation of HTAs and maintain democratic decision-making models.

When the immigrant rights movement achieved national attention, it was the work behind the scenes by labor unions and Latino advocacy organizations that created the possibility for mass mobilization. Recent events are cause for hope, and the possibility of returning to a civil rights era, with immigrant rights at the forefront, is a foreseeable possibility for the first time in 35 years. By placing economic rights at the forefront of the civil rights agenda, the possibilities for inclusiveness are much broader than a single race-based approach. Organized labor is poised to reap the benefits of immigrants who are often organizing themselves and looking to labor unions for representation. For Mexicans in the heartland and hinterlands, the solidarities that arise from a shared marginalization should easily translate into an organized labor movement as unions shed their racist past and move beyond borders and citizenship requirements to truly unite the workers of the world, both in the US and beyond.

The CTW is certainly at the forefront of immigrant worker organizing. Whether the SEIU, UFCW, IBT, UFW, Carpenters, and Laborers decide to follow UNITE-HERE and rejoin the AFL-CIO or not, the organizing-based strategy of CTW represents another source of hope for Mexican immigrant workers. Cross-border networks in the age of NAFTA and globalization are still in their infancy but can build upon the precedent of J4J, CIW, UFW grape boycotts, the drywallers' strike, and FLOC's third-party contracts. It is important to push unions to fully commit to the "immigrant rights = labor rights = civil rights" program and broaden the movement globally under the banner of human rights. Whether as a separate CTW federation and AFL CIO ur via combined forces, the future of the union movement is in its immigrant base, and Mexicans can lead the way. With so much in retreat at the policy and judicial level, the immigrant rights movement and 2006 marches show the real power of unions. Grassroots mobilization and pressure from below lead to far superior outcomes than a sole strategy of special interest lobbying, since the latter's consistent failure to even tread water signals the danger of sacrificing a viable union movement to big labor lobbying tactics.

As forms of work change in the US, forms of labor organizing have also changed. Community-based union approaches, as we have seen with the CTW and FLOC, recognize that as work becomes more flexible, organizers must creatively identify the sites where workers come together. As factories are no longer primary sites of production, worker centers become important spaces for Mexican workers to organize for labor rights and in most cases allow for organizing across racial and ethnic lines. In the authors' community of Ithaca, New York, the Tompkins County Workers' Center fused a Living Wage campaign with an Immigrant Rights Center. As the Workers' Center, its mission is shifting from simply providing informational and referral services to workers facing violations of their labor rights to supporting organizing by workers and poor people. For example, the center won a struggle against a university-area pizzeria by supporting a Latino organizer who helped expose labor violations when Mexican and Central American workers were employed at sub-minimum wages and forced to sleep on the pizzeria basement floor. Connecting these struggles with other successful defenses of immigrant rights is key to our delineation of transformative network politics.

Transformative Network Politics

Today, many progressive organizers and educators advocate for coalition politics, based on organizations that come together to collaborate when issues of shared interest and concern arise. The concept of coalitions suggests that organizations are solid and constant in terms of their ideas and practices; the coalition does not require any changes in intergroup or interpersonal politics. We prefer to envision a concept of network politics because it emphasizes the dynamics of how organizations come together in processes of mutual learning and solidarity. It suggests that new relationships are built through interactions that make central the experiences of historically marginalized or exploited people. Swords (2005, 2007) writes about network politics as the material and cultural practices of neo-Zapatista organizations that challenge procedural democracy and neoliberal development. The Zapatistas and many of their supporters disrupt the territorial and ideological power of state and economic interests by de-centering knowledge production and decision-making. To do so, they center indigenous and poor people's experiences through peace and human rights organizing, caravans, delegations, *Encuentros* (international political gatherings), *Consultas* (popular consultations), elections, community mental health work, struggles for territory, and initial efforts toward autonomy.

Learning from the Zapatistas' network politics suggests that in the US transformative movements must center the experiences of Mexicans, Mexican immigrants, and Mexican Americans, along with the experiences of other historically marginalized and exploited groups. One important element of network politics is the telling of stories of exploitation, discrimination, and neglect. Those who build this country must be seen where they have often been invisible. The people involved in network politics must also come to recognize patterns, the similarities and differences in how exploitation has operated from the Bracero to the post-industrial era. Such patterns include the trends we have documented in Chapters 5 to 11, including anti-immigrant backlash, demographic shifts, and the variety of modes of exploitation, incorporation, and exclusion in different geographic sites. Organizing must include demands for basic survival, as well as rights for workers and immigrants and participation in decision-making about the basic laws that affect health, well-being, integrity, and humanity.

We see the development of legal challenges to the racial and class status quo for Mexican laborers as a window into how liberal adjustments and social democratic reforms can potentially lead to a politics of transformation. Recent class-action lawsuits,[5] state congressional inquiries,[6] and proposed federal legislation[7] have brought the sordid history of the Repatriation Movement and the Bracero Program into the present discourse. What began as essentially a liberal adjustment approach to reparations was based in legal offices and subscribed to the price tag model of just compensation for past wrongs. The lawsuits evolved into a social democratic redress approach in terms of holding corporate and government actors responsible for past events and working to bar them from happening in the future. Of course, laws that secured civil liberties and adherence to the Geneva Convention have been rewritten to allow such abuses as Abu Ghraib and Guantanamo, so activists must avoid the pitfall of assuming that rogue leaders won't rewrite laws and bring on ideologues to rewrite history to justify their plans for committing future atrocities.

We envision the movement developing a transformative politics approach with truth commissions leading to civil society mobilization, rather than with truth commissions as ends in and of themselves. The transformative seeds of the Bracero reparations movement in grassroots organizing may germinate into major social change. Transformative politics does not agree with the liberal reparations model, which claims that monetary compensation fully atones for past transgressions. In contrast, highlighting the grassroots movement, such politics sees the potential for a liberal adjustment to contain the seeds of social democratic reform that, if reorganized and plugged into network politics, could lead to a transformative approach. Solutions to the exploitation of undocumented labor will bring the role of the immigrant rights movement and network politics to the center of recent efforts at improving the conditions of Mexicans residing in the US as well as addressing attempts at collective redress for past historical injustices.

The issue of reparations has taken the liberal center stage for nation-states and supra-governmental authorities. In the US, it has almost always been inextricably tied to the institution of racial slavery, and repeated attempts at making good on past promises have failed. The settlement of the Japanese internment case and particular reparations cases for the victims of the Rosewood, Florida, massacre and most recently the Tulsa Race Riots certainly brings this issue back to the forefront. Reparations cannot fully address what Jürgen Habermas (2001, 45) describes as

... the gruesome features of a century that "invented" the gas chamber, total war, state-sponsored genocide and extermination camps, brain-washing, state security apparatuses, and the panoptic surveillance of entire populations. The twentieth century "generated" more victims, more dead soldiers, more murdered civilians, more displaced minorities, more torture, more dead from cold, from hunger, from maltreatment, more political prisoners and refugees, than could ever have been imagined.

Reparations can never fully remedy past wrongs, and the limited monetary settlements will never make up for pain, suffering, humiliation, and outright physical and psychological torture. However, the positive aspect of this liberal adjustment is that it requires the collective conscience of a nation to come to grips with its sordid history and to allow those who were wronged to express publicly what they endured as the nation-state either looked away or more likely was complicit. The public dialogue on reparations moves offending nations forward by requiring them to deal with a past they deem so easy to forget. The grassroots organizing that has taken place in Mexico and the US requires both nations to seriously examine the historical origins of contemporary racialized predicaments and lingering inequalities.

Alianza Braceroproa, National Assembly of Ex-Braceros/*La Asamblea Nacional de Ex-Braceros*, and the Binational Union of Former Braceros are the more prominently recognized of the social movement organizations placing pressure on the Mexican government for monetary redress. The main means of organizing is to get ex-Braceros together, on a weekly basis, to talk about their shared experiences. Most of these public conversations have focused on the humiliating aspects of the processing centers where Braceros were subjected to the STD and hernia examinations and the DDT delousing ordeal. Recent developments in US courts and Mexican federal decisions have allowed the Mexican government to provide a limited monetary settlement while absolving its culpability for past wrongs. Yet the main contribution of collective action at this point seems to be the shared recognition of past wrongs and ways of remembering, thinking, speaking, and acting that completely counter the subservient roles that the Bracero Program attempted to force on workers.

As ex-Braceros seek redress for past wrongs, the hope is that the act of organizing and sharing stories will unite them into a coherent constituency for future mobilizations in networks of mutual learning. Much of this initial work of articulation has been conducted by the FIOB, which has united indigenous groups to engage in self-education and mobilize to obtain better conditions in Oaxaca and in the US. "Oaxacans have also developed the Frente, which unites different language groups in order to promote community and workplace struggles for social justice" (Bacon 2002). From the beginning, the FIOB approached politics from the perspective that the struggles of other marginalized communities were its struggles as well. "When the Zapatista army rose on January 1, 1994, the *Frente* immediately mounted actions to pressure the Mexican government to refrain from using massive military force in Chiapas. From Fresno to Baja California to Oaxaca, *Frente* activists went on hunger strikes and demonstrated in front of consulates and government offices" (Bacon 2002). Rather than solely subscribing to the HTA model of microbusiness development projects, the FIOB also saw its actions in a global human rights framework that guaranteed expressions of local culture in how it organized its binational community.

The FIOB's organizing strategy is based on the culture of Oaxacan communities, particularly an institution called the *tequio*. "This is the concept that we must participate in collective work to support our community," [Rufino Dominguez] explains. "In our communities we already know one another and can act together. That understanding of mutual assistance makes it easier for us to organize ourselves. Wherever we go, we go united. It's a way of saying that I do not speak alone—we all speak together. We make efforts so that our communities don't lose their culture, their language, and their traditions" (Bacon 2002). The FIOB offers a model for popular education practices that allow communities to collectively prioritize their own sets of concerns while connecting their struggles to end marginalization worldwide.

A transformative model for redressing historical wrongs, identifying presentist concerns, and envisioning future worlds has been the use of truth commissions and the framework of economic human rights for all as political organizing tools by poor people's organizations in the US. The process of organizing a truth commission involves identifying potential local leaders who share their stories of violations of their basic human rights. Truth commissioners are leaders who already work with constituencies that are committed to ensuring a civil society response to these violations. Through telling their stories and hearing each other's experiences, they learn they are not alone in their suffering and gain insights about the social patterns and dynamics that shape their experiences and those of their compatriots. Participants are empowered through the process of inviting leaders to attend, organizing the event, and building relationships among the truth-tellers. Further, the truth commission itself is a public event in a public space where the collective memory of an event like the Bracero Program or the militarization of the border can be recollected and critically challenged based on the knowledge of people directly affected.

Finally, the audience and the truth commissioners listen to the stories and commit themselves to preventing these violations from occurring again. People come together to realize that they are not alone, they did not do something "wrong" to be poor or exploited. Further, they hear how others have survived, resisted, or organized in different ways. Sharing ideas of how to organize makes the truth commissions sites for multiplying lessons from struggle, for realizing "we are all in this together," and for learning how to work together to prevent violations of economic and cultural human rights in the future. In a context where the US government modifies laws that are inconvenient or restrictive to capital, the only assurance of protection for human rights is an engaged, well-networked civil society.

The emphasis in this mode of organizing is on learning from the multiple strategies of survival and resistance that workers deploy, and the collective organizing model grows as more stories are shared. This model draws upon both the *testimonio* tradition in Latin America as well as the Truth and Reconciliation Commissions in South Africa, Peru, and Guatemala. Rather than viewing the truth commission as an end in and of itself, these commissions are designed for organizing and mobilizing—a starting point on the path of transformative politics. It is only by integrating these three broad forms of progressive social change that we can stop the long-standing relationship of exploiting Mexican labor for North American consumption.

Notes

1. We employ the term "discursive closure" in a way that partially revises Laclau and Mouffe's (2001, 121–22) thesis that "... the moment of closure of a discursive totality, which is not given at the 'objective' level of that totality, cannot be established at the level of a 'meaning-giving subject,' since the subjectivity of the agent is penetrated by the same precariousness and absence of suture apparent at any other point of the discursive totality of which it is a part...

Owing to this very absence of a final suture, the dispersion of subject positions cannot constitute a solution: given that none of them manages ultimately to consolidate itself as a *separate position*, there is a game of overdetermination among them that reintroduces the horizon of an impossible totality. It is this game which makes hegemonic articulation possible." In the ensuing discussions on immigration policy, it is always already failed attempts at discursive closure that are driven to maintain social order, but it is the contradictions embedded in said social order that create the spaces available to engage in transformative politics.

2. We take conservative ideologies at face value when they state their purpose is to maintain the status quo, and thus they are not a perspective that advocates for social change.

3. The 1982 decision ruled that the Texas Public Education Department could not restrict undocumented children from attending public school. The US Supreme Court ruled that denying access would impinge upon the students' right for equal protection under the law.

4. See http://www.ndlon.org/.

5. *Isidro Jimenez de la Torre v. US, Attorney General, Secretary of Labor, Secretary of Treasury, Secretary of State, Immigration and Naturalization Service, Secretary of Defense, Secretary of Agriculture, Republic of Mexico, Ministry of Foreign Affairs, Wells Fargo Bank, Banco de Mexico, Banco de Credito Rural*. Two similar class action lawsuits (*Chavez, et al. v. US of America, et al.* and *Barba, et al. v. US of America, et al.*) were moved from Eastern District Courts with *de la Torre* and consolidated in March 2002 with *Senorino Cruz v. US, et al.* to be heard in Northern California District Court by Judge Charles R. Breyer (see Mize 2005).

6. California Senate 2003 Select Committee on Citizen Participation Hearings, "Examination of Unconstitutional Deportations and Coerced Emigration of Legal Residents and US Citizens of Mexican Descent During 1930s," in Balderrama and Rodríguez (2006, 319–26).

7. Bracero Justice Act of 2002 (HR 4918).

Glossary

consumption: The act of buying things or services to satisfy human wants or needs. Consumption is considered in relation to the social processes of production and exploitation, as it requires the exploitation of those who labor to produce goods and services.

exploitation: The social relations in which those who own the means of production or service-provision compensate workers for less than the value of their work. Exploited workers become aware of these unequal relationships and can organize to transform them.

global capital accumulation: Manufacturing, service, and finance industries are controlled by powerful economic groups that accumulate wealth while laborers—the poor and the marginalized—are dispossessed, exploited, or excluded. Corporations are increasingly defined globally in their finance industries, production facilities, and market orientations.

hometown associations: Mexican immigrant remittance and development clubs or organizations that build infrastructure such as roads, churches, or schools in Mexico. They fund these campaigns with remittances and with matching programs from the Mexican government.

maquiladora, or maquila: A factory in Mexico that assembles imported materials without duties or tariffs and re-exports the finished product for distribution primarily in the US. *Maquila* is a short form for *maquiladora*, and both are used interchangeably.

neoliberalism: Policies and practices that promote the ideology of free trade, free markets, individual responsibility, and strong private property to govern political and economic relations. The control of the state and economy is transferred to private elite interests. Neoliberal economic ideology and practices predominate in contemporary politics, as evidenced by NAFTA.

post-Fordist era: Time period beginning in the 1980s and 1990s in which production is less characterized by mass manufacturing, assembly lines, and lifetime union jobs, and more based on value added in the form of information and communication technologies, just-in-time production, and flexible labor to meet niche consumer markets.

production: The creation of goods and services through work. Production requires labor and resources. In North America, production is increasingly of services. Levels of production affect and are affected by levels of consumption, and both shape social consequences including exploitation and environmental degradation.

remittance economy: The economic resources (money) sent by immigrant or migrant workers home to their families or communities of origin.

resistance: Actions to oppose unequal, exploitative, or oppressive social relations to demand respect and dignity for all. Includes building social movements, creating alternative institutions, and labor organizing to (re)build community and cross racial and class lines.

state: All forms of government (judicial, executive, legislative) from the local, state, and national levels to areas of the public domain including education, military, and police that operate within delimited spatial boundaries. State power is embedded in the monopoly of the legitimate use of violence and in its exclusive ability to define who is a citizen.

transnational corporations: Concomitant with the rise of neoliberal globalization, business firms aim to control market share, maximize their scale of production, and squeeze out competition on the global level. Includes companies intimately familiar to most people (e.g., Walmart, Pepsico, Citibank, Dole, etc.).

transnationalism: The increasing prevalence of immigrants living in or identifying with more than one nation simultaneously. Dual citizenship, remittances, hometown associations, and information flows all constitute the phenomenon.

References

Acuña, Rodolfo. 2010. *Occupied America: A history of Chicanos*. 7th ed. New York: Addison Wesley Longman.

Adorno, Theodor W. 2001. *The culture industry*. New York: Routledge.

Alarcón, Rafael. 2003. Skilled immigrants and *cereberos:* Foreign-born engineers and scientists in the high technology industry of Silicon Valley. In *Immigration research for a new century: Multidisciplinary perspectives*, ed. Nancy Foner, Ruben Rumbaut, and Steven J. Gold, 301–21. New York: Russell Sage Foundation.

———. 2007. The free circulation of skilled immigrants in North America. In *Migration without borders: Essays on the free movement of people*, ed. Antoine Pécoud and Paul de Guchteneire, 243–57. Paris: UNESCO Publishing.

Alberta Federation of Labour. 2007. Temporary foreign workers: Alberta's disposable workforce. http://www.afl.org/upload/AFLTFW.pdf (accessed May 5, 2010).

Albright, Jason. 2010. *Cleaners and the mobilization of communities: The 2006 Justice For Janitors campaign at the University of Miami*. Unpublished Master's thesis, Department of Development Sociology, Cornell University: Ithica, NY.

Almaguer, Tomás. 1994. *Racial fault lines: The historical origins of white supremacy in California*. Berkeley: University of California Press.

Althaus, Dudley, and Cynthia Leonor Garza. 2006. Dreams of many ride on boycott: Today's rallies aim to forge a new political reality. *Houston Chronicle*, May 1: A1.

Alvarez, Robert, Jr. 2005. *Mangos, chiles, and truckers: The business of transnationalism*. Minneapolis: University of Minnesota Press.

American Management Association. 2000. Manpower White Paper, May 2006. http://www.manpower.com/mpcom/files?name=Total_Workforce_WhitePaper_31.05.06.pdf (accessed January 31, 2007).

American Staffing Association. 2009. Staffing statistics, American staffing 2009: Looking for growth. http://www.americanstaffing.net/statistics/economic 2009.cfm (accessed May 10, 2010).

Amott, Julie, and Theresa Matthaei. 1996. *Race, gender, and work*. Boston: South End Press.

Andreas, Carol. 1994. *Meatpackers and beefbarons: Company town in a global economy*. Boulder: University Press of Colorado.

Andreas, Peter. 2000. *Border games: Policing the US-Mexico divide.* Ithaca, NY: Cornell University Press.

Anzaldúa, Gloria. 1987. *Borderlands|La Frontera: The new mestiza.* San Francisco: Aunt Lute Books.

Appadurai, Arjun, ed. 1986. *The social life of things: Commodities in cultural perspective.* New York: Cambridge University Press.

——, ed. 1996. *Modernity at large: Cultural dimensions of globalization.* Minneapolis: University of Minnesota Press.

——, ed. 2001. *Globalization.* Durham, NC: Duke University Press.

Arroyo-Picard, Alberto. 2003. *Impacts of the North American Free Trade Agreement in Mexico: Lessons for the free trade area of the Americas negotiation.* Managua: American Friends Service Committee.

Bacon, David. 2002. Grassroots: Cross-border organizing. *Z Magazine Online.* http://zmagsite.zmag.org/Dec2002/bacon1202.htm (accessed January 31, 2007).

Bada, Xóchitl. 2005. Hometown associations. In *The Oxford encyclopedia of Latinas and Latinos in the United States,* ed. Suzanne Oboler and Deena Gonzalez, 310–12. New York: Oxford University Press.

Balderrama, Francisco, and Raymond Rodríguez. 2006. *The great betrayal: Mexican repatriation in the 1930s.* Rev. ed. Albuquerque: University of New Mexico Press.

Banco Interamericano de Desarollo. 2002. *Hagamos la integración Mesoamericana una realidad: Los desafíos de Mesoamérica y el Plan Puebla-Panamá.* Washington: Banco Interamericano de Desarrollo.

Barger, W.K., and Ernesto Reza. 1994. *The farm labor movement in the Midwest.* Austin: University of Texas Press.

Barndt, Deborah. 2007. *Tangled routes: Women, work, and globalization on the tomato trail.* 2nd ed. New York: Rowman and Littlefield.

Bartra, Armando. 1985. *Los herederos de Zapata: Movimientos campesinos posrevolucionarios en México, 1920–1980.* Mexico City: Ediciones Era.

——. 2004. Rebellious cornfields: Toward food and labor self-sufficiency. In *Mexico in transition: Neoliberal globalism, the state and civil society,* ed. Gerardo Otero, 18–36. London: Zed Books.

Basok, Tanya. 2000. He came, he saw, he stayed: Guest worker programs and the issue of non-return. *International Migration* 38: 216–38.

——. 2002. *Tortillas and tomatoes: transmigrant Mexican harvesters in Canada.* Montreal: McGill-Queen's University Press.

Beneria, Lourdes. 1996. The foreign debt crisis and the social costs of adjustment in Latin America. In *Emergences: Women's struggles for livelihood in Latin America,* ed. John Friedman *et al.* Los Angeles: UCLA Latin American Center.

Biemann, Ursula. 1999. *Performing the border.* New York: Women Make Movies Distributor. Documentary.

Binford, Leigh. 2009. From fields of power to fields of sweat: The dual process of constructing temporary migrant labour in Mexico and Canada. *Third World Quarterly* 30: 503–17.

Bonacich, Edna, and Richard Applebaum. 2000. *Behind the label: Inequality in the Los Angeles apparel industry.* Berkeley: University of California Press.

Brady, Mary Pat. 1998. Specular morality, the war on drugs, and anxieties of visibility. In *Making worlds: Gender, metaphor, materiality,* ed. Susan H. Aiken, Ann Brigham, Sallie Marston, and Penny Waterstone, 110–27. Tucson: University of Arizona Press.

Briggs, Vernon M., Jr. 1996. *Mass immigration and the national interest (labor and human resources).* Armonk, NY: M.E. Sharpe.

Broadway, Michael. 2007. Meat packing and the transformation of rural communities: A comparison of Brooks, Alberta and Garden City, Kansas. *Rural Sociology* 72 (4): 560–82.

Burgess, Katrina. 2005. Migrant philanthropy and local governance. In *New patterns for Mexico: Observations on remittances, philanthropic giving, and equitable development,* ed. Barbara J. Merz, 99–124. Cambridge, MA: Harvard University Press.

Bustamante, Jorge A., Guillermina Jasso, J. Edward Taylor, and Paz Triqueros Legarreta. 1998. Characteristics of migrants: Mexicans in the United States. In *Migration between Mexico and the United States,* Vol. 1, 91–162. Austin: Mexican Ministry of Foreign Affairs and the United States Commission on Immigration Reform.

Calavita, Kitty. 1992. *Inside the state: The Bracero Program, immigration, and the INS.* New York: Routledge.

Caldwell, J.T. 2003. Representation and complicity in suburban migrant camps: Reflections of a documentary filmmaker. *Aztlán: A Journal of Chicano Studies* 28: 205–26.

California Institute for Rural Studies. 2002. *In their own words: Farmworker access to healthcare in four California regions.* http://www.cirsinc.org/CPAC.pdf (accessed January 31, 2007).

Call, Wendy. 2002. Resisting the Plan Puebla-Panama: Citizen action in the Americas. Discussion Paper. Americas Program at Interhemispheric Resource Center (IRC): 2.

———. 2003. Mexicans and Central Americans "can't take any more." *NACLA Report on the Americas* 36 (5): 9.

Carranza, Miguel A. 2004. Latinos struggle for equality: A case study of Nebraska's Latino communities. In *La causa: Civil rights, social justice, and the struggle for equality in the Midwest,* ed. Gilberto Cárdenas, 139–76. Houston: Arte Publico Press.

Cason, Jim, and David Brooks. 2002. El rescate de Estados Unidos por México. *La Jornada* (Mexico City). http://migracion.jornada.com.mx/migracion/el-otro-mexico/el-rescate-de-estados-unidos-por-mexico (accessed December 29, 2006).

Castro-Soto, Gustavo. 2001. Plan Puebla Panamá—Quinta parte: Capítulo México: Región Sur-Sureste. *Boletín Chiapas al Día* 246. http://www.ciepac.org/boletines/chiapasaldia.php?id=246#print (accessed June 5, 2005).

Chavez, Leo R. 1992. *Covering immigration*. Berkeley: University of California Press.

———. 2001. *Shadowed lives: Undocumented immigrants in American society*. 2nd ed. Fort Worth: Harcourt Brace College.

Choy, Catherine C. 2003. *Empire of care: Nursing and migration in Filipino American history*. Durham, NC: Duke University Press.

Clawson, Dan. 2003. *The next upsurge: Labor and the new social movements*. Ithaca, NY: ILR Press.

Cohen, Deborah. 2001. Caught in the middle: The Mexican state's relationship with the United States. *Journal of American Ethnic History* 20 (3): 110–32.

Cohen, Jeffrey H. 2001. Transnational migration in rural Oaxaca, Mexico: Dependency, development, and the household. *American Anthropologist* 103: 954–68.

Colby, Catherine. 1997. From Oaxaca to Ontario: Mexican contract labor in Canada and the impact at home. Report for the California Institute for Rural Studies. Davis: California Institute for Rural Studies.

Collier, Robert. 2001. Mourning coffee: World's leading java companies are raking in high profits but growers worldwide face ruin as prices sink to historic low. *San Francisco Chronicle*, May 20: A1.

Collins, Jane. 2003. *Threads: Gender, labor, and power in the global apparel industry*. Chicago: University of Chicago Press.

Colorado Agricultural Experiment Station. 1958. *Annual report*. Fort Collins: Colorado State University.

Comisión Nacional de los Salarios Mínimos (CNSM). 2006. Tabla de salarios mínimos generales y profesionales 2006. http://www.conasami.gob.mx/formatestimonios.aspx?ID=10&int=0 (accessed January 31, 2007).

Compa, Lance. 2005. Blood, sweat, and fears: Workers' rights in US meat and poultry plants. Human Rights Watch Report. http://www.hrw.org/reports/2005/usa0105/ (accessed January 31, 2007).

Coronado, Irasema. 2003. *La vida en las colonias de la frontera*/Life in colonias on the border. *Latino Studies Journal* 1 (1): 193–97.

Critzon, Michael. 2004. Students spend spring break protesting Taco Bell. In *Race, class, and gender in the United States*, ed. Paula S. Rothenberg, 618–20. 6th ed. New York: Worth.

Davis, Mike. 2001. *Magical urbanism: Latinos reinvent the US big city*. New York: Verso.

———. 2007. *Planet of slums*. New York: Verso.

Davy, Megan, and Deborah Meyers. 2005. United States-Canada-Mexico fact sheet on trade and migration. Migration Policy Institute Immigration Facts Series 11. http://www.migrationpolicy.org/pubs/US_Canada_Mexico_1005.pdf (accessed August 31, 2009).

De Genova, Nicholas. 2005. *Working the boundaries: Race, space, and illegality in Mexican Chicago*. Durham, NC: Duke University Press.

Deutsch, Sarah. 1987. *No separate refuge: Culture, class, and gender on an Anglo-Hispanic frontier in the American Southwest, 1880–1940*. New York: Oxford University Press.

DeWind, Josh, Tom Seidl, and Janet Shenk. 1979. Contract labor in US agriculture: The West Indian cane cutters in Florida. In *Peasants and proletarians: The struggles of Third World workers*, ed. Robin Cohen, Peter Gutkind, and Phyllis Brazier, 380–96. New York: Monthly Review Press.

Dickerson, Marla. 2005. From textile city to ghost town. *Los Angeles Times*, December 8. http://articles.latimes.com/2005/dec/08/business/fi-textilecity8 (accessed May 10, 2010).

Driscoll, Barbara A. 1999. *The tracks north: The railroad Bracero Program of World War II*. Austin: University of Texas Press.

du Gay, Paul, Stuart Hall, Linda Janes, Hugh Mackay, and Keith Negus. 1997. *Doing cultural studies: The story of the Sony Walkman*. Newbury Park: Sage.

———. 2009. *Consumption and identity at work*. Newbury Park: Sage.

Dunn, Timothy. 1996. *The militarization of the US-Mexico border*. Austin: University of Texas Press.

Durand, Jorge M. 1994. *Más allá de la línea: Patrones migratorios entre México y Estados Unidos*. Mexico City: Consejo Nacional para la Cultura y las Artes, DF.

Durazo, Marie Elena. 1999. Testimony. Subcommittee on employer-employee relations hearings. http://www.house.gov/ed_workforce/hearings/106th/eer/ud72199/durazo.htm (accessed November 20, 2006).

Eberts, Paul, and Kris Merschrod. 2004. *Socioeconomic trends and well-being indicators in New York State, 1950–2000*. Albany: New York State Legislative Commission on Rural Resources.

Edid, Marilyn. 1994. *Farm labor organizing: Trends and prospects*. Ithaca, NY: ILR-Cornell University Press.

Embriz, Arnulfo. 1993. *Indicadores socioeconómicos de los pueblos indígenas de México, 1990*. Direccion de Investigacion y Promocion Cultural, Subdireccion de Investigacion. Mexico City: Instituto Nacional Indigenista.

Engstrom, James D. 2001. Industry and immigration in Dalton, Georgia. In *Latino workers in the contemporary South*, ed. A.D. Murphy, C. Blanchard, and J. Hill, 44–58. Athens: University of Georgia Press.

Escala-Rabadan, Luis, Gaspar Rivera-Salgado, and Rigoberto Rodriguez. 2006. Linking social capital, human capital, and immigrant groups: Capacity building and organizational development among Mexican and other Latino immigrant hometown associations in California. Paper presented at the Latin American Studies Association Conference. San Juan, Puerto Rico, March 2006.

Eschbach, K., J.M. Hagan, and N.P. Rodríguez. 2004. Deaths during undocumented migration across the Southwestern border. What are the policy implications in the new era of homeland security? *In Defense of the Alien* 26: 37–52.

Fantasia, Rick, and Kim Voss. 2004. *Hard work: Remaking the American labor movement*. Berkeley: University of California Press.

Feliciano, Cynthia. 2001. The benefits of biculturalism: Exposure to immigrant culture and dropping out of school among Asian and Latino youths. *Social Science Quarterly* 82: 865–79.

Fennell, David A. 1999. *Ecotourism: An introduction.* New York: Routledge Press.

Fine, Janice R. 2006. *Worker centers: Organizing communities at the edge of the dream.* Ithaca: ILR Press.

Fink, Deborah. 1998. *Cutting into the meatpacking line: Workers and change in the rural midwest.* Chapel Hill: University of North Carolina Press.

Fisk, Catherine, Daniel Mitchell, and Christopher Erickson. 2000. Union representation of immigrant janitors in Southern California: Economic and legal challenges. In *Organizing immigrants: The challenges for unions in contemporary California,* ed. Ruth Milkman, 199–224. Ithaca: ILR Press.

Foley, Neil. 1997. *The white scourge: Mexicans, Blacks, and poor Whites in Texas cotton culture.* Berkeley: University of California Press.

Gabaccia, Donna. 1992. *Seeking common ground: Multidisciplinary studies of immigrant women in the United States: Contributions in Women's Studies.* Westport, CT: Praeger.

Galan Productions. 2000. The forgotten Americans. Companion website to PBS documentary. http://www.pbs.org/klru/forgottenamericans/index.htm (accessed January 31, 2007).

Galarza, Ernesto. n.d. Collected papers of Ernesto Galarza. Department of Special Collections, Stanford University Libraries, Stanford, CA.

———. 1956. *Strangers in our fields: Based on a report regarding compliance with the contractual, legal, and civil rights of Mexican agricultural contract labor in the United States.* 2nd ed. Washington, DC: United States Section, Joint United States-Mexico Trade Union Committee.

———. 1964. *Merchants of labor: The Mexican Bracero history.* Santa Barbara, CA: McNally and Loftin.

———. 1970. *Spiders in the house and workers in the fields.* South Bend, IN: University of Notre Dame Press.

———. 1977. *Tragedy at Chualar.* Santa Barbara, CA: McNally and Loftin.

Gallagher, Kevin P. 2004. Paying for NAFTA. *NACLA Report on the Americas:* 38–47.

Gamboa, Erasmo. 1990. *Mexican labor and World War II: Braceros in the Pacific Northwest, 1942–1947.* Austin: University of Texas Press.

———. 2000. *Mexican labor and World War II: Braceros in the Pacific Northwest 1942–1947.* 2nd ed. Seattle: University of Washington Press.

Gamboa, Suzanne. 2006. Union hopes to build on Houston success. Associated Press Online. http://www.highbeam.com/doc/1P1–117762054.html (accessed October 1, 2009).

Gamio, Manuel. 1931. *The life story of the Mexican immigrant.* Chicago: University of Chicago Press.

Ganz, Marshall. 2000. Resources and resourcefulness: Strategic capacity in the unionization of California agriculture 1959–1966. *American Journal of Sociology* 105: 1003–63.

Gaouette, Nicole. 2006. Latinos walk out amid firings. *Los Angeles Times,* November 18. http://articles.latimes.com/2006/nov/18/nation/na-protest18 (accessed October 1, 2009).

Garcia, Juan Ramon. 1980. *Operation Wetback: The mass deportation of Mexican undocumented workers in 1954.* Westport, CT: Greenwood Press.

Garcia, María Cristina. 2006. *Seeking refuge: Central American migration to Mexico, the United States, and Canada.* Berkeley: University of California Press.

García, Marío T. 1981. *Desert immigrants.* New Haven, CT: Yale University Press.

Garcia, Matthew. 2001. *A world of their own: Race, labor, and citrus in the making of Greater Los Angeles, 1900–1970.* Chapel Hill: University of North Carolina Press.

Garcia Canclini, Néstor. 1995. *Hybrid cultures.* Minneapolis, MN: University of Minnesota Press.

Garcia y Griego, Manuel. 1983. US importation of Mexican contract laborers. In *The border that joins,* ed. Peter Brown and Henry Shue, 49–98. Totowa: Rowman and Littlefield. Repr. in *Between two worlds: Mexican immigrants in the United States,* ed. David Gutiérrez, 45–88. Wilmington, DE: Scholarly Resources, 1996.

García Zamora, Rodolfo. 2005. The impact of remittances in Jerez, Zacatecas. In *New patterns for Mexico: Observations on remittances, philanthropic giving, and equitable development,* ed. B.J. Merz, 19–32. Cambridge, MA: Harvard University Press.

Gaspar de Alba, Alicia. 2005. *Desert blood: The Juarez murders.* Houston: Arte Publico Press.

Gereffi, Gary. 2005. The new offshoring of jobs and global displacement: Who wins, who loses and who calls the shots? Polson Institute for Global Development Memorial Lecture. Ithaca: Cornell University.

———. 2006. North Carolina in the global economy: Tobacco maps. Center of Globalization, Governance, and Competitiveness, Duke University. http://www.soc.duke.edu/NC_GlobalEconomy/hog/maps.php#map1 (accessed January 31, 2007).

———, and Miguel Korzeniewicz, eds. 1994. *Commodity chains and global capitalism.* Westport, CT: Praeger.

Giannini Foundation of Agricultural Economics. 1982. *1982 census of agriculture economics and statistics.* Davis: California Agricultural Experiment Station.

Gilbert, Alan. 1994. *The Latin American city.* London: The Latin American Bureau.

Gladstone, David L. 2005. *From pilgrimage to package tour: Travel and tourism in the Third World.* New York: Routledge.

Goldring, Luin. 1998. Migration, arrival, and settlement. *The Encyclopedia of Canada's Peoples/Mexicans.* http://www.multiculturalcanada.ca/Encyclopedia/A-Z/m7/2 (accessed August 17, 2009).

———, Carolina Berinstein, and Judith Bernhard. 2007. Institutionalizing precarious immigration status in Canada. The Center for Comparative Immigration Studies Working Paper #158. San Diego: University of California.

Gomez, Jesus. 2000. *Voices from the front lines: Organizing immigrant workers in Los Angeles.* Los Angeles: UCLA Center for Labor Research and Education.

Gonzalez, Juan. 2000. *Harvest of empire: A history of Latinos*. New York: Penguin Books.

Gonzalez Baker, Susan. 1990. *The cautious welcome: The legalization programs of the Immigration Reform and Control Act*. Washington, DC: Rand Corporation and Urban Institute Press.

González de la Rocha, Mercedes. 2006. Vanishing assets: Cumulative disadvantage among the urban poor. *Annals of the American Academy of Political and Social Science* 606: 68–94.

Gordon, Jennifer. 2006. *Suburban sweatshops: The fight for immigrant rights*. Cambridge, MA: Harvard University Press.

Gorz, André. 1973. *Socialism and revolution*. Garden City, NY: Anchor Books.

Gouveia, Lourdes, and Rogelio Saenz. 2000. Global forces and Latino population growth in the Midwest: A regional and subregional analysis. *Great Plains Research* 10: 305–28.

Gouveia, Lourdes, and Donald D. Stull. 1995. Dances with cows: Beefpacking's impact on Garden City, Kansas, and Lexington, Nebraska. In *Any way you cut it: Meat processing and small-town America*, ed. Donald D. Stull, Michael Broadway, and David Griffith, 85–108. Lawrence: University of Kansas Press.

Greenhouse, Steven. 2006. Hundreds, all nonunion, walk out at pork plant in NC. *New York Times*, November 17. http://query.nytimes.com/gst/fullpage.html?res=9B0DE2DA143EF934A25752C1A9609C8B63 (accessed May 10, 2010).

Grey, Mark, and Anne C. Woodrick. 2005. Latinos have revitalized our community: Mexican migration and anglo responses in Marshalltown, Iowa. In *New destinations*, ed. Ruben Hernández-León and Victor Zúñiga, 133–54. New York: Russell Sage Foundation.

Griffith, David 1995. New immigrants in an old industry: Blue crab processing in Pamlico County, North Carolina. In *Any way you cut it: Meat processing and small-town America*, ed. Donald D. Stull, Michael Broadway, and David Griffith, 155–86. Lawrence: University of Kansas Press.

———. 2005. Rural industry and Mexican immigration and settlement in North Carolina. In *New destinations*, ed. Rubén Hernández-León and Victor Zúñiga, 50–75. New York: Russell Sage Foundation.

Grove, Wayne A. 1996. The Mexican Farm Labor Program, 1942–1964: Government-administered labor market insurance. *Agricultural History* 70: 302–20.

Guarnizo, Luis, and Michael Peter Smith. 1998. The locations of transnationalism. *Comparative Urban and Community Research* 6, Special Issue: *Transnationalism from Below*: 3–34.

Guerin-Gonzales, Camille. 1996. *Mexican workers and American dreams*. New Brunswick, NJ: Rutgers University Press.

Guthey, Greig. 2001. Mexican places in southern spaces: Globalization, work, and daily life in and around the North Georgia poultry. In *Latino workers in the contemporary South*, ed. Arthur Murphy, Colleen Blanchard, and Jennifer Hill, 57–67. Athens: University of Georgia Press.

Gutierrez, David. 1995. *Walls and mirrors: Mexican Americans, Mexican immigrants, and the politics of ethnicity.* Berkeley: University of California Press.

———. 2004. *The Columbia history of Latinos since 1960.* New York: Columbia University Press.

Habermas, Jürgen. 2001. *The postnational constellation: Political essays.* Cambridge, MA: MIT Press.

Hall, Stuart 1988. *The hard road to renewal: Thatcherism and the crisis of the Left.* New York: Verso Books.

Ham-Chande, Roberto, and John R. Weeks. 1992. *Demographic dynamics of the US-Mexico border.* El Paso: Texas Western Press.

Hancock, Blackhawk. 2007. Occupational subcultures in the Chicago restaurant industry. University Research Council Grant, Depaul University.

Hanrahan, Jenifer. 1999. Soldiers of the fields, Braceros seek justice, WWII-era guest workers try to reclaim lost wages. *San Diego Union-Tribune,* September 26: A1.

Harvey, David. 2003. *The new imperialism.* New York: Oxford University Press.

Harvey, Neil. 1998. *The Chiapas rebellion: The struggle for land and democracy.* Durham, NC: Duke University Press.

———. 2005a. Inclusion through autonomy: Zapatistas and dissent. *NACLA Report on the Americas* 39 (2): 12–20.

———. 2005b. Zapatismo y sustentabilidad. *La Jornada* (Mexico City): August 14. http://www.jornada.unam.mx/2005/08/14/006a1pol.php (accessed December 30, 2005).

Hellman, Judith Adler. 1997. Structural adjustment in Mexico and the dog that didn't bark. CERLAC Working Paper Series.

———. 1999. *Mexican lives.* 2nd ed. New York: The New Press.

Henriques, Gisele, and Raj Patel. 2004. NAFTA, corn, and Mexico's agricultural trade liberalization. In *Americas Program, Interhemispheric Resource Center.* http://americas.irc-online.org/pdf/reports/0402nafta.pdf (accessed December 30, 2005).

Hernandez, Jose Amaro. 1983. *Mutual aid for survival: The case of the Mexican American.* New York: Krieger Publications.

Hernández-León, Ruben, and Victor Zúñiga. 2000. Making carpet by the mile: The emergence of a Mexican immigrant community in an industrial region of the US historic South. *Social Science Quarterly* 81: 49–66.

Herzog, Lawrence. 1996. Border commuter workers and transfrontier metropolitan structure along the US-Mexico border. In *US-Mexico borderlands: Historical and contemporary perspectives,* ed. Oscar J. Martinez, 176–89. Wilmington, DE: Scholarly Resources.

Hochschild, Arlie, and Barbara Ehrenreich, eds. 2004. *Global woman: Nannies, maids, and sex workers in the new economy.* New York: Holt.

Holmes Norton, E. 1996. Affirmative action in the workplace. In *The affirmative action debate,* ed. George E. Curry, 39–48. Reading, MA: Addison-Wesley.

Hondagneu-Sotelo, Pierrette. 1994. *Gendered transitions: Mexican experiences of immigration.* Berkeley: University of California Press.

————. 2007. *Domestica: Immigrant workers cleaning and caring in the shadows of affluence.* Berkeley: University of California Press.

Horkheimer, Max, and Theodor W. Adorno. 2002. *The dialectic of enlightenment.* Stanford, CA: Stanford University Press.

Instítuto de Geografía (UNAM). 1986. Tenencia de yierra y mano de obra (superficie por municipio). http://www.igeograf.unam.mx/instituto/publi-caciones/atlas/tentierrymanob.jpg (accessed October 30, 2009).

Jayaraman, Sarumathi, and Immanuel Ness. 2005. *New urban immigrant workforce: Innovative models for labor organizing.* New York: M.E. Sharpe.

Jenkins, Craig. 1978. The demand for immigrant workers: Labor scarcity or "social control?" *International Migration Review* 12: 514–35.

Johnson, James H., Jr., W.C. Ferrell, and C. Guinn. 1997. Immigration reform and the browning of America: Tensions, conflicts, and community instability in metropolitan Los Angeles. *International Migration Review* 31(4): 1055–95.

Johnson, Kevin R. 1998. Immigration politics, popular democracy, and California's Proposition 187. In *The Latino condition: A critical reader,* ed. Richard Delgado and Jean Stefancic, 101–24. New York: NYU Press.

————. 2004. *The huddled masses myth: Immigration and civil rights.* Philadelphia: Temple University Press.

Johnson-Webb, Karen. 2003. *Recruiting Hispanic labor: Immigrants in non-traditional areas.* New York: LFB Scholarly Publishing.

Jones, Robert C. 1945. *Mexican war workers in the US: The Mexican-US manpower recruiting program and its operation.* Washington, DC: Pan American Union.

Kandel, William. 2006. Meat-processing firms attract Hispanic workers to rural America. *Amberwaves.* http://www.ers.usda.gov/amberwaves (accessed October 1, 2009).

————, and John Cromartie. 2004. New patterns of Hispanic settlement in rural America. *Rural Development Research Report* 99. Washington, DC: USDA Economic Research Service.

Kazimipur, Abdolmohammed, and Shiva S. Halli. 2001. Immigrants and new poverty: The case of Canada. *International Migration Review* 35: 1129–56.

Kirstein, Peter N. 1977. *Anglo over Bracero: A history of the Mexican worker in the United States from Roosevelt to Nixon.* San Francisco: R and E Research Associates.

Kiser, George C., and Martha W. Kiser. 1979. *Mexican workers in the United States.* Albuquerque: University of New Mexico Press.

Koch, Andrea. 1989. Zapotec migrants: The scheme of a transnational lifestyle. Master's Thesis. University of Amsterdam.

Koval, John P. 2006. Immigrants at work. In *The new Chicago: A social and cultural analysis,* ed. John Koval, *et al.,* 197–212. Philadelphia: Temple University Press.

————, Larry Bennett, Michael I.J. Bennett, Fassil Demissie, Roberta Garner, and Kijoong Kim, eds. 2006. *The new Chicago: A social and cultural analysis.* Philadelphia: Temple University Press.

Kozol, Jonathan. 1991. *Savage inequalities: Children in America's schools.* New York: Harper Perennial.

———. 2005. *The shame of the nation: The restoration of apartheid schooling in America.* New York: Crown.

Krissman, Fred. 2006. *Sin coyote ni patrón:* Why the "migrant network" fails to explain international migration. *International Migration Review* 39 (1): 4–44.

Laclau, Ernesto, and Chantal Mouffe. 2001. *Hegemony and socialist strategy: Towards a radical democratic politics.* 2nd ed. New York: Verso Books.

Lamm, Richard, and Gary Imhoff. 1986. *The immigration time bomb.* New York: Dutton.

Lamphere, Louise, Alex Stepick, and Guillermo Grenier, eds. 1995. *Newcomers in the workplace: Immigrants and the restructuring of the US economy.* Philadelphia: Temple University Press.

Levy, Daniel C., and Kathleen Bruhn. 2001. *Mexico: The struggle for democratic development.* Berkeley: University of California Press.

Lewis, Oscar, and Ruth M. Lewis. 1959. *Five families: Mexican case studies in the culture of poverty.* New York: Basic Books.

Leyva-Solano, Xochitl, and Willibald Sonnleitner. 2000. ¿Qué es el neozapatismo? *Revista Espiral: Estudios Sobre Estado y Sociedad* 6: 163–202.

Lipsitz, George. 1998. *The possessive investment in whiteness: How white people profit from identity politics.* Philadelphia: Temple University Press.

———. 2001. *American Studies in a moment of danger.* Minneapolis: University of Minnesota Press.

Lyon, Richard. 1954. The legal status of American and Mexican migratory farm labor. PhD dissertation. Cornell University, Ithaca, NY.

MacLachlan, Ian. 2001. *Kill and chill: Restructuring Canada's beef commodity chain.* Toronto: University of Toronto Press.

Malone, Scott. 2004. UNITE HERE: Merge to increase organizing clout. *Workers' World Daily* 6: 5.

Manpower. 2006. Engaging the total workforce. Manpower White Paper, May. http://www.manpower.com/mpcom/files?name=Total_Workforce_WhitePaper_31.05.06.pdf, (accessed January 31, 2007).

Martinez, Martha A. 2009. The housing crisis and Latino home ownership in Chicago: Mortgage applications, foreclosures, and property values. Institute for Latino Studies, University of Notre Dame.

Martinez, Oscar J. 1975a. *Border boom town: Cuidad Juarez since 1848.* Austin: University of Texas Press.

———. 1975b. On the size of the Chicano population: New estimates, 1850–1900. *Aztlán* 6: 50–56.

———. 1988. *Troublesome border.* Tucson: University of Arizona Press.

———. 1994. *Border people: Life and society in the U.S.-Mexico borderlands.* Tucson: University of Arizona Press.

Martinez, Rubén. 2001. *Crossing over: A Mexican family on the migrant trail.* New York: Picador.

Marx, Karl. 1976 [1867]. *Capital*. Vol. 1. New York: Penguin Books.

———. 1845. *The German ideology*. http://www.marxists.org/archive/marx/works/1845/german-ideology/ch01a.htm (accessed May 5, 2010).

Mauss, Marcel. 2000. *The gift: The form and reason for exchange in archaic societies*. New York: W.W. Norton.

McCain, Johnny Mac. 1981. Contract labor as a factor in United States-Mexican relations, 1942–1947. PhD Dissertation. University of Texas at Austin.

McMichael, Philip. 2003. *Development and social change: A global perspective*. Thousand Oaks, CA: Pine Forge Press.

McWilliams, Carey. 1990[1948]. *North from Mexico: The Spanish-speaking people of the United States*. Westport, CT: Praeger.

Meyerson, Harold. 2006. The power of the numbers. *Washington Post*, May 3: A23.

Milkman, Ruth. 2001. Organizing immigrant workers: Case studies from southern California. In *Rekindling the movement: Labor's quest for relevance in the 21st century*, ed. Lowell Turner, Henry C. Katz, and Richard Hurd, 99–128. Ithaca, NY: ILR Press.

———.2006. *L.A. story: Immigrant workers and the future of the US labor movement*. New York: Russell Sage Foundation.

———, and Kent Wong. 2000. *Voices from the front lines: Organizing immigrant workers in Los Angeles*. Los Angeles: UCLA Center for Labor Research and Education.

Millard, Ann V., and Jorge Chapa. 2004. *Apple pie and enchiladas: Latino newcomers in the rural Midwest*. Austin: University of Texas Press.

Mize, Ronald. 1996. The economic history of immigration to the United States: Theories, methods, assumptions. Paper presented at the Midwest Sociological Meetings, History and Sociology Session, Chicago.

———. 2003. African Americans and housing. In *State of black Fort Wayne 2002: A statistical profile of the African American community*, 2.1–2.17. Fort Wayne, IN: Urban League. October.

———. 2004. The persistence of workplace identities: Living the effects of the Bracero total institution. In *Immigrant life in the US: Multidisciplinary perspectives*, ed. Donna Gabaccia and Colin W. Leach, 133–51. New York: Routledge Press.

———. 2005. Reparations for Mexican Braceros? Lessons learned from Japanese and African American attempts at redress. LatCrit VIII Symposium Issue. *Cleveland State Law Review* 52: 273–95.

———. 2006. Mexican contract workers and the US capitalist agricultural labor process: The formative era, 1942–1964. *Rural Sociology* 71: 85–107.

———, and Craig Leedham. 2000. Manufacturing bias: An analysis of newspaper coverage of Latino immigration issues. *Latino Studies Journal* 11: 88–107.

Montejano, David. 1987. *Anglos and Mexicans in the making of Texas*. Austin: University of Texas Press.

Montwieler, Nancy H. 1987. *The immigration reform law of 1986: Analysis, text, and legislative history*. Washington, DC: Bureau of National Affairs.

Moody, Kim. 1988. *An injury to all*. New York: Verso.

Mooney, Patrick, and Theo J. Majka. 1995. *Farmers' and farm workers' movements: Social protest in American agriculture*. New York: Twayne.

Morales, Maria Cristina. 2009. The acclimatization of immigrant social networks to economic restructuring: Social capital in the construction industry. Paper presented at the American Sociological Association Annual Meetings, New Latino Destinations Paper Session, San Francisco.

Muñoz Ríos, P. 2006. El salario mínimo de México, el más deteriorado de América Latina: Expertos. *La Jornada*, January 2. http://www.jornada.unam. mx/2006/01/02/index.php?section=sociedad&article=032n1soc (accessed June 25, 2006).

Murray, Douglas. 1982. The abolition of *el cortito*, the short-handled hoe: A case study in social conflict and state policy in California agriculture. *Social Problems* 30: 26–39.

Mutabaruka. 1996. *The Ultimate Collection*. Shanachie Records.

Ness, Immanuel. 1998. Organizing immigrant communities: UNITE's workers center strategy. In *Organizing to win: New research on union strategies*, ed. K. Brofenbrenner, Sheldon Friedman, Richard Hurd, Rudolph Oswald, and Ronald Seeber, 87–102. Ithaca, NY: Cornell University Press.

———. 2005. *Immigrants, unions, and the new US labor market*. Philadelphia: Temple University Press.

Ngai, Mae. 2004. *Impossible subjects: Illegal aliens and the making of modern America*. Princeton, NJ: Princeton University Press.

Nora, Amaury. 2003. Access to higher education for Hispanic Studies: Real or illusory? In *The majority in the minority: Expanding the representation of Latina/o faculty, administrators, and students in higher education*, ed. Jeanett Castellanos and Lee Brown, 47–68. Sterling, VA: Stylus.

Ono, Kent A., and John M. Sloop. 2002. *Shifting borders: Rhetoric, immigration, and California's Proposition 187*. Philadelphia: Temple University Press.

OECD (Organization for Economic Co-Operation and Development). 2001. National tourism policy review of Mexico. http://www.oecd.org/dataoecd /43/54/33650486.pdf (accessed June 1, 2008).

Orozco, Manuel. 2002. *Latino hometown associations as agents of development in sending money home: Hispanic remittances and community development*. New York: Rowman and Littlefield.

Oxfam America. 2004. Like machines in the fields: Workers without rights in American agriculture. http://fr.oxfamamerica.org/en/newsandpublications/ publications/research_reports/art7011.html (accessed October 1, 2009).

Parra, Ricardo. 2004. Latinos in the Midwest: Civil rights and community action. In *Latinos in the Midwest: Civil rights and community action*, ed. Gilberto Cárdenas, 1–18. Houston: Arte Publico Press.

Peña, Devon. 1997. *The terror of the machine*. Austin: University of Texas Press.

Pfeffer, Max, and Pilar Parra. 2004. Immigrants and the community, rural New York initiative. http://devsoc.cals.cornell.edu/cals/devsoc/outreach/cardi/

publications/upload/11–2004-immigrants_community.pdf (accessed January 14, 2009).

Pickard, Miguel. 2003. El gobierno Mexicano frente al PPP: Se busca una nueva estrategia ante el rechazo Popular. *Boletin Chiapas al Dia* 329: 1–4.

Piore, Michael. 1979. *Birds of passage: Migrant labor and industrial societies.* New York: Cambridge University Press.

Portes, Alejandro, and Ruben Rumbaut. 1996. *Immigrant America: A portrait.* 2nd ed. Berkeley: University of California Press.

Portillo, Lourdes. 2001. *Señorita extraviada.* New York: Women Make Movies Distributor. Documentary.

Preibisch, Kerry. 2007. Globalizing work, globalizing citizenship: Community-migrant worker alliances in Southwestern Ontario. In *Organizing the transnational: Labour, politics, and social change,* ed. Luin Goldring and Sailana Krishnamurti, 97–114. Vancouver: University of British Columbia Press.

———, and Leigh Binford. 2007. Interrogating racialized global labour supply: An exploration of the ethnic replacement of foreign agricultural workers in Canada. *The Canadian Review of Sociology and Anthropology* 44 (1): 5–36.

———, and Luz María Hermoso Santamaria. 2006. Engendering labour migration: The case of foreign workers in Canadian agriculture. In *Women, migration and citizenship: Making local, national, and transnational connections,* ed. Evangelia Tastsoglou and Alexandra Dobrowolsky, 107–30. Burlington, VT: Ashgate.

———, and Stan Raper. 2007. Forcing governments to govern in defense of noncitizen workers: A story about the Canadian labour movement's alliance with agricultural migrants. In *Organizing the transnational: Labour, politics, and social change,* ed. Luin Goldring and Sailana Krishnamurti, 115–28. Vancouver: University of British Columbia Press.

Presidencia de la República. 2001. *Plan Puebla-Panamá documento base.* Vol. 2003. México, D.F.: Oficina del Presidente.

Preston, Julia, and Samuel Dillon. 2004. *Opening Mexico: The making of a democracy.* New York: Farrar, Strauss, and Giroux.

Pritchard, Justin. 2004. AP investigation: Mexican worker deaths rise sharply even as overall US job safety improves. *Ithaca Journal,* March 15: C1.

Rasmussen, Wayne D. 1951. *A history of the Emergency Farm Labor Supply Program: Agriculture monograph 13.* Washington, DC: US Department of Agriculture, Bureau of Agricultural Economics.

Ravenstein, Ernst. 1889. The laws of migration. *Journal of the Royal Statistical Society* 52: 241–305.

Reimers, David. 1985. *Still the golden door: The Third World comes to America.* New York: Columbia University Press.

Reisler, Mark. 1976. *By the sweat of their brow: Mexican immigrant labor in the United States.* Westport, CT: Greenwood Press.

———. 1979. Always the laborer, never the citizen: Anglo perceptions of the Mexican immigrant during the 1920's. *The Pacific Historical Review* 45: 231–54.

Ricourt, Milagros, and Ruby Danta. 2002. *Hispanas de Queens: Latino panethnicity in a New York City neighborhood*. Ithaca, NY: Cornell University Press.

Ritzer, George. 2004. *The McDonaldization of society*. Thousand Oaks, CA: Pine Forge Press.

Rivera-Lyles, Jeannette. 2004. US growers in Mexico partly to blame for migrants in Pompano Beach, FL. *The Miami Herald*, December 6.

Rivera-Salgado, Gaspar. 1999. Welcome to Oaxacalifornia. *Cultural Survival Quarterly* 23: 59–61.

———, and L. Escala Rabadán. 2004. Collective identity and organizational strategies of indigenous and mestizo Mexican migrants. In *Indigenous Mexican migrants in the United States*, ed. Jonathan Fox and Gaspar Rivera-Salgado. Boulder, CO: Lynne Rienner.

Rodríguez, Néstor. 1997. The social construction of the US-Mexico border. In *Immigrants out! The new nativism and the anti-immigrant impulse in the United States*, ed. Juan Perea, 223–43. New York: New York University Press.

Roediger, David. 2005. *Working toward whiteness: How America's immigrants become white*. New York: Basic Books.

Roett, Riordan. 1995. Mexico political update: Chase Manhattan's emerging markets group memo. Washington, DC: Chase Manhattan Bank, Institute for Policy Studies.

Romero, Mary. 1992. *Maid in the USA*. New York: Routledge.

———, and Marwa Serag. 2005. Violation of Latino civil rights resulting from INS and local police's use of race, culture, and class profiling: The case of the Chandler Roundup in Arizona. *Cleveland State Law Review* 52: 75–96.

Ruiz, Vicki. 1987. *Cannery women, cannery lives: Mexican women, unionization, and the California food processing industry, 1930–1950*. Albuquerque: University of New Mexico Press.

Salazar Parreñas, Rhacel. 2001. *Servants of globalization: Women, migration, and domestic work*. Stanford, CA: Stanford University Press.

Sanchez, George J. 1993. *Becoming Mexican American*. New York: Oxford University Press.

SANDAG. 1992. Baja California demographic profile. San Diego: INFO Update Newsletter.

Sandoval, Carlos, and Catherine Tambini. 2003. *Farmingville*. Amagansett, NY: Camino Bluff Productions. Documentary.

Sassen, Saskia. 2005. Global cities and processes. In *The Oxford encyclopedia of Latinos and Latinas in the United States*, ed. Suzanne Oboler and Deena Gonzalez, 203–9. New York: Oxford University Press.

Satzewich, Vic. 1991. *Racism and the incorporation of foreign labour: Farm labour migration to Canada since 1945*. New York: Routledge.

———. 2007. Business or bureaucratic dominance in immigration policymaking in Canada: Why was Mexico included in the Caribbean Seasonal Agricultural Workers Program in 1974? *International Migration & Integration* 8: 255–75.

Schlosser, Eric. 2002. *Fast food nation*. Scranton, PA: Harper Collins.

Schor, Juliet. 1999. *The overspent American: Why we want what we don't need.* New York: Harper Perennial Books.

Scruggs, Otey. M. 1960. Evolution of the Mexican Farm Labor Agreement of 1942. *Agricultural History* 34: 140–49.

——. 1962. Texas, good neighbor? *Southwestern Social Science Quarterly* 43 (2): 118–25.

——. 1979. Texas and the Bracero Program, 1942–1947. In *Mexican workers in the United States,* ed. George C. Kiser and Martha Kiser, 85–96. Albuquerque: University of New Mexico Press.

Secretaría de Trabajo y Provisión Social. 1946. *Los Braceros.* México, D.F.: Dirección de Previsión Social, Secretaría de Trabajo y Provisión Social.

Sharma, Nandita. 2006. *Home economics: Nationalism and the making of migrant workers in Canada.* Toronto: University of Toronto Press.

Shostak, Arthur. 1991. *Robust unionism: Innovations in the labor market.* Ithaca, NY: ILR Press.

Sifuentes, Edward. 2006. Some migrants still in canyon: Offers evicted workers few options. *North County Times Online.* http://www.nctimes.com/articles/2006/11/25/news/top_stories/20_56_3311_24_06.txt (accessed January 31, 2007).

Simmel, Georg. 1972. *On individuality and social forms.* Chicago: University of Chicago Press.

Simpson, Audra. 2006. Enunciating citizenship and nationhood: Mohawk border crossing, the Jay Treaty of 1794, and the terrific meaning of Iroquois inconvenience. Paper presented at the Transnational Turn in American Studies Colloquium, American Studies Program, Cornell University, Ithaca. March.

Sinclair, Upton. 1985 [1906]. *The jungle.* New York: Penguin Books.

Skaggs, Sheryl, Donald Tomaskovic-Devey, and Jeffrey Leiter. 2006. Latino/a employment growth in North Carolina: Ethnic displacement or replacement? http://sasw.chass.ncsu.edu/jeff/latinos/eeoc.pdf (accessed January 31, 2007).

Sklar, Leslie. 1989. *Assembling for development: The maquila industry in Mexico and the United States.* Boston: Unwin Hyman.

Smith, Robert Courtney. 2005. Racialization and Mexicans in New York City. In *New destinations,* ed. Ruben Hernández-León and Victor Zúñiga, 220–43. New York: Russell Sage Foundation.

——. 2006a. Globalization and transnationalism. In *The Oxford encyclopedia of Latinas and Latinos in the United States,* ed. Suzanne Oboler and Deena Gonzalez, 209–15. New York: Oxford University Press.

——. 2006b. *Mexican New York: Transnational lives of new immigrants.* Berkeley: University of California Press.

Speed, Shannon, and Melissa Forbis. 2005. Embodying alternative logics: Everyday leaders and the diffusion of power in Zapatista autonomous regions. *LASA Forum* 36 (1): 19–21.

Stahler-Sholk, Richard. 2000. A world in which many worlds fit: Zapatista responses to globalization. Paper presented at Latin American Studies Association meeting, Miami.

Statistics Canada. 2006. Facts and figures: Immigration overview, permanent and temporary residents. Ottawa: Citizenship and Immigration Canada.

Steinberg, Stephen. 2001. *Turning black: The retreat from racial justice in American thought and policy.* Boston: Beacon Press.

Stephen, Lynn. 2000. The construction of indigenous suspects: Militarization and the gendered and ethnic dynamics of human rights abuses in Southern Mexico. *American Ethnologist* 26 (4): 822–42.

Striffler, Steven. 2005. *Chicken: The dangerous transformation of America's favorite food.* New Haven, CT: Yale University Press.

Stull, Donald, and Michael Broadway. 2004. *Slaughterhouse blues: The meat and poultry industry in North America.* New York: Wadsworth.

———, and Ken Erickson. 1992. The price of a good steak: Beef packing and its consequences for Garden City, Kansas. In *Structuring diversity: Ethnographic perspectives on the new immigration,* ed. Louise Lamphere, 35–64. Chicago: University of Chicago Press.

———, and David Griffith, eds. 1995. *Any way you cut it: Meat processing and small-town America.* Lawrence: University of Kansas Press.

Suro, Roberto, and Audrey Singer. 2002. Latino growth in metropolitan America: Changing patterns, new locations. http://www.brook.edu/es/urban/publications/surosinger.pdf (accessed May 10, 2010).

Swords, Alicia C.S. 2005. The power of networks: Popular political education among neo-Zapatista organizations in Chiapas, Mexico. PhD dissertation. Cornell University, Ithaca.

———. 2007. Neo-Zapatista network politics: Transforming democracy and development. *Latin American Perspectives* 34 (2): 1–16.

———, and Ronald L. Mize. 2008. Beyond tourist gazes and performances: US consumption of land and labor in Puerto Rican and Mexican destinations. *Latin American Perspectives* 35 (3): 53–69.

Tadiar, Neferti. 2009. *Things fall away: Philippine historical experience and the makings of globalization.* Durham, NC: Duke University Press.

Tait, Vanessa. 2005. *Poor workers' unions: Rebuilding labor from below.* Boston: South End Press.

Tatalovich, Raymond. 1997. Official English as nativist backlash. In *Immigrants out! The new nativism and the anti-immigrant impulse in the United States,* ed. Juan Perea, 78–104. New York: New York University Press.

Taylor, Paul S. 1931. *Mexican labor in the United States.* Berkeley: University of California Press.

———. 1983. *On the ground in the thirties.* Layton, UT: Gibbs Smith.

Tepeyac, Centro de Derechos Humanos. 2002. Intereses y resistencias: El Plan Puebla-Panamá y el corredor carretero Oaxaca-Istmo-Huatulco. In *Tehuantepec: Centro de derechos humanos Tepeyac del Istmo de Tehuantepec with La Neta,* 1–61. Austin: Texas Center for Policy Studies.

Thomas, Robert J. 1992. *Citizenship, gender, and work: Social organization of industrial agriculture.* Berkeley: University of California Press.

United Farm Workers (UFW). 1966. *El Malcriado: Trade journal of the United Farm Workers* 1 (29).

———. 2006. UFW: The official website of the United Farm Workers of America. http://www.ufw.org (accessed October 1, 2009).

United Food and Commercial Workers (UFCW) Canada. 2006. The status of migrant farm workers in Canada, 2005. Fifth Annual National Report. http://www.ufcw.ca/Default.aspx?SectionID=a3b41eb1-f567-4f3b-8a8b-e70050308832&LanguageId=1 (accessed October 1, 2007).

US Bureau of Labor Statistics. 2003. Consumer Expenditures. *Statistical Abstract of the United States.* Washington, DC: US Government Printing Office.

———. 2006. Consumer Expenditures. *Statistical Abstract of the United States.* Washington, DC: US Government Printing Office.

US Census. 1990. *Census of population and housing.* Washington, DC: US Government Printing Office.

———. 2000. *Census of population and housing.* Washington, DC: US Government Printing Office.

———. 2005. American community survey 2004. http://factfinder.census.gov/ (accessed January 31, 2007).

———. 2006. *Statistical abstract of the United States.* 125 ed. Washington, DC: US Government Printing Office. http://www.census.gov/statab/www/.

US Department of Homeland Security. 2003. *2002 yearbook of immigration statistics.* Washington, DC: Office of Immigration Statistics.

US Department of Labor. 1993. *US farmworkers in the post-IRCA period, based on data from the National Agricultural Workers Survey (NAWS) Research Report No. 4.* Washington, DC: US Government Printing Office.

———. 2003a. *H-2A annual report.* Washington, DC: US Government Printing Office.

———. 2003b. *H-2A crop activity summary, FY2002.* Washington, DC: Employment and Training Administration.

———. 2007. Agricultural labor exemptions, wage and hour division. http://www:dol/gov/programs/whd/state/agriemp2.htm (accessed October 1, 2009).

US English. 2006. States with official English laws. http://www.ujs-english.org/inc/official/states.asp (accessed June 14, 2009).

US Federal Reserve. 1999. H10. Foreign exchange rates (weekly). http://www.federalreserve.gov/releases/h10/hist/dat96_mx.htm, (accessed January 31, 2007).

———. 2006. H10. Foreign exchange rates (weekly). http://www.federalreserve.gov/releases/h10/hist/dat00.mx.htm (accessed January 31, 2007).

US President's Commission on Migratory Labor. 1951. *Migratory labor in American agriculture.* Washington, DC: US Government Printing Office,

Urrea, Luis Alberto. 1993. *Across the wire: Life and hard times on the Mexican border.* New York: Anchor Books, Doubleday.

————. 1996. *By the lake of sleeping children: The secret life of the Mexican border.* New York: Anchor Books, Doubleday.

Valdes, Dennis Nodin. 1991. *Al Norte: Agricultural workers in the Great Lakes Region, 1917–1970.* Austin: University of Texas Press.

Valenzuela, Abel, Jr., N. Theodore, E. Meléndez, and A.L. Gonzalez. 2006. *On the corner: Day labor in the United States.* http://www.sscnet.ucla.edu/issr/csup/index.php (accessed January 31, 2007).

Valle, Isabel. 1994. *Fields of toil: A migrant family's story.* Pullman: Washington State University Press.

Vargas, Zaragosa. 1999. *Proletarians of the north: Mexican industrial workers in Detroit and the Midwest, 1917–1933.* Berkeley: University of California Press.

————. 2007. *Labor rights are civil rights: Mexican American workers in twentieth-century America.* Princeton, NJ: Princeton University Press.

Veblen, Thorstein. 1994[1899]. *The theory of the leisure class.* New York: Dover Publications.

Vite Pérez, Miguel Ángel, and Roberto Rico Martínez. 2001. *Qué solos están los pobres: Neoliberalismo y urbanización popular en la zona etropolitana de la Ciudad de México.* Mexico City: Plaza y Valdés.

Vosko, Leah F., ed. 2006. *Precarious employment: Understanding labour market insecurity in Canada.* Montreal: McGill-Queen's University Press.

Waldinger, Roger. 1996. From Ellis Island to LAX: Immigrant prospects in the American city. *International Migration Review* 30 (4): 1078–87.

————, Christopher Erickson, Ruth Milkman, Daniel Mitchell Jr., Abel Valenzuela, Kent Wong, and Maurice Zietlin. 1997. Justice for Janitors: Organizing in difficult times. *Dissent* 44: 37–44.

Walia, Harsha, 2005. No one is illegal! February 1. http://www.leftturn.org (accessed July 1, 2005).

Weber, Devra. 1996. *Dark sweat, white gold: California farm workers, cotton, and the New Deal.* Berkeley: University of California Press.

Weinberg, William. 2004. NAFTA at ten; tragic toll for Mexican Maize. *Native Americas* 21 (2): 52.

Weisman, Jonathan. 2006. With Senate vote, Congress passes border fence bill: Barrier trumps immigration overhaul. http://www.washingtonpost.com/wp-dyn/content/article/2006/09/29/AR2006092901912.html (accessed July 7, 2007).

Wells, Miriam J. 2000. Immigration and unionization in the San Francisco hotel industry. In *Organizing immigrants: The challenges for unions in contemporary California,* ed. Ruth Milkman, 109–29. Ithaca, NY: ILR Press.

Willis, Paul E. 1978. *Profane culture.* New York: Routledge Falmer.

Woodruff, Elizabeth. 2003. *American Congo: The African American freedom struggle in the delta.* Cambridge, MA: Harvard University Press.

Workplace Project. 2006. *Annual report: 13 years fighting for immigrant rights.* Hempstead, NY: Workplace Project.

Yanz, Lynda, and David Smith. 1983. Women as a reserve army of labor: A critique. *Review of Radical Political Economics* 15: 92–106.

Zavella, Patricia. 1987. *Women's work and Chicano families: Cannery workers of the Santa Clara Valley.* Ithaca, NY: Cornell University Press.

Zepeda, J. Chris. 2006. Beyond solidarity: Zapatismo and Chicanos in Los Angeles. Paper presented at the National Association of Chicana and Chicano Studies National Conference, Guadalajara, Mexico.

Zinn, Howard. 1995. *A people's history of the United States: 1492–Present.* New York: Harper.

Index